1811
DICTIONARY
OF THE
VULGAR TONGUE.

THE

CANTING ACADEMY;

OR,

VILLANIES DISCOVERED:

WHEREIN ARE SHEWN

The Myſterious and Villanous Practices of that Wicked Crew, commonly known by the Names of

HECTORS, TRAPANNERS, GILTS, &c.

With ſeveral NEW CATCHES and SONGS.

ALSO A

COMPLEAT CANTING DICTIONARY,

BOTH OF

Old Words, and ſuch as are *now moſt in Uſe*.

A Book very uſeful and neceſſary (to be known, but not practiſed) for all People.

THE SECOND EDITION.

LONDON:

Printed by F. LEACH, for MAT. DREW; and are to be ſold by the Bookſellers.

N. B. The Dedication is ſigned, R. HEAD.

Advertisement reproduced from the second edition of "A Classical Dictionary Of The Vulgar Tongue," 1788.

1811
DICTIONARY
OF THE
VULGAR TONGUE.

A
DICTIONARY
OF
Buckish Slang, University Wit,
AND
PICKPOCKET ELOQUENCE.

Unabridged from the
original 1811 edition with a foreword by
MAX HARRIS

BIBLIOPHILE BOOKS

33 Maiden Lane
Covent Garden
London WC2E 7JS

Printed and bound in England

ISBN 0 900123 34 6

FOREWORD.

It is all ironic, but predictable. The age in which we have advanced to all manner of instant communication systems was bound to be the age in which the individual capacity to communicate would atrophy.

Language is now something other people use. They use it on television. Execrably. They use it on radio. Execrably. They use it on computers. Cryptically. They use it on word processors. Abstractly.

Since words are not very important, communication being fabricated for us by an outside world, the teaching system has bypassed its once insistent emphasis on linguistic expression.

The cultural loss thereby is enormous, and for the most part people have become sad anonymous creatures. Not quite zombies. But nearly.

Language is the method by which we identify ourselves to each other.

To communicate by the present method of grunts, cliches, stammers, "y'knows", "likes", painful lurching illiteracies is to define ourselves as spastic personalities.

The great glory of human language communication is that it is not an elitist skill, more easily available to the privileged or the educated. Or at least it once wasn't. The language of the British aristocracy was a feeble colourless, stylised product of dim intellects, as Wodehouse spent a lifetime informing us. The community language of the London Cockney was a miracle of quick-witted creative invention. Language belonged to the workers, not the nobs.

Australia, perhaps because of its Irish component, was once a language-rich country. Such genius as we once possessed was more concerned with a passion for metaphor, rather than the introduction of neologisms, the latter being a special talent of the Americans. But once again, one was more likely to pick up a living Australian language at Flemington Race Course than within the portals of the Melbourne Club. "Bernborough is off like a bride's nightie". This was once un-exceptional for a racing commentator's introduction to the start of a horse-race.

It is instructive now to look at such an encyclopaedic publication as Sidney Baker's "The Australian Language". It records a large number of words and idioms which were obsolescent when the work was issued a couple of decades ago. But in that period the whole compilation is a record of obsolescence. Scarcely an idiom or richly emotive word survives.

Language as a personal resource is dying out. We live life now with a minimal language, presented to us by the media, and geared to the lowest common denominator of comprehension.

I am not sure whether it is a hopeless rear-guard action by the surviving word-lovers, or, the battle lost, curiosity motivates a nostalgia market for the world of vanished words.

Captain Francis Grose's Dictionary of the Vulgar Tongue is either, a crusading or nostalgic purpose.

It is the fun dictionary of all dictionaries. It was so in its own time. It remains so . .

'Vulgar Tongue' was last revived by Robert Cromie of the Chicago Tribune, using the 1811 edition, which pays scant regard to the 1785 original.

Robert Cromie clarifies the matter.

"Capt. Grose, to be sure, is granted a modest credit for his book. "Buckish Slang, University Wit, and Pickpocket Eloquence" (London, 1811) does mention Grose in one slim line on the title page ("Compiled originally by Captain Grose"), and the preface declares, somewhat condescendingly, that although Grose's dictionary has enjoyed considerable vogue, "its circulation was confined almost exclusively to the lower orders of society"."

"While I have not made an exhaustive comparison between Grose's lexicon and the Lexicon Balatronicum, or Jester's Lexicon, turned out by "a member of the Whip Club" and several other worthies, among them "Hell Fire" Dick, there is no doubt whatever that the major portion of "Buckish Slang" should be credited to Grose, who died in Dublin in 1791, three years after a second edition of his "Classical Dictionary" had appeared."

There is a great temptation to pre-empt the reader's joy and surprise in making his or her own discoveries from the pages of Vulgar Tongue. A few examples will do no harm, since the dictionary is full of startling riches.

Radiant youth thinks it invented 'pig' as an offensive term for the police. The term was in use in 1785, presumably going underground in the United States for nearly two centuries, to re-emerge in the 1960s. "Screw" has always struck me as a rather nasty and very American word for copulation. I would have dated it as a neologism of the 1930s. The term is entirely english and familiar in the rogue's vocabulary of the 18th Century.

The word that most delights me is nincumpoop. Innocuous? I can't imagine a more insulting obscenity.

Enough. The temptation to divulge the contents is really quite compulsive. I must get my catch-fart to bring me a mug of scandal broth.

MAX HARRIS
October 1980.

Lexicon Balatronicum.

A

DICTIONARY

OF

Buckish Slang, University Wit,

AND

PICKPOCKET ELOQUENCE.

Compiled originally by Captain Grose.

AND NOW CONSIDERABLY ALTERED AND ENLARGED,

WITH

THE MODERN CHANGES AND IMPROVEMENTS,

BY A

MEMBER OF THE WHIP CLUB.

ASSISTED BY

Hell-Fire Dick, and James Gordon, Esqrs. of Cambridge; and William Soames, Esq. of the Hon. Society of Newman's Hotel.

LONDON:

PRINTED FOR C. CHAPPEL,

Pall-Mall;

SOLD BY J. JOHNSTON, CHEAPSIDE; GODDARD, PALL-MALL, AND ALL OTHER BOOKSELLERS.

1811.

PREFACE.

THE merit of Captain Grose's Dictionary of the Vulgar Tongue has been long and universally acknowledged. But its circulation was confined almost exclusively to the lower orders of society: he was not aware, at the time of its compilation, that our young men of fashion would at no very distant period be as distinguished for the vulgarity of their jargon as the inhabitants of Newgate; and he therefore conceived it superfluous to incorporate with his work the few examples of fashionable slang that might occur to his observation.

But our Jehus of rank have a phraseology not less peculiar to themselves, than the disciples of Barrington: for the uninitiated to understand their modes of expression, is as impossible as for a Buxton to construe the Greek Testament. To sport an Upper Benjamin, and to swear with a good grace, are qualifications easily attainable by their cockney imitators; but without the aid of our additional definitions, neither the cits of Fish-street, nor the boors of Brentford would be able to attain the language of whippism. We trust, therefore, that the whole tribe of second-rate Bang ups, will feel grateful for our endeavour to render this part of the work as complete as possible. By an occasional reference to our pages, they may be initiated into all the peculiarities of language by which the man of spirit is distinguished from the man of worth. They may now talk bawdy before their papas, without the fear of detection, and abuse their less spirited companions, who prefer a good dinner at home to a glorious *up-shot* in the highway, without the hazard of a cudgelling.

But we claim not merely the praise of gratifying curiosity, or affording assistance to the ambitious ; we are very sure that the moral influence of the Lexicon Balatronicum will be more certain and extensive than that of any methodist sermon that has ever been delivered within the bills of mortality. We need not descant on the dangerous impressions that are made on the female mind, by the remarks that fall incidentally from the lips of the brothers or servants of a family ; and we have before observed, that improper topics can with our assistance be discussed, even before the ladies, without raising a blush on the cheek of modesty. It is impossible that a female should understand the meaning of *twiddle diddles*, or rise from table at the mention of *Buckinger's boot*. Besides, Pope assures us, that "*vice to be hated needs but to be seen ;*" in this volume it cannot be denied, that she is seen very plainly ; and a love of virtue is, therefore, the necessary result of perusing it.

The propriety of introducing the *University slang* will be readily admitted ; it is not less curious than that of the College in the Old Bailey, and is less generally understood. When the number and accuracy of our additions are compared with the price of the volume, we have no doubt that its editors will meet with the encouragement that is due to learning, modesty, and virtue.

DICTIONARY

OF THE

VULGAR TONGUE.

ABBESS, or LADY ABBESS, A bawd, the mistress of a brothel.

ABEL-WACKETS. Blows given on the palm of the hand with a twisted handkerchief, instead of a ferula ; a jocular punishment among seamen, who sometimes play at cards for wackets, the loser suffering as many strokes as he has lost games.

ABIGAIL. A lady's waiting-maid.

ABRAM. Naked. *Cant.*

ABRAM COVE. A cant word among thieves, signifying a naked or poor man ; also a lusty, strong rogue.

ABRAM MEN. Pretended mad men.

TO SHAM ABRAM. To pretend sickness.

ACADEMY, or PUSHING SCHOOL. A brothel. The Floating Academy ; the lighters on board of which those persons are confined, who by a late regulation are condemned to hard labour, instead of transportation.—Campbell's Academy ; the same, from a gentleman of that name, who had the contract for victualling the hulks or lighters.

ACE OF SPADES. A widow.

ACCOUNTS. To cast up one's accounts ; to vomit.

ACORN. You will ride a horse foaled by an acorn, i. e. the gallows, called also the Wooden and Three-legged Mare. You will be hanged.—See THREE-LEGGED MARE.

ACT OF PARLIAMENT. A military term for small beer, five pints of which, by an act of parliament, a landlord was formerly obliged to give to each soldier gratis.

ACTEON. A cuckold, from the horns planted on the head of Acteon by Diana.

Active Citizen. A louse.

Adam's Ale. Water.

Adam Tiler. A pickpocket's associate, who receives the stolen goods, and runs off with them. *Cant.*

Addle Pate. An inconsiderate foolish fellow.

Addle Plot. A spoil-sport, a mar-all.

Admiral of the Blue, who carries his flag on the main-mast. A landlord or publican wearing a blue apron, as was formerly the custom among gentlemen of that vocation.

Admiral of the Narrow Seas. One who from drunkenness vomits into the lap of the person sitting opposite to him. *Sea phrase.*

Adrift. Loose, turned adrift, discharged. *Sea phrase.*

Egrotat, (*Cambridge*), A certificate from the apothecary that you are *indisposed,* (i. e.) to go to chapel. He sports an Ægrotat, he is sick, and unable to attend Chapel, or Hall. It does not follow, however, but that he can *Strum a piece,* or sport a pair of oars.

Affidavit Men. Knights of the post, or false witnesses, said to attend Westminster Hall, and other courts of justice, ready to swear any thing for hire.

After-Clap. A demand after the first given in has been discharged; a charge for pretended omissions; in short, any thing disagreeable happening after all consequences of the cause have been thought at an end.

Against the Grain. Unwilling. It went much against the grain with him, i. e. it was much against his inclination, or against his pluck.

Agog, All-a-gog. Anxious, eager, impatient: from the Italian *agogare,* to desire eagerly.

Aground. Stuck fast, stopped, at a loss, ruined; like a boat or vessel aground.

Air and Exercise. He has had air and exercise, i. e. he has been whipped at the cart's tail; or, as it is generally, though more vulgarly, expressed, at the cart's a-se.

Alderman. A roasted turkey garnished with sausages; the latter are supposed to represent the gold chain worn by those magistrates.

Aldgate. A draught on the pump at Aldgate; a bad bill of exchange, drawn on persons who have no effects of the drawer.

Ale Draper. An alehouse keeper.

Ale Post. A may-pole.

All-a-mort. Struck dumb, confounded. What, sweet one, all-a-mort? *Shakespeare.*

All Holiday. It is all holiday at Peckham, or it is all holiday

liday with him; a saying signifying that it is all over with the business or person spoken of or alluded to.

All Hollow. He was beat all hollow, i. e. he had no chance of conquering: it was all hollow, or a hollow thing, it was a decided thing from the beginning. See Hollow.

All Nations. A composition of all the different spirits sold in a dram-shop, collected in a vessel into which the drainingsof the bottles and quartern pots are emptied.

Alls. The five alls is a country sign, representing five human figures, each having a motto under him. The first is a king in his regalia; his motto, I govern all: the second, a bishop in pontificals; motto, I pray for all: third, a lawyer in his gown; motto, I plead for all: fourth: a soldier in his regimentals, fully accoutred; motto, I fight for all: fifth, a poor countryman with his scythe and rake; motto, I pay for all.

Altamel. A verbal or lump account, without particulars, such as is commonly produced at bawdy-houses, spunging-houses, &c. Vide Dutch Reckoning.

Altitudes. The man is in his altitudes, i. e. he is drunk.

Ambassador. A trick to duck some ignorant fellow or landsman, frequently played on board ships in the warm latitudes. It is thus managed: A large tub is filled with water, and two stools placed on each side of it. Over the whole is thrown a tarpaulin, or old sail: this is kept tight by two persons, who are to represent the king and queen of a foreign country, and are seated on the stools. The person intended to be ducked plays the Ambassador, and after repeating a ridiculous speech dictated to him, is led in great form up to the throne, and seated between the king and queen, who rising suddenly as soon as he is seated, he falls backwards into the tub of water.

Ambassador of Morocco. A Shoemaker. (See Mrs. Clarke's Examination.)

Ambidexter. A lawyer who takes fees from both plaintiff and defendant, or that goes snacks with both parties in gaming.

Amen Curler. A parish clerk.

Amen. He said Yes and Amen to every thing; he agreed to every thing.

Aminadab. A jeering name for a Quaker.

Ames Ace. Within ames ace; nearly, very near.

To Amuse. To fling dust or snuff in the eyes of the person intended to be robbed; also to invent some plausible tale, to delude shop-keepers and others, thereby to put them off their guard. *Cant.*

Amusers. Rogues who carried snuff or dust in their poc-

 kets,

kets, which they threw into the eyes of any person they intended to rob; and running away, their accomplices (pretending to assist and pity the half-blinded person) took that opportunity of plundering him.

ANABAPTIST. A pickpocket caught in the fact, and punished with the discipline of the pump or horse-pond.

ANCHOR. Bring your a-se to an anchor, i. e. sit down. To let go an anchor to the windward of the law; to keep within the letter of the law. *Sea wit.*

ANGLERS. Pilferers, or petty thieves, who, with a stick having a hook at the end, steal goods out of shop-windows, grates, &c.; also those who draw in or entice unwary persons to prick at the belt, or such like devices.

ANGLING FOR FARTHINGS. Begging out of a prison window with a cap, or box, let down at the end of a long string.

ANKLE. A girl who is got with child, is said to have sprained her ankle.

ANODYNE NECKLACE. A halter.

ANTHONY or TANTONY PIG. The favourite or smallest pig in the litter.—To follow like a tantony pig, i. e. St. Anthony's pig; to follow close at one's heels. St. Anthony the hermit was a swineherd, and is always represented with a swine's bell and a pig. Some derive this saying from a privilege enjoyed by the friars of certain convents in England and France (sons of St. Anthony), whose swine were permitted to feed in the streets. These swine would follow any one having greens or other provisions, till they obtained some of them; and it was in those days considered an act of charity and religion to feed them.

TO KNOCK ANTHONY. Said of an in-kneed person, or one whose knees knock together; to cuff Jonas. See JONAS.

APE LEADER. An old maid; their punishment after death, for neglecting increase and multiply, will be, it is said, leading apes in hell.

APOSTLES. To manœuvre the apostles, i. e. rob Peter to pay Paul; that is, to borrow money of one man to pay another.

APOSTLES. (*Cambridge.*) Men who are plucked, refused their degree.

APOTHECARY. To talk like an apothecary; to use hard or gallipot words: from the assumed gravity and affectation of knowledge generally put on by the gentlemen of this profession, who are commonly as superficial in their learning as they are pedantic in their language.

APOTHECARY'S BILL. A long bill.

Apothecary's, or Law Latin. Barbarous Latin, vulgarly called Dog Latin, in Ireland Bog Latin.

Apple Cart. Down with his apple-cart; knock or throw him down.

Apple Dumplin Shop. A woman's bosom.

Apple-pye Bed. A bed made apple-pye fashion, like what is called a turnover apple-pye, where the sheets are so doubled as to prevent any one from getting at his length between them: a common trick played by frolicsome country lasses on their sweethearts, male relations, or visitors.

April Fool. Any one imposed on, or sent on a bootless errand, on the first of April; which day it is the custom among the lower people, children, and servants, by dropping empty papers carefully doubled up, sending persons on absurd messages, and such like contrivances, to impose on every one they can, and then to salute them with the title of April Fool. This is also practised in Scotland under the title of Hunting the Gowke.

Apron String Hold. An estate held by a man during his wife's life.

Aqua Pumpaginis. Pump water. *Apothecaries Latin.*

Arbor Vitæ. A man's penis.

Arch Duke. A comical or eccentric fellow.

Arch Rogue, Dimber Damber Upright Man. The chief of a gang of thieves or gypsies.

Arch Dell, or Arch Doxy, signifies the same in rank among the female canters or gypsies.

Ard. Hot. *Cant.*

Armour. In his armour, pot valiant: to fight in armour; to make use of Mrs. Philips's ware. See C--d--m.

Ark. A boat or wherry. Let us take an ark and winns, let us take a sculler. *Cant.*

Ark Ruffians. Rogues who, in conjunction with watermen, robbed, and sometimes murdered, on the water, by picking a quarrel with the passengers in a boat, boarding it, plundering, stripping, and throwing them overboard, &c. A species of badger. *Cant.*

Arrah now. An unmeaning expletive, frequently used by the vulgar Irish.

Ars Musica. A bum fiddlle.

Arse. To hang an arse; to hang back, to be afraid to advance. He would lend his a--e, and sh-te through his ribs; a saying of any one who lends his money inconsiderately. He would lose his a--e if it was loose; said of a careless person. A--e about; turn round.

Arsy varsey. To fall arsy varsey, i. e. head over heels.

Arthur,

Arthur; King Arthur. A game used at sea, when near the line, or in a hot latitude. It is performed thus: A man who is to represent king Arthur, ridiculously dressed, having a large wig made out of oakum, or some old swabs, is seated on the side, or over a large vessel of water. Every person in his turn is to be ceremoniously introduced to him, and to pour a bucket of water over him, crying, hail, king Arthur! if during this ceremony the person introduced laughs or smiles (to which his majesty endeavours to excite him, by all sorts of ridiculous gesticulations), he changes place with, and then becomes, king Arthur, till relieved by some brother tar, who has as little command over his muscles as himself.

Articles. Breeches; coat, waistcoat, and articles.

Article. A wench. A prime article. A handsome girl. She's a a prime article (*Whip slang*), she's a devilish good piece, a hell of a *goer*.

Ask, or Ax my A--e. A common reply to any question; still deemed wit at sea, and formerly at court, under the denomination of selling bargains. See **Bargain.**

Assig. An assignation.

Athanasian Wench, or Quicunque vult. A forward girl, ready to oblige every man that shall ask her.

Aunt. Mine aunt; a bawd or procuress: a title of eminence for the senior dells, who serve for instructresses, midwives, &c. for the dells. *Cant*. See **Dells.**

Avoir du pois Lay. Stealing brass weights off the counters of shops. *Cant.*

Autem. A church.

Autem Bawler. A parson. *Cant.*

Autem Cacklers. } Dissenters of every denomination.
Autem Prickears. } *Cant.*

Autem Cackle Tub. A conventicle or meeting-house for dissenters. *Cant.*

Autem Dippers. Anabaptists. *Cant.*

Autem Divers. Pickpockets who practice in churches; also churchwardens and overseers of the poor. *Cant.*

Autem Goglers. Pretended French prophets. *Cant.*

Autem Mort. A married woman; also a female beggar with several children hired or borrowed to excite charity. *Cant.*

Autem Quavers. Quakers.

Autem Quaver Tub. A Quakers' meeting-house. *Cant.*

Awake. Acquainted with, knowing the business. Stow the books, the culls are awake; hide the cards, the fellows know what we intended to do.

BABES IN THE WOOD. Criminals in the stocks, or pillory

BABBLE. Confused, unintelligible talk, such as was used at the building the tower of Babel.

BACK BITER. One who slanders another behind his back, i. e. in his absence. His bosom friends are become his back biters, said of a lousy man.

BACKED. Dead. He wishes to have the senior, or old square-toes, backed; he longs to have his father on six men's shoulders; that is, carrying to the grave.

BACK UP. His back is up, i. e. he is offended or angry; an expression or idea taken from a cat; that animal, when angry, always raising its back. An allusion also sometimes used to jeer a crooked man; as, So, Sir, I see somebody has offended you, for your back is up.

BACON. He has saved his bacon; he has escaped He has a good voice to beg bacon; a saying in ridicule of a bad voice.

BACON-FACED. Full-faced.

BACON FED. Fat, greasy.

BACK GAMMON PLAYER. A sodomite.

BACK DOOR (USHER, or GENTLEMAN OF THE). The same.

BAD BARGAIN. One of his majesty's bad bargains; a worthless soldier, a malingeror. See MALINGEROR.

BADGE. A term used for one burned in the hand. He has got his badge, and piked; he was burned in the hand, and is at liberty. *Cant.*

BADGE-COVES. Parish Pensioners. *Cant.*

BADGERS. A crew of desperate villains who robbed near rivers, into which they threw the bodies of those they murdered. *Cant.*

BAG. He gave them the bag, i. e. left them.

BAG OF NAILS. He squints like a bag of nails; i. e. his eyes are directed as many ways as the points of a bag of nails. The old BAG OF NAILS at Pimlico; originally the BACCHANALS.

BAGGAGE. Heavy baggage; women and children. Also a familiar epithet for a woman; as, cunning baggage, wanton baggage, &c.

BAKERS DOZEN. Fourteen; that number of rolls being allowed to the purchasers of a dozen.

BAKER-KNEE'D. One whose knees knock together in walking, as if kneading dough.

BALDERDASH. Adulterated wine.

BALLOCKS. The testicles of a man or beast; also a vulgar nick name for a parson. His brains are in his ballocks, a cant saying to designate a fool.

BALUM RANCUM. A hop or dance, where the women are all prostitutes. N. B. The company dance in their birthday suits.

BALSAM.

Balsam. Money.

Bam. A jocular imposition, the same as a humbug. See Humbug.

To Bam. To impose on any one by a falsity; also to jeer or make fun of any one.

To Bamboozle. To make a fool of any one, to humbug or impose on him.

Banaghan. He beats Banaghan; an Irish saying of one who tells wonderful stories. Perhaps Banaghan was a minstrel famous for dealing in the marvellous.

Bandbox. Mine a-se on a bandbox; an answer to the offer of any thing inadequate to the purpose for which it is proffered, like offering a bandbox for a seat.

Banbury Story of a Cock and a Bull. A round-about, nonsensical story.

Bandog. A bailiff or his follower; also a very fierce mastiff: likewise, a bandbox. *Cant.*

Bang Up. (*Whip.*) Quite the thing, hellish fine. Well done. Compleat. Dashing. In a handsome stile. A bang up cove; a dashing fellow who spends his money freely. To bang up prime: to bring your horses up in a dashing or fine style: as the swell's rattler and prads are bang up prime; the gentleman sports an elegant carriage and fine horses.

To Bang. To beat.

Banging. Great; a fine banging boy.

Bang Straw. A nick name for a thresher, but applied to all the servants of a farmer.

Bankrupt Cart. A one-horse chaise, said to be so called by a Lord Chief Justice, from their being so frequently used on Sunday jaunts by extravagant shopkeepers and tradesmen.

Banks's Horse. A horse famous for playing tricks, the property of one Banks. It is mentioned in Sir Walter Raleigh's Hist. of the World, p. 178; also by Sir Kenelm Digby and Ben Jonson.

Bantling. A young child.

Banyan Day. A sea term for those days on which no meat is allowed to the sailors: the term is borrowed from the Banyans in the East Indies, a cast that eat nothing that had life.

Baptized, or Christened. Rum, brandy, or any other spirits, that have been lowered with water.

Barber's Chair. She is as common as a barber's chair, in which a whole parish sit to be trimmed; said of a prostitute.

Barber's Sign. A standing pole and two wash balls.

Bargain. To sell a bargain; a species of wit, much in vogue about the latter end of the reign of Queen Anne, and frequently alluded to by Dean Swift, who says the maids of honour often amused themselves with it. It consisted in the seller naming his or her hinder parts, in answer to the question, What? which the buyer was artfully led to ask. As a specimen, take the following instance: A lady would come into a room full of company, apparently in a fright, crying out, It is white, and follows me! On any of the company asking, What? she sold him the bargain, by saying, Mine a--e.

Bargees. (*Cambridge.*) Barge-men on the river.

Barker. The shopman of a bow-wow shop, or dealer in second hand clothes, particularly about Monmouth-Street, who walks before his master's door, and deafens every passenger with his cries of---Clothes, coats, or gowns—what d'ye want, gemmen?---what d'ye buy? See Bow-wow Shop.

Barkshire. A member or candidate for Barkshire, said of one troubled with a cough, vulgarly styled barking.

Barking Irons. Pistols, from their explosion resembling the bow-wow or barking of a dog. *Irish.*

Barn. A parson's barn; never so full but there is still room for more. Bit by a barn mouse, tipsey, probably from an allusion to barley.

Barnaby. An old dance to a quick movement. See Cotton, in his Virgil Travesti; where, speaking of Eolus he has these lines,

> Bounce cry the port-holes, out they fly,
> And make the world dance Barnaby.

Barnacle. A good job, or snack easily got: also shellfish growing at the bottoms of ships; a bird of the goose kind; an instrument like a pair of pincers, to fix on the noses of vicious horses whilst shoeing; a nick name for spectacles, and also for the gratuity given to grooms by the buyers and sellers of horses.

Barrel Fever. He died of the barrel fever; he killed himself by drinking.

Barrow Man. A man under sentence of transportation; alluding to the convicts at Woolwich, who are principally employed in wheeling barrows full of brick or dirt.

Bartholomew Baby. A person dressed up in a tawdry manner, like the dolls or babies sold at Bartholomew fair.

Basket. An exclamation frequently made use of in cock-pits, at cock-fightings, where persons refusing or unable to pay their losings, are adjudged by that respectable assembly

sembly to be put into a basket suspended over the pit, there to remain during that day's diversion: on the least demur to pay a bet, Basket is vociferated in terrorem. He grins like a basket of chips: a saying of one who is on the broad grin.

Basket-making. The good old trade of basket-making; copulation, or making feet for children's stockings.

Bastard. The child of an unmarried woman.

Bastardly Gullion. A bastard's bastard.

To baste. To beat. I'll give him his bastings, I'll beat him heartily.

Basting. A beating.

Bastonading. Beating any one with a stick; from baton, a stick, formerly spelt baston.

Bat. A low whore: so called from moving out like bats in the dusk of the evening.

Batch. We had a pretty batch of it last night; we had a hearty dose of liquor. Batch originally means the whole quantity of bread baked at one time in an oven.

Battner. An ox: beef being apt to batten or fatten those that eat it. The cove has hushed the battner; i. e. has killed the ox.

Batchelor's Fare. Bread and cheese and kisses.

Batchelor's Son. A bastard.

Battle-Royal. A battle or bout at cudgels or fisty-cuffs, wherein more than two persons are engaged: perhaps from its resemblance, in that particular, to more serious engage ments fought to settle royal disputes.

Bawbee. A halfpenny. *Scotch.*

Bawbels, or Bawbles. Trinkets; a man's testicles.

Bawd. A female procuress.

Bawdy Basket. The twenty-third rank of canters, who carry pins, tape, ballads, and obscene books to sell, but live mostly by stealing. *Cant.*

Bawdy-house Bottle. A very small bottle; short measure being among the many means used by the keepers of those houses, to gain what they call an honest livelihood: indeed this is one of the least reprehensible; the less they give a man of their infernal beverages for his money, the kinder they behave to him.

Bay Fever. A term of ridicule applied to convicts, who sham illness, to avoid being sent to Botany Bay.

Bayard of Ten Toes. To ride bayard of ten toes, is to walk on foot. Bayard was a horse famous in old romances.

Beak. A justice of peace, or magistrate. Also a judge or chairman who presides in court. I clapp'd my peepers full of tears, and so the old beak set me free; I began to weep, and the judge set me free.

Bean. A guinea. Half bean; half a guinea.

Bear. One who contracts to deliver a certain quantity or sum of stock in the public funds, on a future day, and at stated price; or, in other words, sells what he has not got, like the huntsman in the fable, who sold the bear's skin before the bear was killed. As the bear sells the stock he is not possessed of, so the bull purchases what he has not money to pay for; but in case of any alteration in the price agreed on, either party pays or receives the difference. *Exchange Alley.*

Bear-garden Jaw or Discourse. Rude, vulgar language, such as was used at the bear-gardens.

Bear Leader. A travelling tutor.

Beard Splitter. A man much given to wenching.

Bearings. I'll bring him to his bearings; I'll bring him to reason. *Sea term.*

Beast. To drink like a beast, i. e. only when thirsty.

Beast with Two Backs. A man and woman in the act of copulation. *Shakespeare in Othello.*

Beater Cases. Boots. *Cant.*

Beau-nasty. A slovenly fop; one finely dressed, but dirty.

Beau Trap. A loose stone in a pavement, under which water lodges, and on being trod upon, squirts it up, to the great damage of white stockings; also a sharper neatly dressed, lying in wait for raw country squires, or ignorant fops.

Becalmed. A Piece of sea wit, sported in hot weather. I am becalmed, the sail sticks to the mast; that is, my shirt sticks to my back. His prad is becalmed; his horse knocked up.

Beck. A beadle. See Hermanbeck.

Bed. Put to bed with a mattock, and tucked up with a spade; said of one that is dead and buried. You will go up a ladder to bed, i. e. you will be hanged. In many country places, persons hanged are made to mount up a ladder, which is afterwards turned round or taken away, whence the term, "Turned off."

Bedfordshire. I am for Bedfordshire, i.e. for going to bed.

Bedizened. Dressed out, over-dressed, or awkwardly ornamented.

Bed-Maker. Women employed at Cambridge to attend on the Students. sweep his room, &c. They will put their hands to any thing, and are generally blest with a pretty family of daughters: who unmake the beds. as fast as they are made by their mothers.

Beef. To cry beef; to give the alarm. They have cried beef on us. *Cant.*—To be in a man's beef; to wound him with

a sword

a sword. To be in a woman's beef; to have carnal knowledge of her. Say you bought your beef of me, a jocular request from a butcher to a fat man, implying that he credits the butcher who serves him.

BEEF EATER. A yeoman of the guards, instituted by Henry VII. Their office was to stand near the bouffet, or cupboard, thence called Bouffetiers, since corrupted to Beef Eaters. Others suppose they obtained this name from the size of their persons, and the easiness of their duty, as having scarce more to do than to eat the king's beef.

BEETLE-BROWED. One having thick projecting eyebrows.

BEETLE-HEADED. Dull, stupid.

BEGGAR MAKER. A publican, or ale-house keeper.

BEGGAR'S BULLETS. Stones. The beggar's bullets began to fly, i. e. they began to throw stones.

BEILBY'S BALL. He will dance at Beilby's ball, where the sheriff pays the music; he will be hanged. Who Mr. Beilby was, or why that ceremony was so called, remains with the quadrature of the circle, the discovery of the philosopher's stone, and divers other desiderata yet undiscovered.

BELCH. All sorts of beer; that liquor being apt to cause eructation.

BELCHER. A red silk handkerchief, intermixed with yellow and a little black. The kiddey flashes his belcher; the young fellow wears a silk handkerchief round his neck.

BELL, BOOK, AND CANDLE. They cursed him with bell, book, and candle; an allusion to the popish form of excommunicating and anathematizing persons who had offended the church.

TO BEAR THE BELL. To excel or surpass all competitors, to be the principal in a body or society; an allusion to the fore horse or leader of a team, whose harness is commonly ornamented with a bell or bells. Some suppose it a term borrowed from an ancient tournament, where the victorious knights bore away the *belle* or *fair lady*. Others derive it from a horse-race, or other rural contentions, where bells were frequently given as prizes.

BELLOWS. The lungs.

BELLOWER. The town crier.

BELLOWSER. Transportation for life: i. e. as long.

BELLY. His eye was bigger than his belly; a saying of a person at a table, who takes more on his plate than he can eat.

BELLYFULL. A hearty beating, sufficient to make a man yield or give out. A woman with child is also said to have got her belly full.

Belly Cheat. An apron.

Belly Plea. The plea of pregnancy, generally adduced by female felons capitally convicted, which they take care to provide for, previous to their trials; every gaol having, as the Beggar's Opera informs us, one or more child getters, who qualify the ladies for that expedient to procure a respite.

Belly Timber. Food of all sorts.

Bell Swagger. A noisy bullying fellow.

Bell Wether. The chief or leader of a mob; an idea taken from a flock of sheep, where the wether has a bell about his neck.

Bene. Good—**Benar.** Better. *Cant.*

Bene Bowse. Good beer, or other strong liquor. *Cant.*

Bene Cove. A good fellow. *Cant.*

Bene Darkmans. Good night. *Cant.*

Bene Feakers. Counterfeiters of bills. *Cant.*

Bene Feakers of Gybes. Counterfeiters of passes. *Cant.*

Beneshiply. Worshipfully. *Cant.*

Ben. A fool. *Cant.*

Benish. Foolish.

Benison. The beggar's benison: May your ***** and purse never fail you.

Bermudas. A cant name for certain places in London, privileged against arrests, like the Mint in Southwark. *Ben. Jonson.* These privileges are abolished.

Bess, or Betty. A small instrument used by house-breakers to force open doors. Bring bess and glym; bring the instrument to force the door, and the dark lantern. Small flasks, like those for Florence wine, are also called betties.

Bess. See **Brown Bess.**

Best. To the best in Christendom: i. e. the best **** in Christendom; a health formerly much in vogue.

Bet. A wager.—**To Bet.** To lay a wager.

Betty Martin. That's my eye, Betty Martin; an answer to any one that attempts to impose or humbug.

Betwattled. Surprised, confounded, out of one's senses; also bewrayed.

Bever. An afternoon's luncheon; also a fine hat; beaver's fur making the best hats.

Beverage. Garnish money, or money for drink, demanded of any one having a new suit of clothes.

Bible. A boatswain's great axe. *Sea term.*

Bible Oath. Supposed by the vulgar to be more binding than an oath taken on the Testament only, as being the bigger book, and generally containing both the Old and New Testament.

Biddy, or Chick-a-biddy. A chicken, and figuratively a young wench.

Bidet, commonly pronounced **Biddy.** A kind of tub, contrived for ladies to wash themselves, for which purpose they bestride it like a French poney, or post-horse, called in French bidets.

Bienly. Excellently. She wheedled so bienly; she coaxed or flattered so cleverly. *French.*

Bill at Sight. To pay a bill at sight; to be ready at all times for the venereal act.

Bilboa. A sword. Bilboa in Spain was once famous for well-tempered blades: these are quoted by Falstaff, where he describes the manner in which he lay in the buck-basket. Bilboes, the stock; prison. *Cant.*

To Bilk. To cheat. Let us bilk the rattling cove; let us cheat the hackney coachman of his fare. *Cant.* Bilking a coachman, a box-keeper, and a poor whore, were formerly, among men of the town, thought gallant actions.

Bill of Sale. A widow's weeds. See **House to let.**

Billingsgate Language. Foul language, or abuse. Billingsgate is the market where the fishwomen assemble to purchase fish; and where, in their dealings and disputes, they are somewhat apt to leave decency and good manners a little on the left hand.

Bing. To go. *Cant.* Bing avast; get you gone. Binged avast in a darkmans; stole away in the night. Bing we to Rumeville: shall we go to London?

Bingo. Brandy or other spirituous liquor. *Cant.*

Bingo Boy. A dram drinker. *Cant.*

Bingo Mort. A female dram drinker. *Cant.*

Binnacle Word. A fine or affected word, which sailors jeeringly offer to chalk up on the binnacle.

Bird and Baby. The sign of the eagle and child.

Bird-witted. Inconsiderate, thoughtless, easily imposed on.

Birds of a Feather. Rogues of the same gang.

Birth-day Suit. He was in his birth-day suit, that is, stark naked.

Bishop. A mixture of wine and water, into which is put a roasted orange. Also one of the largest of Mrs. Philips's purses, used to contain the others.

Bishoped, or To bishop. A term used among horse-dealers, for burning the mark into a horse's tooth, after he has lost it by age; by bishoping, a horse is made to appear younger than he is. It is a common saying of milk that is burnt too, that the bishop has set his foot in it. Formerly, when a bishop passed through a village, all the inhabitants ran out of their houses to solicit his blessing, even leaving their milk, &c. on the fire, to take its chance : which, went burnt to, was said to be bishoped.

To **Bishop** the balls, a term used among printers, to water them.

Bit. Money. He grappled the cull's bit ; he seized the man's money. A bit is also the smallest coin in Jamaica, equal to about sixpence sterling.

Bitch. A she dog, or doggess; the most offensive appellation that can be given to an English woman, even more provoking than that of whore, as may be gathered from the regular Billinsgate or St. Giles's answer---" I may be a whore, but can't be a bitch."

To **Bitch.** To yield, or give up an attempt through fear. To stand bitch ; to make tea, or do the honours of the tea-table, performing a female part : bitch there standing for woman, species for genius.

Bitch Booby. A country wench. *Military term.*

Bite. A cheat ; also a woman's privities. The cull wapt the mort's bite ; the fellow enjoyed the wench heartily. *Cant.*

To **Bite.** To over-reach, or impose ; also to steal.---*Cant.* ---Biting was once esteemed a kind of wit, similar to the humbug. An instance of it is given in the Spectator : A man under sentence of death having sold his body to a surgeon rather below the market price, on receiving the money, cried, A bite! I am to be hanged in chains.—To bite the roger ; to steal a portmanteau. To bite the wiper, to steal a handkerchief. To bite on the bridle ; to be pinched or reduced to dfiiculties. Hark ye, friend, whether do they bite in the collar or the cod-piece ? *Water wit to anglers.*

Biter. A wench whose **** is ready to bite her a-se : a lascivious, rampant wench.

Blab. A tell-tale, or one incapable of keeping a secret.

Black and white. In writing. I have it in black and white ; I have written evidence.

Black Art. The art of picking a lock. *Cant.*

Black A-se. A copper or kettle. The pot calls the kettle black a-se. *Cant.*

Black Book. He is down in the black book, i. e. has a stain in his character. A black book is keep in most regiments, wherein the names of all persons sentenced to punishment are recorded.

Black Box. A lawyer. *Cant.*

Black Eye. We gave the bottle a black eye, i. e. drank it almost up. He cannot say black is the white of my eye ; he cannot point out a blot in my character.

Black

Black Fly. The greatest drawback on the farmer is the black fly, i. e. the parson who takes tithe of the harvest.

Black Guard. A shabby, mean fellow; a term said to be derived from a number of dirty, tattered roguish boys, who attended at the Horse Guards, and Parade in St. James's Park, to black the boots and shoes of the soldiers, or to do any other dirty offices. These, from their constant attendance about the time of guard mounting, were nick-named the black-guards.

Black Jack. A nick name given to the Recorder by the Thieves.

Black Jack. A jug to drink out of, made of jacked leather.

Black Joke. A popular tune to a song, having for the burden, "Her black joke and belly so white:" figuratively the black joke signifies the monosyllable. See Monosyllable.

Black Indies. Newcastle upon Tyne, whose rich coal mines prove an Indies to the proprietors.

BlackLegs. A gambler or sharper on the turf or in the cock-pit: so called, perhaps, from their appearing generally in boots; or else from game-cocks whose legs are always black.

Black Monday. The first Monday after the school-boys holidays, or breaking up, when they are to go to school, and produce or repeat the tasks set them.

Black Psalm. To sing the black psalm; to cry: a saying used to children.

Black Spice Racket. To rob chimney sweepers of their soot, bag and soot.

Black Spy. The Devil.

Black Strap. Bene Carlo wine; also port. A task of labour imposed on soldiers at Gibraltar, as a punishment for small offences.

Blank. To look blank; to appear disappointed or confounded.

Blanket Hornpipe. The amorous congress.

Blarney. He has licked the blarney stone; he deals in the wonderful, or tips us the traveller. The blarney stone is a triangular stone on the very top of an ancient castle of that name in the county of Cork in Ireland, extremely difficult of access; so that to have ascended to it, was considered as a proof of perseverance, courage, and agility, whereof many are supposed to claim the honour, who never atchieved the adventure: and to tip the blarney, is figuratively used telling a marvellous story, or falsity; and also sometimes to express flattery. *Irish.*

A blasted Fellow or Brimstone. An abandoned rogue or prostitute. *Cant.*

To blast,

To Blast. To curse.

Blater. A calf. *Cant.*

Bleached Mort. A fair-complexioned wench.

Bleaters. Those cheated by Jack in a box. *Cant.*—See **Jack in a Box.**

Bleating Cheat. A sheep. *Cant.*

Bleating Rig. Sheep stealing. *Cant.*

Bleeders. Spurs. He clapped his bleeders to his prad; he put spurs to his horse.

Bleeding Cully. One who parts easily with his money, or bleeds freely.

Bleeding new. A metaphor borrowed from fish, which will not bleed when stale.

Blessing. A small quantity over and above the measure, usually given by hucksters dealing in peas, beans, and other vegetables.

Blind. A feint, pretence, or shift.

Blind Cheeks. The breech. Buss blind cheeks; kiss mine a-se.

Blind Excuse. A poor or insufficient excuse. A blind ale-house, lane, or alley; an obscure, or little known or frequented ale-house, lane, or alley.

Blind Harpers. Beggars counterfeiting blindness, playing on fiddles, &c.

Blindman's Buff. A play used by children, where one being blinded by a handkerchief bound over his eyes, attempts to seize any one of the company, who all endeavour to avoid him; the person caught must be blinded in his stead.

Blind Cupid. The backside.

Blindman's Holiday. Night, darkness.

Block Houses. Prisons, houses of correction, &c.

Blocked at both ends. Finished. The game is blocked at both ends; the game is ended.

Blood. A riotous disorderly fellow.

Blood for Blood. A term used by tradesmen for bartering the different commodities in which they deal. Thus a hatter furnishing a hosier with a hat, and taking payment in stockings, is said to deal blood for blood.

Blood Money. The reward given by the legislature on the conviction of highwaymen, burglars, &c.

Bloody Back. A jeering appellation for a soldier, alluding to his scarlet coat.

Bloody. A favourite word used by the thieves in swearing, as bloody eyes, bloody rascal.

Bloss or Blowen. The pretended wife of a bully, or shoplifter. *Cant.*

To Blot the Skrip and jar it. To stand engaged or bound for any one. *Cant.*

Blow. He has bit the blow, i. e. he has stolen the goods. *Cant.*

Blowen. A mistress or whore of a gentleman of the scamp. The blowen kidded the swell into a snoozing ken, and shook him of his dummee and thimble; the girl inveigled the gentleman into a brothel and robbed him of his pocket book and watch.

Blower. A pipe. How the swell funks his blower and lushes red tape: what a smoke the gentleman makes with his pipe, and drinks brandy.

To Blow the Grounsils. To lie with a woman on the floor. *Cant.*

To Blow the Gab. To confess, or impeach a confederate. *Cant.*

Blow-up. A discovery, or the confusion occasioned by one.

A Blowse, or Blowsabella. A woman whose hair is dishevelled, and hanging about her face; a slattern.

Blubber. The mouth.—I have stopped the cull's blubber: I have stopped the fellow's mouth, meant either by gagging or murdering him.

To Blubber. To cry.

To sport Blubber. Said of a large coarse woman, who exposes her bosom.

Blubber Cheeks. Large flaccid cheeks, hanging like the fat or blubber of a whale.

Blue. To look blue; to be confounded, terrified, or disappointed. Blue as a razor; perhaps, blue as azure.

Blue Boar. A venereal bubo.

Blue Devils. Low spirits.

Blue Flag. He has hoisted the blue flag; he has commenced publican, or taken a public house, an allusion to the blue aprons worn by publicans. See Admiral of the Blue.

Blue Pigeons. Thieves who steal lead off houses and churches. *Cant.* To fly a blue pigeon; to steal lead off houses or churches.

Blue Plumb. A bullet.—Surfeited with a blue plumb; wounded with a bullet. A sortment of George R—'s blue plumbs: a volley of ball, shot from soldiers' firelocks.

Blue Skin. A person begotten on a black woman by a white man. One of the blue squadron; any one having a cross of the black breed, or, as it is termed, a lick of the tar brush.

Blue Tape, or **Sky Blue**. Gin.

Blue Ruin. Gin. Blue ribband; gin.

Bluff. Fierce, surly. He looked as bluff as bull beef.

Bluffer. An inn-keeper. *Cant.*

Blunderbuss. A short gun, with a wide bore, for carrying slugs; also a stupid, blundering fellow.

Blunt. Money. *Cant.*

To Bluster. To talk big, to hector or bully.

Boarding School. Bridewell, Newgate, or any other prison, or house of correction.

Bob. A shoplifter's assistant, or one that receives and carries off stolen goods. All is bob; all is safe. *Cant.*

Bob. A shilling.

Bobbed. Cheated, tricked, disappointed.

Bobbish. Smart, clever, spruce.

Bob stay. A rope which holds the bowsprit to the stem or cutwater. Figuratively, the frenum of a man's yard.

Bob Tail. A lewd woman, or one that plays with her tail; also an impotent man, or an eunuch. Tag, rag, and bob-tail; a mob of all sorts of low people, To shift one's bob; to move off, or go away. To bear a bob; to join in chorus with any singers. Also a term used by the sellers of game, for a partridge.

Body Snatchers. Bum bailiffs.

Body of Divinity bound in Black Calf. A parson.

Bog Lander. An Irishman; Ireland being famous for its large bogs, which furnish the chief fuel in many parts of that kingdom.

Bog Trotter. The same.

Bog House. The necessary house. To go to bog; to go to stool.

Bog Latin. Barbarous Latin. *Irish.*—See **Dog Latin**, and **Apothecaries Latin**.

Bogy. Ask bogy, i. e. ask mine a-se. *Sea wit.*

Boh. Said to be the name of a Danish general, who so terrified his opponent Foh, that he caused him to bewray himself. Whence, when we smell a stink, it is custoto exclaim, Foh! i. e. I smell general Foh. He cannot say Boh to a goose; i. e. he is a cowardly or sheepish fellow. There is a story related of the celebrated Ben Jonson, who always dressed very plain; that being introduced to the presence of a nobleman, the peer, struck by his homely appearance and awkward manner, exclaimed, as if in doubt, "you Ben Johnson! why you look as if you could not say Boh to a goose!" "Boh!" replied the wit.

Bold. Bold as a miller's shirt, which every day takes a rogue by the collar.

Bolt. A blunt arrow.

Bolt Upright. As erect, or straight up, as an arrow set on its end.

To Bolt. To run suddenly out of one's house, or hiding place, through fear; a term borrowed from a rabbit-warren, where the rabbits are made to bolt, by sending ferrets into their burrows: we set the house on fire, and made him bolt. To bolt, also means to swallow meat without chewing: the farmer's servants in Kent are famous for bolting large quantities of pickled pork.

Bones. Dice.

Bone Box. The mouth. Shut your bone box; shut your mouth.

Bone Picker. A footman.

Boned. Seized, apprehended, taken up by a constable. *Cant.*

Bolus. A nick name for an apothecary.

Bone Setter. A hard-trotting horse.

Booby, or Dog Booby. An awkward lout, clodhopper, or country fellow. See Clodhopper and Lout. A bitch booby; a country wench.

Booby Hutch. A one-horse chaise, noddy, buggy, or leathern bottle.

Books. Cards to play with. To plant the books; to place the cards in the pack in an unfair manner.

Book-keeper. One who never returns borrowed books. Out of one's books; out of one's favor. Out of his books; out of debt.

Boot Catcher. The servant at an inn whose business it is to clean the boots of the guest.

Boots. The youngest officer in a regimental mess, whose duty it is to skink, that is, to stir the fire, snuff the candles, and ring the bell. See Skink.---To ride in any one's old boots; to marry or keep his cast-off mistress.

Booty. To play booty; cheating play, where the player purposely avoids winning.

Bo-peep. One who sometimes hides himself, and sometimes appears publicly abroad, is said to play at bo-peep. Also one who lies perdue, or on the watch.

Borachio. A skin for holding wine, commonly a goat's; also a nick name for a drunkard.

Borde. A shilling. A half borde; a sixpence.

Bordello. A bawdy house.

Bore. A tedious, troublesome man or woman, one who bores the ears of his hearers with an uninteresting tale; a term much in fashion about the years 1780 and 1781.

Born under a Threepenny Halfpenny Planet,

NEVER TO BE WORTH A GROAT. Said of any person remarkably unsuccessful in his attempts or profession.

BOTCH. A nick name for a taylor.

BOTHERED or BOTH-EARED. Talked to at both ears by different persons at the same time, confounded, confused. *Irish phrase.*

BOTHERAMS. A convivial society.

BOTTLE-HEADED. Void of wit.

BOTTOM. A polite term for the posteriors. Also, in the sporting sense, strength and spirits to support fatigue; as a bottomed horse. Among bruisers it is used to express a hardy fellow, who will bear a good beating.

BOTTOMLESS PIT. The monosyllable.

BOUGHS. Wide in the boughs, with large hips and posteriors.

BOUGHS. He is up in the boughs; he is in a passion.

TO BOUNCE. To brag or hector; also to tell an improbable story. To bully a man out of any thing. The kiddey bounced the swell of the blowen; the lad bullied the gentleman out of the girl.

BOUNCER. A large man or woman; also a great lie.

BOUNCING CHEAT. A bottle; from the explosion in drawing the cork. *Cant.*

BOUNG. A purse. *Cant.*

BOUNG NIPPER. A cut purse. *Cant.*—Formerly purses were worn at the girdle, from whence they were cut.

BOOSE, or BOUSE. Drink.

BOOSEY. Drunk.

BOWSING KEN. An ale-house or gin-shop.

BOWSPRIT. The nose, from its being the most projecting part of the human face, as the bowsprit is of a ship.

BOW-WOW. The childish name for a dog; also a jeering appellation for a man born at Boston in America.

BOW-WOW MUTTON. Dog's flesh.

BOW-WOW SHOP. A salesman's shop in Monmouth-street; so called because the servant barks, and the master bites. See BARKER.

BOWYER. One that draws a long bow, a dealer in the marvellous, a teller of improbable stories, a liar: perhaps from the wonderful shots frequently boasted of by archers.

TO BOX THE COMPASS. To say or repeat the mariner's compass, not only backwards or forwards, but also to be able to answer any and all questions respecting its divisions. *Sea term.*

TO BOX THE JESUIT, AND GET COCK ROACHES. A sea term for masturbation; a crime, it is said, much practised by the reverend fathers of that society.

BRACE. The Brace tavern; a room in the S. E. corner of the King's

King's Bench, where, for the convenience of prisoners residing thereabouts, beer purchased at the tap-house was retailed at a halfpenny per pot advance. It was kept by two brothers of the name of Partridge, and thence called the *Brace.*

BRACKET-FACED. Ugly, hard-featured.

BRAGGET. Mead and ale sweetened with honey.

BRAGGADOCIA. A vain-glorious fellow, a boaster.

BRAINS. If you had as much brains as guts, what a clever fellow you would be! a saying to a stupid fat fellow. To have some guts in his brains; to know something.

BRAN-FACED. Freckled. He was christened by a baker, he carries the bran in his face.

BRANDY-FACED. Red-faced, as if from drinking brandy.

BRANDY. Brandy is Latin for a goose; a memento to prevent the animal from rising in the stomach by a glass of the good creature.

BRAT. A child or infant.

BRAY. A vicar of Bray; one who frequently changes his principles, always siding with the strongest party: an allusion to a vicar of Bray, in Berkshire, commemorated in a well-known ballad for the pliability of his conscience.

BRAZEN-FACED. Bold-faced, shameless, impudent.

BREAD AND BUTTER FASHION. One slice upon the other. John and his maid were caught lying bread and butter fashion.—To quarrel with one's bread and butter; to act contrary to one's interest. To know on which side one's bread is buttered; to know one's interest, or what is best for one. It is no bread and butter of mine; I have no business with it; or rather, I won't intermeddle, because I shall get nothing by it.

BREAK-TEETH WORDS. Hard words, difficult to pronounce.

BREAKING SHINS. Borrowing money; perhaps from the figurative operation being, like the real one, extremely disagreeable to the patient.

BREAD. Employment. Out of bread; out of employment. In bad bread; in a disagreeable scrape, or situation.

BREAD BASKET. The stomach; a term used by boxers. I took him a punch in his bread basket; i. e. I gave him a blow in the stomach.

BREAST FLEET. He or she belongs to the breast fleet; i.e. is a Roman catholic; an appellation derived from their custom of beating their breasts in the confession of their sins.

BREECHED. Money in the pocket: the swell is well breeched, let's draw him; the gentleman has plenty of money in his pocket, let us rob him.

BREECHES. To wear the breeches; a woman who governs her husband is said to wear the breeches.

BREECHES BIBLE. An edition of the Bible printed in 1598, wherein it is said that Adam and Eve sewed fig-leaves together, and made themselves breeches.

BREEZE. To raise a breeze; to kick up a dust or breed a disturbance.

BRIDGE. To make a bridge of any one's nose; to push the bottle past him, so as to deprive him of his turn of filling his glass; to pass one over. Also to play booty, or purposely to avoid winning.

BRIM. (Abbreviation of Brimstone.) An abandoned woman; perhaps originally only a passionate or irascible woman, compared to brimstone for its inflammability.

BRISKET BEATER. A Roman catholic. See BREAST FLEET, and CRAW THUMPER.

BRISTOL MILK. A Spanish wine called sherry, much drunk at that place, particularly in the morning.

BRISTOL MAN. The son of an Irish thief and a Welch whore.

BRITISH CHAMPAIGNE. Porter.

BROGANIER. One who has a strong Irish pronunciation or accent.

BROGUE. A particular kind of shoe without a heel, worn in Ireland, and figuratively used to signify the Irish accent.

BROTHER OF THE
- BLADE. A soldier.
- BUSKIN. A player.
- BUNG. A brewer.
- COIF. A serjeant at law.
- GUSSET. A pimp.
- QUILL. An author.
- STRING. A fiddler.
- WHIP. A coachman.

BROTHER STARLING. One who lies with the same woman, that is, builds in the same nest.

BROUGHTONIAN. A boxer: a disciple of Broughton, who was a beef-eater, and once the best boxer of his day.

BROWN BESS. A soldier's firelock. To hug brown Bess; to carry a firelock, or serve as a private soldier.

BROWN GEORGE. An ammunition loaf. A wig without powder; similar to the undress wig worn by his majesty.

BROWN MADAM, or MISS BROWN. The monosyllable.

BROWN STUDY. Said of one absent, in a reverie, or thoughtful.

BRUISER. A boxer; one skilled in the art of boxing; also an inferior workman among chasers.

Brewes, or Browes. The fat scum from the pot in which salted beef is boiled.

To Brush. To run away. Let us buy a brush and lope; let us go away or off. To have a brush with a woman; to lie with her. To have a brush with a man; to fight with him. The cove cracked the peter and bought a brush; the fellow broke open the trunk, and then ran away.

Brusher. A bumper, a full glass. See Bumper.

Bub. Strong beer.

Bubber. A drinking bowl; also a great drinker; a thief that steals plate from public houses. *Cant.*

The Bubble. The party cheated, perhaps from his being like an air bubble, filled with words, which are only wind, instead of real property.

To Bubble. To cheat.

To Bar the Bubble. To except against the general rule, that he who lays the odds must always be adjudged the loser: this is restricted to betts laid for liquor.

Bubbly Jock. A turkey cock. *Scotch.*

Bubble and Squeak. Beef and cabbage fried together. It is so called from its bubbling up and squeaking whilst over the fire.

Bube. The venereal disease.

Buck. A blind horse; also a gay debauchee.

To run a Buck. To poll a bad vote at an election.—*Irish term.*

Buck Bail. Bail given by a sharper for one of the gang.

A Buck of the first Head. One who in debauchery surpasses the rest of his companions, a blood or choice spirit. There are in London divers lodges or societies of Bucks, formed in imitation of the Free Masons: one was held at the Rose, in Monkwell-street, about the year 1705. The president is styled the Grand Buck. A buck sometimes signifies a cuckold.

Buck's Face. A cuckold.

Buck Fitch. A lecherous old fellow.

Buckeen. A bully. *Irish.*

Bucket. To kick the bucket; to die.

Buckinger's Boot. The monosyllable. Matthew Buckinger was born without hands and legs; notwithstanding which he drew coats of arms very neatly, and could write the Lord's Prayer within the compass of a shilling; he was married to a tall handsome woman, and traversed the country, shewing himself for money.

Buckles. Fetters.

Budge, or Sneaking Budge. One that slips into houses in

in the dark, to steal cloaks or other clothes. Also lambs' fur formerly used for doctors' robes, whence they were called budge doctors. Standing budge; a thief's scout or spy.

To **Budge**. To move, or quit one's station. Don't budge from hence; i. e. don't move from hence, stay here.

Budget. A wallet. To open the budget; a term used to signify the notification of the taxes required by the minister for the expences of the ensuing year; as To-morrow the minister will go to the house, and open the budget.

Bufe. A dog. Bufe's nob; a dog's head. *Cant.*

Bufe Nabber. A dog stealer. *Cant.*

Buff. All in buff; stript to the skin, stark naked.

Buff. To stand buff; to stand the brunt. To swear as a witness. He buffed it home; and I was served; he swore hard against me, and I was found guilty.

Buffer. One that steals and kills horses and dogs for their skins; also an inn-keeper: in Ireland it signifies a boxer.

Buffer. A man who takes an oath: generally applied to Jew bail.

Buffle-headed. Confused, stupid.

Bug. A nick name given by the Irish to Englishmen; bugs having, as it is said, been introduced into Ireland by the English.

To **Bug**. A cant word among journeymen hatters, signifying the exchanging some of the dearest materials of which a hat is made for others of less value. Hats are composed of the furs and wool of divers animals among which is a small portion of beavers' fur. Bugging, is stealing the beaver, and substituting in lieu thereof an equal weight of some cheaper ingredient.—Bailiffs who take money to postpone or refrain the serving of a writ, are said to bug the writ.

Bug-Hunter. An upholsterer.

Bugaboe. A scare-babe, or bully-beggar.

Bugaroch. Comely, handsome. *Irish.*

Buggy. A one-horse chaise.

Bugger. A blackguard, a rascal, a term of reproach. Mill the bloody bugger; beat the damned rascal.

Bulk and File. Two pickpockets; the bulk jostles the party to be robbed, and the file does the business.

Bulker. One who lodges all night on a bulk or projection before old-fashioned shop windows.

Bull. An Exchange Alley term for one who buys stock on

on speculation for time, i. e. agrees with the seller, called a Bear, to take a certainsum of stock at a future day, at a stated price: if at that day stock fetches more than the price agreed on, he receives the difference; if it falls or is cheaper, he either pays it, or becomes a lame duck, and waddles out of the Alley. See LAME DUCK and BEAR.

BULL. A blunder; from one Obadiah Bull, a blundering lawyer of London, who lived in the reign of Henery VII.: by a bull, is now always meant a blunder made by an Irishman. A bull was also the name of false hair formerly much worn by women. To look like bull beef, or as bluff as bull beef; to look fierce or surly. Town bull, a great whore-master.

BULL. A crown piece. A half bull; half a crown.

BULL BEGGAR, or BULLY BEGGAR. An imaginary being with which children are threatened by servants and nurses, like raw head and bloody bones.

BULL CALF. A great hulkey or clumsy fellow. See HULKEY.

BULL CHIN. A fat chubby child.

BULL DOGS. Pistols.

BULL HANKERS. Persons who over-drive bulls, or frequent bull baits.

BULL'S EYE. A crown-piece.

BULL'S FEATHER. A horn: he wears the bull's feather; he is a cuckold.

TO BULLOCK. To hector, bounce, or bully.

BULLY. A cowardly fellow, who gives himself airs of great bravery. A bully huff cap; a hector. See HECTOR.

BULLY BACK. A bully to a bawdy-house; one who is kept in pay, to oblige the frequenters of the house to submit to the impositions of the mother abbess, or bawd; and who also sometimes pretends to be the husband of one of the ladies, and under that pretence extorts money from greenhorns, or ignorant young men, whom he finds with her. See GREENHORN.

BULLY COCK. One who foments quarrels in order to rob the persons quarrelling.

BULLY RUFFIANS. Highwaymen who attack passengers with oaths and imprecations.

BULLY TRAP. A brave man with a mild or effeminate appearance, by whom bullies are frequently taken in.

BUM. the breech, or backside.

TO BUM. To arrest a debtor. The gill bummed the swell for a thimble; the tradesman arrested the gentleman for a watch.

BUM TRAP. A sheriff's officer who arrests debtors.

Ware

Ware hawke! the bum traps are fly to our panney; keep a good look out, the bailiffs know where our house is situated.

Bum Bailiff. A sheriff's officer, who arrests debtors; so called perhaps from following his prey, and being at their bums, or, as the vulgar phrase is, hard at their a-ses. Blackstone says, it is a corruption of bound bailiff, from their being obliged to give bond for their good behaviour.

Bum Brusher. A schoolmaster.

Bum Boat. A boat attending ships to retail greens, drams, &c. commonly rowed by a woman; a kind of floating chandler's shop.

Bum Fodder. Soft paper for the necessary house or torchecul.

Bumfiddle. The backside, the breech. See Ars Musica.

Bumbo. Brandy, water, and sugar; also the negro name for the private parts of a woman.

Bumkin. A raw country fellow.

Bummed. Arrested.

Bumper. A full glass; in all likelihood from its convexity or bump at the top: some derive it from a full glass formerly drunk to the health of the pope—*au bon pere.*

Bumping. A ceremony performed on boys perambulating the bounds of the parish on Whit-monday, when they have their posteriors bumped against the stones marking the boundaries, in order to fix them in their memory.

Bun. A common name for a rabbit, also for the monosyllable. To touch bun for luck; a practice observed among sailors going on a cruize.

Bundling. A man and woman sleeping in the same bed, he with his small clothes, and she with her petticoats on; an expedient practised in America on a scarcity of beds, where, on such an occasion, husbands and parents frequently permitted travellers to bundle with their wives and daughters. This custom is now abolished. See Duke of Rochefoucalt's Travels in America.

Bung upwards. Said of a person lying on his face.

Bung your eye. Drink a dram; strictly speaking, to drink till one's eye is bunged up or closed.

Bunt. An apron.

Bunter. A low dirty prostitute, half whore and half beggar.

Buntlings. Petticoats. *Cant.*

Burn Crust. A jocular name for a baker.

Burn the Ken. Strollers living in an alehouse without paying their quarters, are said to burn the ken. *Cant.*

Burning Shame. A lighted candle stuck into the parts of a woman, certainly not intended by nature for a candlestick.

Burner. A clap. The blowen tipped the swell a burner; the girl gave the gentleman a clap.

Burner. He is no burner of navigable rivers; i. e. he is no conjuror, or man of extraordinary abilities; or rather, he is but a simple fellow. See Thames.

Burnt. Poxed or clapped. He was sent out a sacrifice, and came home a burnt offering; a saying of seamen who have caught the venereal disease abroad. He has burnt his fingers; he has suffered by meddling.

Burr. A hanger on, or dependant; an allusion to the field burrs, which are not easily got rid of. Also the Northumbrian pronunciation: the people of that country, but chiefly about Newcastle and Morpeth, are said to have a burr in their throats, particularly called the Newcastle burr.

Bushel Bubby. A full breasted woman.

Busk. A piece of whalebone or ivory, formerly worn by women, to stiffen the fore part of their stays: hence the toast—Both ends of the busk.

Buss Beggar. An old superannuated fumbler, whom none but beggars will suffer to kiss them.

Bus-napper. A constable. *Cant.*

Bus-napper's Kenchin. A watchman. *Cant.*

Busy. As busy as the devil in a high wind; as busy as a hen with one chick.

Butcher's Dog. To be like a butcher's dog, i. e. lie by the beef without touching it; a simile often applicable to married men.

Butcher's Horse. That must have been a butcher's horse, by his carrying a calf so well; a vulgar joke on an awkward rider.

Butt. A dependant, poor relation, or simpleton, on whom all kinds of practical jokes are played off; and who serves as a butt for all the shafts of wit and ridicule.

Butter Box. A Dutchman, from the great quantity of butter eaten by the people of that country.

Buttered Bun. One lying with a woman that has just lain with another man, is said to have a buttered bun.

Butter and Eggs Trot. A kind of short jogg trot, such as is used by women going to market, with butter and eggs.—She looks as if butter would not melt in her mouth, yet I warrant you cheese would not choak her; a saying of a demure looking woman, of suspected character. Don't make butter dear; a gird at the patient angler.

Buttock. A whore. *Cant.*

Buttock Broker. A bawd, or match-maker. *Cant.*

But-

BUTTOCK BALL. The amorous congress. *Cant.*

BUTTOCK AND FILE. A common whore and a pickpocket. *Cant.*

BUTTOCK AND TWANG, or DOWN BUTTOCK AND SHAM FILE. A common whore, but no pickpocket.

BUTTOCK AND TONGUE. A scolding wife.

BUTTOCKING SHOP. A brothel.

BUTTON. A bad shilling, among coiners. His a-se makes buttons; he is ready to bewray himself through fear. *Cant.*

BUZMAN. A pickpocket. *Cant.*

BUZZARD. A simple fellow. A blind buzzard: a purblind man or woman.

BYE BLOW. A bastard.

CAB

CABBAGE. Cloth, stuff, or silk purloined by taylors from their employers, which they deposit in a place called *hell*, or their *eye*: from the first, when taxed, with their knavery, they equivocally swear, that if they have taken any, they wish they may find it in *hell*; or, alluding to the second, protest, that what they have over and above is not more than they could put in their *eye*.—When the scrotum is relaxed or whiffled, it is said they will not cabbage.

CAB. A brothel. Mother: how many tails have you in your cab? how many girls have you in your bawdy house?

CACAFEUGO. A sh-te-fire, a furious braggadocio or bully huff.

CACKLE. To blab, or discover secrets. The cull is leaky, and cackles; the rogue tells all. *Cant.* See LEAKY.

CACKLER. A hen.

CACKLER'S KEN. A hen roost. *Cant.*

CACKLING CHEATS. Fowls. *Cant.*

CACKLING FARTS. Eggs. *Cant.*

CADDEE. A helper. An under-strapper.

CADGE. To beg. Cadge the swells; beg of the gentlemen.

CAFFAN. Cheese. *Cant.*

CAGG. To cagg; a military term used by the private soldiers, signifying a solemn vow or resolution not to get drunk for a certain time; or, as the term is, till their cagg is out: which vow is commonly observed with the strictest

est exactness. Ex. I have cagg'd myself for six months. Excuse me this time, and I will cagg myself for a year. This term is also used in the same sense among the common people of Scotland, where it is performed with divers ceremonies.

CAG. To be cagged. To be sulky or out of humour. The cove carries the cag; the man is vexed or sullen.

CAG MAGG. Bits and scraps of provisions. Bad meat.

CAGG MAGGS. Old Lincolnshire geese, which having been plucked ten or twelve years, are sent up to London to feast the cockneys.

CAKE, or CAKEY. A foolish fellow.

CALF-SKIN FIDDLE. A drum. To smack calf's skin; to kiss the book in taking an oath. It is held by the St. Giles's casuists, that by kissing one's thumb instead of smacking calf's skin, the guilt of taking a false oath is avoided.

CALVES. His calves are gone to grass; a saying of a man with slender legs without calves. Veal will be cheap, calves fall; said of a man whose calves fall away.

CALVES HEAD CLUB. A club instituted by the Independents and Presbyterians, to commemorate the decapitation of King Charles I. Their chief fare was calves heads; and they drank their wine and ale out of calves skulls.

CALIBOGUS. Rum and spruce beer, American beverage.

CALLE. A cloak or gown. *Cant.*

CAMBRIDGE FORTUNE. A wind-mill and a water-mill, used to signify a woman without any but personal endowments.

CAMBRIDGE OAK. A willow.

CAMBRADE. A chamber fellow; a Spanish military term. Soldiers were in that country divided into chambers, five men making a chamber, whence it was generally used to signify companion.

CAMESA. A shirt or shift. *Cant. Spanish.*

CAMP CANDLESTICK. A bottle, or soldier's bayonet.

CAMPBELL'S ACADEMY. The hulks or lighters, on board of which felons are condemned to hard labour. Mr. Campbell was the first director of them. See ACADEMY and FLOATING ACADEMY.

CANARY BIRD. A jail bird, a person used to be kept in a cage; also, in the canting sense, guineas.

CANDLESTICKS. Bad, small, or untunable bells. Hark! how the candlesticks rattle.

CANDY. Drunk. *Irish.*

Cane. To lay Cane upon Abel; to beat any one with a cane or stick.

Cank. Dumb.

Cannister. The head. To mill his cannister; to break his head.

Canniken. A small can: also, in the canting sense, the plague.

Cant. An hypocrite, a double-tongue palavering fellow. See Palaver.

Cant. To cant; to toss or throw: as, Cant a slug into your bread room; drink a dram. *Sea wit.*

Canticle. A parish clerk.

Canting. Preaching with a whining, affected tone, perhaps a corruption of chaunting; some derive it from Andrew Cant, a famous Scotch preacher, who used that whining manner of expression. Also a kind of gibberish used by thieves and gypsies, called likewise pedlar's French, the slang, &c. &c.

Canters, or The Canting Crew. Thieves, beggars, and gypsies, or any others using the canting lingo. See Lingo.

Canterbury Story. A long roundabout tale.

To Cap. To take one's oath. I will cap downright; I will swear home. *Cant.*

To Cap. To take off one's hat or cap. To cap the quadrangle; a lesson of humility, or rather servility, taught undergraduates at the university, where they are obliged to cross the area of the college cap in hand, in reverence to the fellows who sometimes walk there. The same ceremony is observed on coming on the quarter deck of ships of war, although no officer should be on it.

To Cap. To support another's assertion or tale. To assist a man in cheating. The file kidded the joskin with sham books, and his pall capped; the deep one cheated the countryman with false cards, and his confederate assisted in the fraud.

Cap Acquaintance. Persons slightly acquainted, or only so far as mutually to salute with the hat on meeting. A woman who endeavours to attract the notice of any particular man, is said to set her cap at him.

Caper Merchant. A dancing master, or hop merchant; marchand des capriolles. *French term.*—To cut papers; to leap or jump in dancing. See Hop Merchant.

Capping Verses. Repeating Latin Verses in turn, beginning with the letter with which the last speaker left off.

Capon. A castrated cock, also an eunuch.

Capricornified. Cuckolded, hornified.

Capsize. To overturn or reverse. He took his broth till he capsized; he drank till he fell out of his chair. *Sea term.*

Captain. Led captain; an humble dependant in a great family, who for a precarious subsistence, and distant hopes of preferment, suffers every kind of indignity, and is the butt of every species of joke or ill-humour. The small provision made for officers of the army and navy in time of peace, obliges many in both services to occupy this wretched station. The idea of the appellation is taken from a led horse, many of which for magnificence appear in the retinues of great personages on solemn occasions, such as processions, &c.

Captain Copperthorne's Crew. All officers; a saying of a company where every one strives to rule.

Captain Lieutenant. Meat between veal and beef, the flesh of an old calf; a military simile, drawn from the officer of that denomination, who has only the pay of a lieutenant, with the rank of captain; and so is not entirely one or the other, but between both.

Captain Podd. A celebrated master of a puppet-shew, in Ben Johnson's time, whose name became a common one to signify any of that fraternity.

Captain Queernabs. A shabby ill-dressed fellow.

Captain Sharp. A cheating bully, or one in a set of gamblers, whose office is to bully any pigeon, who, suspecting roguery, refuses to pay what he has lost. *Cant.*

Captain Tom. The leader of a mob; also the mob itself.

Caravan. A large sum of money; also, a person cheated of such sum. *Cant.*

Carbuncle Face. A red face, full of pimples.

Cardinal. A cloak in fashion about the year 1760.

To Carouse. To drink freely or deep: from the German word expressing *all out.*

Carriers. A set of rogues who are employed to look out and watch upon the roads, at inns, &c. in order to carry information to their respective gangs, of a booty in prospect.

Carriers. Pigeons which carry expresses.

Carrion Hunter. An undertaker; called also a cold cook, and death hunter. See Cold Cook and Death Hunter.

Carrots. Red hair.

Carrotty-pated. Ginger-hackled, red-haired. See Ginger-hackled.

Carry Witchet. A sort of conundrum, puzzlewit, or riddle.

Cart.

Cart. To put the cart before the horse; to mention the last part of a story first. To be flogged at the cart's a-se or tail; persons guilty of petty larceny are frequently sentenced to be tied to the tail of a cart, and whipped by the common executioner, for a certain distance: the degree of severity in the execution is left to the discretion of the executioner, who, it is said, has cats of nine tails of all prices.

Carting. The punishment formerly inflicted on bawds, who were placed in a tumbrel or cart, and led through a town, that their persons might be known.

Carvel's Ring. The private parts of a woman. Ham Carvel, a jealous old doctor, being in bed with his wife, dreamed that the Devil gave him a ring, which, so long as he had it on his finger, would prevent his being made a cuckold: waking he found he had got his finger the Lord knows where. See Rabelais, and Prior's versification of the story.

To Cascade. To vomit.

Case. A house; perhaps from the Italian *casa.* In the canting lingo it meant store or ware house, as well as a dwelling house. Tout that case; mark or observe that house. It is all bob, now let's dub the gig of the case; now the coast is clear, let us break open the door of the house.

Case Vrow. A prostitute attached to a particular bawdy house.

Cash, or Caffan. Cheese. *Cant.* See Caffan.

Caster. A cloak. *Cant.*

Castor. A hat. To prig a castor; to steal a hat.

Casting up one's Accounts. Vomiting.

Cat. A common prostitute. An old cat; a cross old woman.

Cat-Heads. A woman's breasts. *Sea phrase.*

To Cat, or Shoot the Cat. To vomit from drunkenness.

Cat and Bagpipean Society. A society which met at their office in the great western road: in their summons, published in the daily papers, it was added, that the kittens might come with the old cats without being scratched.

Cat Call. A kind of whistle, chiefly used at theatres, to interrupt the actors, and damn a new piece. It derives its name from one of its sounds, which greatly resembles the modulation of an intriguing boar cat.

Cat harping Fashion. Drinking cross-ways, and not, as usual, over the left thumb. *Sea term.*

Cat in Pan. To turn cat in pan, to change sides or parties; supposed originally to have been to turn *cate* or *cake* in pan.

Cat's Foot. To live under the cat's foot; to be under the dominion of a wife hen-pecked. To live like dog and cat; spoken of married persons who live unhappily together. As many lives as a cat; cats, according to vulgar naturalists, have nine lives, that is one less than a woman. No more chance than a cat in hell without claws; said of one who enters into a dispute or quarrel with one greatly above his match.

Cat Lap. Tea, called also scandal broth. See Scandal Broth.

Cat Match. When a rook or cully is engaged amongst bad bowlers.

Cat of nine Tails. A scourge composed of nine strings of whip-cord, each string having nine knots.

Cat's Paw. To be made a cat's paw of; to be made a tool or instrument to accomplish the purpose of another: an allusion to the story of a monkey, who made use of a cat's paw to scratch a roasted chesnut out of the fire.

Cat's Sleep. Counterfeit sleep: cats often counterfeiting sleep, to decoy their prey near them, and then suddenly spring on them.

Cat Sticks. Thin legs, compared to sticks with which boys play at cat. See Trapsticks.

Cat whipping, or Whipping the cat. A trick often practised on ignorant country fellows, vain of their strength, by laying a wager with them that they may be pulled through a pond by a cat. The bet being made, a rope is fixed round the waist of the party to be catted, and the end thrown across the pond, to which the cat is also fastened by a packthread, and three or four sturdy fellows are appointed to lead and whip the cat; these on a signal given, seize the end of the cord, and pretending to whip the cat, haul the astonished booby through the water. ---To whip the cat, is also a term among tailors for working jobs at private houses, as practised in the country.

Catamaran. An old scraggy woman; from a kind of float made of spars and yards lashed together, for saving shipwrecked persons.

Catch Club. A member of the catch club; a bum bailiff.

Catch Fart. A footboy; so called from such servants commonly following close behind their master or mistress.

Catch Penny. Any temporary contrivance to raise a contribution on the public.

Catch Pole. A bum bailiff, or sheriff's officer.

Catching Harvest. A dangerous time for a robbery, when many persons are on the road, on account of a horse-race, fair, or some other public meeting.

Cater Cousins. Good friends. He and I are not cater cousins,

cousins, i. e. we are not even cousins in the fourth degree, or four times removed; that is, we have not the least friendly connexion.

Caterpillar. A nick name for a soldier. In the year 1745, a soldier quartered at a house near Derby, was desired by his landlord to call upon him, whenever he came that way; for, added he, soldiers are the pillars of the nation. The rebellion being finished, it happened the same regiment was quartered in Derbyshire, when the soldier resolved to accept of his landlord's invitation, and accordingly obtained leave to go to him: but, on his arrival, he was greatly surprised to find a very cold reception; whereupon expostulating with his landlord, he reminded him of his invitation, and the circumstance of his having said, soldiers were the pillars of the nation. If I did, answered the host, I meant *cater*pillars.

Caterwauling. Going out in the night in search of intrigues, like a cat in the gutters.

Cathedral. Old-fashioned. An old cathedral-bedstead, chair, &c.

Cattle. Sad cattle: whores or gypsies. Black cattle, bugs. *Cant.*

Cavaulting School. A Bawdy-house.

Caudge-Pawed. Left-handed.

Cauliflower. A large white wig, such as is commonly worn by the dignified clergy, and was formerly by physicians. Also the private parts of a woman; the reason for which appellation is given in the following story: A woman, who was giving evidence in a cause wherein it was necessary to express those parts, made use of the term cauliflower; for which the judge on the bench, a peevish old fellow, reproved her, saying she might as well call it artichoke. Not so, my lord, replied she; for an artichoke has a bottom, but a **** and a cauliflower have none.

Cautions. The four cautions: I. Beware of a woman before.---II. Beware of a horse behind.---III. Beware of a cart side-ways.---IV. Beware of a priest every way.

Caw-handed, or caw-pawed. Awkward, not dextrous, ready, or nimble.

Caxon. An old weather-beaten wig.

Cent per Cent. An usurer.

Chafed. Well beaten; from *chauffé*, warmed.

Chalkers. Men of wit, in Ireland, who in the night amuse themselves with cutting inoffensive passengers across the face with a knife. They are somewhat like those facetious gentlemen some time ago known in England by the title of Sweaters and Mohocks.

Chalking. The amusement above described.

Chap. A fellow. An odd chap; A strange fellow.

Chaperon. The cicisbeo, or gentleman usher to a lady: from the French.

Chapt. Dry or thirsty.

Charactered, or Lettered. Burnt in the hand. They have palmed the character upon him; they have burned him in the hand. *Cant.*---See Lettered.

Charm. A picklock. *Cant.*

Charren. The smoke of Charren.--His eyes water from the smoke of Charren; a man of that place coming out of his house weeping, because his wife had beat him, told his neighbours the smoke had made his eyes water.

Chatter Box. One whose tongue runs twelve score to the dozen, a chattering man or woman.

Chatter Broth. Tea. See Cat Lap and Scandal Broth.

Chatts. Lice: perhaps an abbreviation of chattels, lice being the chief live stock or chattels of beggars, gypsies, and the rest of the canting crew. *Cant.*—Also, according to the canting academy, the gallows.

Chates. The gallows. *Cant.*

Chaunter Culls. Grub-street writers, who compose songs, carrols, &c. for ballad-singers. *Cant.*

Chaunt. A song.

To Chaunt. To sing. To publish an account in the newspapers. The kiddey was chaunted for a toby; his examination concerning a highway robbery was published in the papers.

Chaw Bacon. A countryman. A stupid fellow.

Cheapside. He came at it by way of Cheapside; he gave little or nothing for it, he bought it cheap.

Cheats. Sham sleeves to put over a dirty shift or shirt. See Shams.

Cheek by Jowl. Side by side, hand to fist.

Cheeks. Ask cheeks near cunnyborough; the repartee of a St. Gilse's fair one, who bids you ask her backside, *anglicè* her a-se. A like answer is current in France: any one asking the road or distance to Macon, a city near Lyons, would be answered by a French lady of easy virtue, 'Mettez votre nez dans mon cul, & vous serrez dans les Fauxbourgs.'

Cheese-toaster. A sword.

Cheese it. Be silent, be quiet, don't do it. Cheese it, the coves are fly; be silent, the people understand our discourse.

Cheeser. A strong smelling fart.

Chelsea. A village near London, famous for the military hospital. To get Chelsea; to obtain the benefit of that hospital.

pital. Dead Chelsea, by G-d! an exclamation uttered by a grenadier at Fontenoy, on having his leg carried away by a cannon-ball.

CHEST OF TOOLS. A shoe-black's brush and wig, &c. *Irish.*

CHERRY-COLOURED CAT. A black cat, there being black cherries as well as red.

CHERUBIMS. Peevish children, because cherubims and seraphims continually do cry.

CHESHIRE CAT. He grins like a Cheshire cat; said of any one who shews his teeth and gums in laughing.

CHICK-A-BIDDY. A chicken, so called to and by little children.

CHICKEN-BREASTED. Said of a woman with scarce any breasts.

CHICKEN BUTCHER. A poulterer.

CHICKEN-HAMMED. Persons whose legs and thighs are bent or archward outwards.

CHICKEN-HEARTED. Fearful, cowardly.

CHICKEN NABOB. One returned from the East Indies with but a moderate fortune of fifty or sixty thousand pounds, a diminutive nabob: a term borrowed from the chicken turtle.

CHILD. To eat a child; to partake of a treat given to the parish officers, in part of commutation for a bastard child: the common price was formerly ten pounds and a greasy chin. See GREASY CHIN.

CHIMNEY CHOPS. An abusive appellation for a negro.

CHINK. Money.

CHIP. A child. A chip of the old block; a child who either in person or sentiments resembles its father or mother.

CHIP. A brother chip; a person of the same trade or calling.

CHIPS. A nick name for a carpenter.

CHIRPING MERRY. Exhilarated with liquor. Chirping glass, a cheerful glass, that makes the company chirp like birds in spring.

CHIT. An infant or baby.

CHITTERLINS. The bowels. There is a rumpus among my bowels, i. e. I have the colic. The frill of a shirt.

CHITTY-FACED. Baby-faced; said of one who has a childish look.

CHIVE, or CHIFF. A knife, file, or saw. To chive the darbies; to file off the irons or fetters. To chive the boungs of the frows; to cut off women's pockets.

CHIVEY. I gave him a good chivey; I gave him a hearty scolding.

CHIVING LAY. Cutting the braces of coaches behind, on which the coachman quitting the box, an accomplice robs the

the boot; also, formerly, cutting the back of the coach to steal the fine large wigs then worn.

CHOAK. Choak away, the churchyard's near; a jocular saying to a person taken with a violent fit of coughing, or who has swallowed any thing, as it is called the wrong way; Choak, chicken, more are hatching: a like consolation.

CHOAK PEAR. Figuratively, an unanswerable objection: also a machine formerly used in Holland by robbers; it was of iron, shaped like a pear; this they forced into the mouths of persons from whom they intended to extort money; and on turning a key, certain interior springs thrust forth a number of points, in all directions, which so enlarged it, that it could not be taken out of the mouth: and the iron, being case-hardened, could not be filed: the only methods of getting rid of it, were either by cutting the mouth, or advertizing a reward for the key. These pears were also called pears of agony.

CHOAKING PYE, or COLD PYE. A punishment inflicted on any person sleeping in company: it consists in wrapping up cotton in a case or tube of paper, setting it on fire, and directing the smoke up the nostrils of the sleeper. See HOWELL'S COTGRAVE.

CHOCOLATE. To give chocolate without sugar; to reprove. *Military term.*

CHOICE SPIRIT. A thoughtless, laughing, singing, drunken fellow.

CHOP. A blow. *Boxing term.*

TO CHOP AND CHANGE. To exchange backwards and forwards. To chop, in the canting sense, means making dispatch, or hurrying over any business: ex. The *autem bawler* will soon quit the *hums*, for he *chops up* the *whiners*; the parson will soon quit the pulpit, for he hurries over the prayers. See AUTEM BAWLER, HUMS, and WHINERS.

CHOP CHURCHES. Simoniacal dealers in livings, or other ecclesiastical preferments.

CHOPPING. Lusty. A chopping boy or girl; a lusty child.

CHOPS. The mouth. I gave him a wherrit, or a souse, across the chops; I gave him a blow over the mouth. See WHERRIT.

CHOP-STICK. A fork.

CHOUDER. A sea-dish, composed of fresh fish, salt pork, herbs, and sea-biscuits, laid in different layers, and stewed together.

TO CHOUSE. To cheat or trick: he choused me out of it. Chouse is also the term for a game like chuck-farthing.

CHRIST-CROSS ROW. The alphabet in a horn-book: called Christ-cross Row, from having, as an Irishman observed, Christ's cross *prefixed* before and *after* the twenty-four letters.

CHRISTENING. Erasing the name of the true maker from a stolen watch, and engraving a fictitious one in its place.

CHRISTIAN PONEY. A chairman.

CHRISTIAN. A tradesman who has faith, i. e. will give credit.

CHRISTMAS COMPLIMENTS. A cough, kibed heels, and a snotty nose.

CHUB. He is a young chub, or a mere chub; i. e. a foolish fellow, easily imposed on: an illusion to a fish of that name, easily taken.

CHUBBY. Round-faced, plump.

CHUCK. My chuck; a term of endearment.

CHUCK FARTHING. A parish clerk.

CHUCKLE-HEADED. Stupid, thick-headed.

CHUFFY. Round-faced, chubby.

CHUM. A chamber-fellow, particularly at the universities and in prison.

CHUMMAGE. Money paid by the richer sort of prisoners in the Fleet and King's Bench, to the poorer, for their share of a room. When prisons are very full, which is too often the case, particularly on the eve of an insolvent act, two or three persons are obliged to sleep in a room. A prisoner who can pay for being alone, chuses two poor chums, who for a stipulated price, called chummage, give up their share of the room, and sleep on the stairs, or, as the term is, ruff it.

CHUNK. Among printers, a journeyman who refuses to work for legal wages; the same as the flint among taylors. See FLINT.

CHURCH WARDEN. A Sussex name for a shag, or cormorant, probably from its voracity.

CHURCH WORK. Said of any work that advances slowly.

CHURCHYARD COUGH. A cough that is likely to terminate in death.

CHURK. The udder.

CHURL. Originally, a labourer or husbandman: figuratively a rude, surly, boorish fellow. To put a churl upon a gentleman; to drink malt liquor immediately after having drunk wine.

CINDER GARBLER. A servant maid, from her business of sifting the ashes from the cinders. *Custom-house wit.*

CIRCUMBENDIBUS. A roundabout way, or story. He took such a circumbendibus; he took such a circuit.

Cit. A citizen of London.

City College. Newgate.

Civility Money. A reward claimed by bailiffs for executing their office with civility.

Civil Reception. A house of civil reception; a bawdy-house, or nanny-house. See Nanny-house.

Clack. A tongue, chiefly applied to women; a simile drawn from the clack of a water-mill.

Clack-loft. A pulpit, so called by orator Henley.

Clammed. Starved.

Clan. A family's tribe or brotherhood; a word much used in Scotland. The head of the clan; the chief: an allusion to a story of a Scotchman, who, when a very large louse crept down his arm, put him back again, saying he was the head of the clan, and that, if injured, all the rest would resent it.

Clank. A silver tankard. *Cant.*

Clank Napper. A silver tankard stealer. See Rum Bubber.

Clanker. A great lie.

Clap. A venereal taint. He went out by Had'em, and came round by Clapham home; i. e. he went out a wenching, and got a clap.

Clap on the Shoulder. An arrest for debt; whence a bum bailiff is called a shoulder-clapper.

Clapper. The tongue of a bell, and figuratively of a man or woman.

Clapper Claw. To scold, to abuse, or claw off with the tongue.

Clapperdogeon. A beggar born. *Cant.*

Claret. French red wine; figuratively, blood. I tapped his claret; I broke his head, and made the blood run. Claret-faced; red-faced.

Clawed off. Severely beaten or whipped; also smartly poxed or clapped.

Clear. Very drunk. The cull is clear, let's bite him; the fellow is very drunk, let's cheat him. *Cant.*

Cleaver. One that will cleave; used of a forward or wanton woman.

Clean. Expert; clever. Amongst the knuckling coves he is reckoned very clean; he is considered very expert as a pickpocket.

Clerked. Soothed, funned, imposed on. The cull will not be clerked; i. e. the fellow will not be imposed on by fair words.

Cleymes. Artificial sores, made by beggars to excite charity.

CLICK. A blow. A click in the muns; a blow or knock in the face. *Cant.*

To CLICK. To snatch. To click a nab; to snatch a hat. *Cant.*

CLICKER. A salesman's servant; also, one who proportions out the different shares of the booty among thieves.

CLICKET. Copulation of foxes; and thence used, in a canting sense, for that of men and women: as, The cull and the mort are at clicket in the dyke; the man and woman are copulating in the ditch.

CLIMB. To climb the three trees with a ladder; to ascend the gallows.

CLINCH. A pun or quibble. To clinch, or to clinch the nail; to confirm an improbable story by another: as, A man swore he drove a tenpenny nail through the moon; a bystander said it was true, for he was on the other side and clinched it.

CLINK. A place in the Borough of Southwark, formerly privileged from arrests; and inhabited by lawless vagabonds of every denomination, called, from the place of their residence, clinkers. Also a gaol, from the clinking of the prisoners' chains or fetters: he is gone to clink.

CLINKERS. A kind of small Dutch bricks; also irons worn by prisoners; a crafty fellow.

To CLIP. To hug or embrace: to clip and cling. To clip the coin; to diminish the current coin. To clip the king's English; to be unable to speak plain through drunkenness.

CLOAK TWITCHERS. Rogues who lurk about the entrances into dark alleys, and bye-lanes, to snatch cloaks from the shoulders of passengers.

CLOD HOPPER. A country farmer, or ploughman.

CLOD PATE. A dull, heavy booby.

CLOD POLE. The same.

CLOSE. As close as God's curse to a whore's a-se: close as shirt and shitten a-se.

CLOSE-FISTED. Covetous or stingy.

CLOSH. A general name given by the mobility to Dutch seamen, being a corruption of *Claus,* the abbreviation of Nicholas, a name very common among the men of that nation.

CLOTH MARKET. He is just come from the cloth market, i. e. from between the sheets, he is just risen from bed.

CLOUD. Tobacco. Under a cloud; in adversity.

CLOVEN, CLEAVE, or CLEFT. A term used for a woman who passes for a maid, but is not one.

CLOVEN FOOT. To spy the cloven foot in any business; to

discover

discover some roguery or something bad in it: a saying that alludes to a piece of vulgar superstition, which is, that, let the Devil transform himself into what shape he will, he cannot hide his cloven foot.

To Chuck. To shew a propensity for a man. The mors chucks; the wench wants to be doing.

Clout. A blow. I'll give you a clout on your jolly nob; I'll give you a blow on your head. It also means a handkerchief. *Cant.* Any pocket handkerchief except a silk one.

Clouted Shoon. Shoes tipped with iron.

Clouting Lay. Picking pockets of handkerchiefs.

Clover. To be, or live, in clover; to live luxuriously. Clover is the most desirable food for cattle.

Clowes. Rogues.

Cloy. To steal. To cloy the clout; to steal the handkerchief. To cloy the lour; to steal money. *Cant.*

Cloyes. Thieves, robbers, &c.

Club. A meeting or association, where each man is to spend an equal and stated sum, called his club.

Club Law. Argumentum bacculinum, in which an oaken stick is a better plea than an act of parliament.

Clump. A lump. Clumpish; lumpish, stupid.

Clunch. An awkward clownish fellow.

To Clutch the Fist. To clench or shut the hand. Clutch fisted; covetous, stingy. See Close-fisted.

Clutches. Hands, gripe, power.

Clutter. A stir, noise, or racket: what a confounded clutter here is!

Cly. Money; also a pocket. He has filed the cly; he has picked a pocket. *Cant.*

Cly the Jerk. To be whipped. *Cant.*

Clyster Pipe. A nick name for an apothecary.

Coach Wheel. A half crown piece is a fore coach wheel, and a crown piece a hind coach wheel; the fore wheels of a coach being less than the hind ones.

To Coax. To fondle, or wheedle. To coax a pair of stockings; to pull down the part soiled into the shoes, so as to give a dirty pair of stockings the appearance of clean ones. Coaxing is also used, instead of darning, to hide the holes about the ancles.

Cob. A Spanish dollar.

Cob, or Cobbing. A punishment used by the seamen for petty offences, or irregularities, among themselves: it consists in bastonadoing the offender on the posteriors with a cobbing stick, or pipe staff; the number usually inflicted is a dozen. At the first stroke the executioner repeats the

the word *watch*, on which all persons present are to take off their hats, on pain of like punishment: the last stroke is always given as hard as possible, and is called *the purse*. Ashore, among soldiers, where this punishment is sometimes adopted, *watch* and *the purse* are not included in the number, but given over and above, or, in the vulgar phrase, free gratis for nothing. This piece of discipline is also inflicted in Ireland, by the school-boys, on persons coming into the school without taking off their hats; it is there called school butter.

COBBLE. A kind of boat.

TO COBBLE. To mend, or patch; likewise to do a thing in a bungling manner.

COBBLE COLTER. A turkey.

COBBLER. A mender of shoes, an improver of the understandings of his customers; a translator.

COBBLERS PUNCH. Treacle, vinegar, gin, and water.

COCK, or CHIEF COCK OF THE WALK. The leading man in any society or body; the best boxer in a village or district.

COCK ALE. A provocative drink.

COCK ALLEY or COCK LANE. The private parts of a woman.

COCK AND A BULL STORY. A roundabout story, without head or tail, i.e. beginning or ending.

COCK OF THE COMPANY. A weak man, who from the desire of being the head of the company associates with low people, and pays all the reckoning.

COCK-A-WHOOP. Elevated, in high-spirits, transported with joy.

COCK BAWD. A male keeper of a bawdy-house.

COCK HOIST. A cross buttock.

COCKISH. Wanton, forward. A cockish wench; a forward coming girl.

COCKLES. To cry cockles; to be hanged: perhaps from the noise made whilst strangling. *Cant.*—This will rejoice the cockles of one's heart · a saying in praise of wine, ale or spirituous liquors.

COCK PIMP. The supposed husband of a bawd.

COCK ROBIN. A soft, easy fellow.

COCK-SURE. Certain: a metaphor borrowed from the cock of a firelock, as being much more certain to fire than the match.

COCK YOUR EYE. Shut one eye: thus translated into apothecaries Latin.---*Gallus tuus ego.*

COCKER. One fond of the diversion of cock-fighting.

COCKNEY. A nick name given to the citizens of London, or

or persons born within the sound of Bow bell, derived from the following story: A citizen of London being in the country, and hearing a horse neigh, exclaimed, Lord! how that horse laughs! A by-stander telling him that noise was called *neighing*, the next morning, when the cock crowed, the citizen to shew he had not forgot what was told him, cried out, Do you hear how the *cock neighs?* The king of the cockneys is mentioned among the regulations for the sports and shows formerly held in the Middle Temple on Childermas Day, where he had his officers, a marshal, constable, butler, &c. See Dugdale's Origines Juridiciales, p. 247.---Ray says, the interpretation of the word Cockney, is, a young person coaxed or conquered, made wanton; or a nestle cock, delicately bred and brought up, so as, when arrived at man's estate, to be unable to bear the least hardship. Whatever may be the origin of this appellation, we learn from the following verses, attributed to Hugh Bigot, Earl of Norfolk, that it was in use. in the time of king Henry II.

> Was I in my castle at Bungay,
> Fast by the river Waveney,
> I would not care for the king of Cockney;

i. e. the king of London.

COCKSHUT TIME. The evening, when fowls go to roost.

COD. A cod of money: a good sum of money.

CODDERS. Persons employed by the gardeners to gather peas.

CODGER. An old codger; an old fellow.

COD PIECE. The fore flap of a man's breeches. Do they bite, master? where, in the cod piece or collar?---a jocular attack on a patient angler by watermen, &c.

CODS. The scrotum. Also a nick name for a curate: a rude fellow meeting a curate, mistook him for the rector, and accosted him with the vulgar appellation of Bol---ks the rector, No, Sir, answered he; only Cods the curate, at your service.

COD'S HEAD. A stupid fellow.

COFFEE HOUSE. A necessary house. To make a coffee-house of a woman's ****; to go in and out and spend nothing.

COG. The money, or whatsoever the sweeteners drop to draw in a bubble.

COG. A tooth. A queer cog; a rotten tooth. How the cull flashes his queer cogs; how the fool shews his rotten teeth.

TO COG. To cheat with dice; also to coax or wheedle. To cog

cog a die; to conceal or secure a die. To cog a dinner; to wheedle one out of a dinner.

COGUE. A dram of any spirituous liquor.

COKER. A lie.

COKES. The fool in the play of Bartholomew Fair: perhaps a contraction of the word *coxcomb*.

COLCANNON. Potatoes and cabbage pounded together in a mortar, and then stewed with butter: an Irish dish.

COLD. You will catch cold at that; a vulgar threat or advice to desist from an attempt. He caught cold by lying in bed barefoot; a saying of any one extremely tender or careful of himself.

COLD BURNING. A punishment inflicted by private soldiers on their comrades for trifling offences, or breach of their mess laws; it is administered in the following manner: The prisoner is set against the wall, with the arm which is to be burned tied as high above his head as possible. The executioner then ascends a stool, and having a bottle of cold water, pours it slowly down the sleeve of the delinquent, patting him, and leading the water gently down his body, till it runs out at his breeches knees: this is repeated to the other arm, if he is sentenced to be burned in both.

COLD COOK. An undertaker of funerals, or carrion hunter. See CARRION HUNTER.

COLD IRON. A sword, or any other weapon for cutting or stabbing. I gave him two inches of cold iron into his beef.

COLD MEAT. A dead wife is the best cold meat in a man's house.

COLD PIG. To give cold pig is a punishment inflicted on sluggards who lie too long in bed: it consists in pulling off all the bed clothes from them, and throwing cold water upon them.

COLD PUDDING. This is said to settle one's love.

COLE. Money. Post the cole: pay down the money.

COLIANDER, or CORIANDER SEEDS. Money.

COLLAR DAY. Execution day.

COLLEGE. Newgate, or any other prison. New College; the Royal Exchange. King's College: the King's Bench prison. He has been educated at the steel, and took his last degree at college; he has received his education at the house of correction, and was hanged at Newgate.

COLLEGE COVE. The College cove has numbered him, and if he is knocked down he'll be twisted; the turnkey of Newgate has told the judge how many times the prisoner has been tried before, and therefore if he is found guilty, he certainly will be hanged. It is said to be the custom of the Old Bailey for one of the turnkeys of Newgate to give information to the

the judge how many times an old offender has been tried, by holding up as many fingers as the number of times the prisoner has been before arraigned at that bar.

COLLEGIATES. Prisoners of the one, and shopkeepers of the other of those places.

COLLECTOR. A highwayman.

TO COLLOGUE. To wheedle or coax.

COOK RUFFIAN, who roasted the devil in his feathers. A bad cook.

COOL CRAPE. A shroud.

COOLER. A woman.

COOLER. The backside. Kiss my cooler. Kiss my a-əs. It is principally used to signify a woman's posteriors.

COOL LADY. A female follower of the camp, who sells brandy.

COOL NANTS. Brandy.

COOL TANKARD. Wine and water, with lemon, sugar, and burrage.

COLQUARRON. A man's neck. His colquarron is just about to be twisted; he is just going to be hanged. *Cant.*

COLT. One who lets horses to highwaymen; also a boy newly initiated into roguery; a grand or petty juryman on his first assize. *Cant.*

COLTAGE. A fine or beverage paid by colts on their first entering into their offices.

COLT BOWL. Laid short of the jack by a colt bowler, i. e. a person raw or unexperienced in the art of bowling.

COLT'S TOOTH. An old fellow who marries or keeps a young girl, is said to have a colt's tooth in his head.

COLT VEAL. Coarse red veal, more like the flesh of a colt than that of a calf.

COMB. To comb one's head; to clapperclaw, or scold any one: a woman who lectures her husband, is said to comb his head. She combed his head with a joint stool; she threw a stool at him.

COME. To come; to lend. Has he come it; has he lent it? To come over any one; to cheat or over reach him. Coming wench; a forward wench, also a breeding woman.

COMING! SO IS CHRISTMAS. Said of a person who has long been called, and at length answers, Coming!

COMFORTABLE IMPORTANCE. A wife.

COMMISSION. A shirt. *Cant.*

COMMODE. A woman's head dress.

COMMODITY. A woman's commodity; the private parts of a modest woman, and the public parts of a prostitute.

COMMONS. The house of commons; the necessary house.

COMPANY. To see company; to enter into a course of prostitution.

COMPLIMENT. See CHRISTMAS.

COMUS'S COURT. A social meeting formerly held at the Half Moon tavern Cheapside.

CONFECT. Counterfeited.

CONGER. To conger; the agreement of a set or knot of booksellers of London, that whosoever of them shall buy a good copy, the rest shall take off such a particular number, in quires, at a stated price; also booksellers joining to buy either a considerable or dangerous copy.

CONGO. Will you lap your congo with me? will you drink tea with me?

CONNY WABBLE. Eggs and brandy beat up together. *Irish.*

CONSCIENCE KEEPER. A superior, who by his influence makes his dependants act as he pleases.

CONTENT. The cull's content; the man is past complaining: a saying of a person murdered for resisting the robbers. *Cant.*

CONTENT. A thick liquor, in imitation of chocolate, made of milk and gingerbread.

CONTRA DANCE. A dance where the dancers of the different sexes stand opposite each other, instead of side by side, as in the minuet, rigadoon, louvre, &c. and now corruptly called a country dance.

CONUNDRUMS. Enigmatical conceits.

CONVENIENT. A mistress. *Cant.*

CONVENIENCY. A necessary. A leathern conveniency, a coach.

COOPED UP. Imprisoned, confined like a fowl in a coop.

COQUET. A jilt.

CORINTH. A bawdy-house. *Cant.*

CORINTHIANS. Frequenters of brothels. Also an impudent, brazen-faced fellow, perhaps from the Corinthian brass.

CORK-BRAINED. Light-headed, foolish.

CORNED. Drunk.

CORNISH HUG. A particular lock in wrestling, peculiar to the people of that county.

CORNY-FACED. A very red pimpled face.

CORPORAL. To mount a corporal and four; to be guilty of onanism: the thumb is the corporal, the four fingers the privates.

CORPORATION. A large belly. He has a glorious corporation; he has a very prominent belly.

CORPORATION. The magistrates, &c. of a corporate town. *Corpus sine ratione.* Freemen of a corporation's work; neither strong nor handsome.

Cosset. A foundling. Cosset colt or lamb; a colt or lamb brought up by hand.

Costard. The head. I'll smite your costard; I'll give you a knock on the head.

Costard Monger. A dealer in fruit, particularly apples.

Cot, or Quot. A man who meddles with women's household business, particularly in the kitchen. The punishment commonly inflicted on a quot, is pinning a greasy dishclout to the skirts of his coat.

Cove. A man, a fellow, a rogue. The cove was bit; the rogue was outwitted. The cove has bit the cole; the rogue has got the money. *Cant.*

Covent, or Convent Garden, vulgarly called **Common Garden.** Anciently, the garden belonging to a dissolved monastery; now famous for being the chief market in London for fruit, flowers, and herbs. The theatres are situated near it. In its environs are many brothels, and not long ago, the lodgings of the second order of ladies of easy virtue were either there, or in the purlieus of Drury Lane.

Covent Garden Abbess. A bawd.

Covent Garden Ague. The venereal disease. He broke his shins against Covent Garden rails; he caught the venereal disorder.

Covent Garden Nun. A prostitute.

Coventry. To send one to Coventry; a punishment inflicted by officers of the army on such of their brethren as are testy, or have been guilty of improper behaviour, not worthy the cognizance of a court martial. The person sent to Coventry is considered as absent; no one must speak to or answer any question he asks, except relative to duty, under penalty of being also sent to the same place. On a proper submission, the penitent is recalled, and welcomed by the mess, as just returned from a journey to Coventry.

Covey. A collection of whores. What a fine covey here is, if the Devil would but throw his net!

To Couch a Hogshead. To lie down to sleep *Cant.*

Counterfeit Crank. A general cheat, assuming all sorts of characters; one conterfeiting the falling sickness.

Country Harry. A waggoner. *Cant.*

Country Put. An ignorant country fellow.

County Work. Said of any work that advances slowly.

Court Card. A gay fluttering coxcomb.

Court Holy Water. } Fair speeches and promises,
Court Promises. } without performance.

Court of Assistants. A court often applied to by young women who marry old men.

Cow. To sleep like a cow, with a **** at one's a-se; said of a married man; married men being supposed to sleep with their backs towards their wives, according to the following proclamation:

> All you that in your beds do lie,
> Turn to your wives, and occupy:
> And when that you have done your best,
> Turn a-se to a-se, and take your rest.

Cow Juice. Milk.

Cow's Baby. A calf.

Cow's Courant. Gallop and sh---e.

Cow-handed. Awkward.

Cow-hearted. Fearful.

Cow Itch. The product of a sort of bean, which excites an insufferable itching, used chiefly for playing tricks.

Cow's Spouse. A bull.

Cow's Thumb. Done to a cow's thumb; done exactly.

Coxcomb. Anciently, a fool. Fools, in great families, wore a cap with bells, on the top of which was a piece of red cloth, in the shape of a cock's comb. At present, coxcomb signifies a fop, or vain self-conceited fellow.

Crab. To catch a crab; to fall backwards by missing one's stroke in rowing.

Crab Lanthorn. A peevish fellow.

Crab Louse. A species of louse peculiar to the human body; the male is denominated a cock, the female a hen.

Crab Shells. Shoes. *Irish.*

Crabs. A losing throw to the main at hazard.

Crabbed. Sour, ill-tempered, difficult.

Crack. A whore.

To Crack. To boast or brag; also to break. I cracked his napper; I broke his head.

The Crack, or All the Crack. The fashionable theme, the go. The Crack Lay, of late is used, in the cant language, to signify the art and mystery of house-breaking.

Cracker. Crust, sea biscuit, or ammunition loaf; also the backside. Farting crackers; breeches.

Crackish. Whorish.

Cracking Tools. Implements of house-breaking, such as a crow, a center bit, false keys, &c.

Crackmans. Hedges. The cull thought to have loped by breaking through the crackmans, but we fetched him back by a nope on the costard, which stopped his jaw; the man thought to have escaped by breaking through the hedge,

but

but we brought him back by a great blow on the head, which laid him speechless.

CRACKSMAN. A house-breaker. The kiddy is a clever cracksman; the young fellow is a very expert house-breaker.

CRAG. The neck.

CRAMP RINGS. Bolts, shackles, or fetters. *Cant.*

CRAMP WORDS. Sentence of death passed on a criminal by a judge. He has just undergone the cramp word; sentence has just been passed on him. *Cant.*

CRANK. Gin and water; also, brisk, pert.

CRANK. The falling sickness. *Cant.*

TO CRASH. To kill. Crash that cull; kill that fellow. *Cant.*

CRASHING CHEATS. Teeth.

CRAW THUMPERS. Roman catholics, so called from their beating their breasts in the confession of their sins. See BRISKET BEATER, and BREAST FLEET.

CREAM-POT LOVE. Such as young fellows pretend to dairy-maids, to get cream and other good things from them.

TO CREEME. To slip or slide any thing into the hands of another. *Cant.*

CREEPERS. Gentlemen's companions, lice.

CREW. A knot or gang; also a boat or ship's company. The canting crew are thus divided into twenty-three orders, which see under the different words:

MEN.

1 Rufflers
2 Upright Men
3 Hookers or Anglers
4 Rogues
5 Wild Rogues
6 Priggers of Prancers
7 Palliardes
8 Fraters
9 Jarkmen, or Patricoes
10 Fresh Water Mariners, or Whip Jackets
11 Drummerers
12 Drunken Tinkers
13 Swadders, or Pedlars
14 Abrams.

WOMEN.

1 Demanders for Glimmer or Fire
2 Bawdy Baskets
3 Morts
4 Autem Morts
5 Walking Morts
6 Doxies
7 Delles
8 Kinching Morts
9 Kinching Coes

CRIB. A house. To crack a crib: to break open a house.

TO CRIB. To purloin, or appropriate to one's own use, part of any thing intrusted to one's care.

TO FIGHT A CRIB. To make a sham fight. *Bear Garden term.*

CRIBBAGE-

Cribbage-faced. Marked with the small pox, the pits bearing a kind of resemblance to the holes in a cribbage-board.

Cribbeys, or Cribby Islands. Blind alleys, courts, or bye-ways; perhaps from the houses built there being cribbed out of the common way or passage; and islands, from the similarity of sound to the Caribbee Islands.

Crim. Con. Money. Damages directed by a jury to be paid by a convicted adulterer to the injured husband, for criminal conversation with his wife.

Crimp. A broker or factor, as a coal crimp, who disposes of the cargoes of the Newcastle coal ships; also persons employed to trapan or kidnap recruits for the East Indian and African companies. To crimp, or play crimp; to play foul or booty: also a cruel manner of cutting up fish alive, practised by the London fishmongers, in order to make it eat firm; cod, and other crimped fish, being a favourite dish among voluptuaries and epicures.

Crinkum Crankum. A woman's commodity. See Spectator.

Crinkums. The foul or venereal disease.

Cripple. Sixpence, that piece being commonly much bent and distorted.

Crispin. A shoemaker: from a romance, wherein a prince of that name is said to have exercised the art and mystery of a shoemaker, thence called the gentle craft: or rather from the saints Crispinus and Crispianus, who according to the legend, were brethren born at Rome, from whence they travelled to Soissons in France, about the year 303, to propagate the Christian religion; but, because they would not be chargeable to others for their maintenance, they exercised the trade of shoemakers: the governor of the town discovering them to be Christians, ordered them to be beheaded, about the year 303; from which time they have been the tutelar saints of the shoemakers.

Crispin's Holiday. Every Monday throughout the year, but most particularly the 25th of October, being the anniversary of Crispinus and Crispianus.

Crispin's Lance. An awl.

Croaker. One who is always foretelling some accident or misfortune: an allusion to the croaking of a raven, supposed ominous.

Croakumshire. Northumberland, from the particular croaking in the pronunciation of the people of that county, especially about Newcastle and Morpeth, where they are said to be born with a burr in their throats, which prevents their pronouncing the letter *r*.

Croakers. Forestallers, called also Kidders and Tranters.

Crocodile's Tears. The tears of a hypocrite. Crocodiles are fabulously reported to shed tears over their prey before they devour it.

Crocus, or Crocus Metallorum. A nick name for a surgeon of the army and navy.

Croker. A groat, or four pence.

Crone. An old ewe whose teeth are worn out; figuratively, a toothless old beldam.

Crony. An intimate companion, a comrade; also a confederate in a robbery.

Crook. Sixpence.

Crook Back. Sixpence: for the reason of this name, see Cripple.

Crook your Elbow. To crook one's elbow, and wish it may never come straight, if the fact then affirmed is not true—according to the casuists of Bow-street and St. Giles's, adds great weight and efficacy to an oath.

Crook Shanks. A nick name for a man with bandy legs. He buys his boots in Crooked Lane, and his stockings in Bandy-legged Walk; his legs grew in the night, therefore could not see to grow straight: jeering sayings of men with crooked legs.

Crop. A nick name for a presbyterian: from their cropping their hair, which they trimmed close to a bowl-dish, placed as a guide on their heads; whence they were likewise called roundheads. See Roundheads.

Crop. To be knocked down for a crop; to be condemned to be hanged. Cropped, hanged.

Cropping Drums. Drummers of the foot guards, or Chelsea hospital, who find out weddings, and beat a point of war to serenade the new married couple, and thereby obtain money.

Croppen. The tail. The croppen of the rotan; the tail of the cart. Croppen ken: the necessary house. *Cant.*

Cropsick. Sickness in the stomach, arising from drunkenness.

Cross. To come home by weeping cross; to repent at the conclusion.

Cross Dishonest. A cross cove; any person who lives by stealing or in a dishonest manner.

Cross Bite. One who combines with a sharper to draw in a friend; also, to counteract or disappoint. *Cant.*—This is peculiarly used to signify entrapping a man so as to obtain *crim. con.* money, in which the wife, real or supposed, conspires with the husband.

Cross Buttock. A particular lock or fall in the Broughtonian

tonian art, which, as Mr. Fielding observes, conveyed more pleasant sensations to the spectators than the patient.

CROSS PATCH A peevish boy or girl, or rather an unsocial ill-tempered man or woman.

TO CROW. To brag, boast, or triumph. To crow over any one; to keep him in subjection: an image drawn from a cock, who crows over a vanquished enemy. To pluck a crow; to reprove any one for a fault committed, to settle a dispute. To strut like a crow in a gutter; to walk proudly, or with an air of consequence.

CROWD. A fiddle: probably from *crooth*, the Welch name for that instrument.

CROWDERO. A fiddler.

CROWDY. Oatmeal and water, or milk; a mess much eaten in the north.

CROW FAIR. A visitation of the clergy. See REVIEW OF THE BLACK CUIRASSIERS.

CROWN OFFICE. The head. I fired into her keel upwards; my eyes and limbs Jack, the crown office was full; I s—k-d a woman with her a--e upwards, she was so drunk, that her head lay on the ground.

CRUISERS. Beggars, or highway spies, who traverse the road, to give intelligence of a booty; also rogues ready to snap up any booty that may offer, like privateers or pirates on a cruise.

CRUMMY. Fat, fleshy. A fine crummy dame; a fat woman. He has picked up his crumbs finely of late; he has grown very fat, or rich, of late.

CRUMP. One who helps solicitors to affidavit men, or false witnesses.---'I wish you had, Mrs. Crump;' a Gloucestershire saying, in answer to a wish for any thing; implying, you must not expect any assistance from the speaker. It is said to have originated from the following incident: One Mrs. Crump, the wife of a substantial farmer, dining with the old Lady Coventry, who was extremely deaf, said to one of the footmen, waiting at table, 'I wish I had a draught of small beer,' her modesty not permitting her to desire so fine a gentleman to bring it: the fellow, conscious that his mistress could not hear either the request or answer, replied, without moving, 'I wish you had, Mrs. Crump.' These wishes being again repeated by both parties, Mrs. Crump got up from the table to fetch it herself; and being asked by my lady where she was going, related what had passed. The story being told abroad, the expression became proverbial.

CRUMP-BACKED. Hump-backed.

CRUSTY BEAU. One that uses paint and cosmetics, to obtain a fine complexion.

Crusty Fellow. A surly fellow.

Cub. An unlicked cub; an unformed, ill-educated young man, a young nobleman or gentleman on his travels: an allusion to the story of the bear, said to bring its cub into form by licking. Also, a new gamester.

Cuckold. The husband of an incontinent wife: cuckolds, however, are Christians, as we learn by the following story: An old woman hearing a man call his dog Cuckold, reproved him sharply, saying, 'Sirrah, are not you ashamed to call a dog by a Christian's name?' To cuckold the parson; to bed with one's wife before she has been churched.

Cucumbers. Taylors, who are jocularly said to subsist, during the summer, chiefly on cucumbers.

Cuff. An old cuff; an old man. To cuff Jonas; said of one who is knock-kneed, or who beats his sides to keep himself warm in frosty weather; called also Beating the booby.

Cuffin. A man.

Cull. A man, honest or otherwise. A bob cull; a good-natured, quiet fellow. *Cant.*

Cullability. A disposition liable to be cheated, an unsuspecting nature, open to imposition.

Cully. A fop or fool: also, a dupe to women: from the Italian word *coglione*, a blockhead.

Culp. A kick or blow: from the words *mea culpa*, being that part of the popish liturgy at which the people beat their breasts; or, as the vulgar term is, thump their craws.

Cundum. The dried gut of a sheep, worn by men in the act of coition, to prevent venereal infection; said to have been invented by one colonel Cundum. These machines were long prepared and sold by a matron of the name of Philips, at the Green Canister, in Half-moon-street, in the Strand. That good lady having acquired a fortune, retired from business; but learning that the town was not well served by her successors, she, out of a patriotic zeal for the public welfare, returned to her occupation; of which she gave notice by divers hand-bills, in circulation in the year 1776. Also a false scabbard over a sword, and the oil-skin case for holding the colours of a regiment.

Cunningham. A punning appellation for a simple fellow.

Cunning Man. A cheat, who pretends by his skill in astrology to assist persons in recovering stolen goods: and also to tell them their fortunes, and when, how often, and to whom they shall be married; likewise answers all lawful questions, both by sea and land. This profession is frequently occupied by ladies.

Cunning Shaver. A sharp fellow, one that trims close, i. e. cheats ingeniously.

Cunny-thumbed. To double one's fist with the thumb inwards, like a woman.

Ct.** The κοννος of the Greek, and the *cunnus* of the Latin dictionaries; a nasty name for a nasty thing: *un con Miege.*

Cup of the Creature. A cup of good liquor.

Cup-shot. Drunk.

Cupboard Love. Pretended love to the cook, or any other person, for the sake of a meal. My guts cry cupboard; i. e. I am hungry

Cupid, Blind Cupid. A jeering name for an ugly blind man: Cupid, the god of love, being frequently painted blind. See **Blind Cupid.**

Cur. A cut or curtailed dog. According to the forest laws, a man who had no right to the privilege of the chase, was obliged to cut or law his dog: among other modes of disabling him from disturbing the game, one was by depriving him of his tail: a dog so cut was called a cut or curtailed dog, and by contraction a cur. A cur is figuratively used to signify a surly fellow.

Curbing Law. The act of hooking goods out of windows: the curber is the thief, the curb the hook. *Cant.*

Cure A-se. A dyachilón plaister, applied to the parts galled by riding.

Curle. Clippings of money, which curls up in the operation. *Cant.*

Curmudgeon. A covetous old fellow, derived, according to some, from the French term *cœur mechant.*

Curry. To curry favour; to obtain the favour of a person be coaxing or servility. To curry any one's hide; to beat him.

Curse of Scotland. The nine of diamonds; diamonds, it is said, imply royalty, being ornaments to the imperial crown; and every ninth king of Scotland has been observed for many ages, to be a tyrant and a curse to that country. Others say it is from its similarity to the arms of Argyle; the Duke of Argyle having been very instrumental in bringing about the union, which, by some Scotch patricts, has been considered as detrimental to their country.

Curse of God. A cockade.

Cursitors. Broken petty-fogging attornies, or Newgate solicitors. *Cant.*

Curtails. Thieves who cut off pieces of stuff hanging out of-shop windows, the tails of women's gowns, &c.; also, threves wearing short jackets.

Curtain Lecture. A woman who scolds her husband when in bed, is said to read him a curtain lecture.

Curtezan. A prostitute.

Cushion. He has deserved the cushion; a saying of one whose wife is brought to bed of a boy: implying, that having done his business effectually, he may now indulge or repose himself.

Cushion Thumper, or Duster. A parson; many of whom in the fury of their eloquence, heartily belabour their cushions.

Custard Cap. The cap worn by the sword-bearer of the city of London, made hollow at the top like a custard.

Custom-house Goods. The stock in trade of a prostitute, because fairly entered.

Cut. Drunk. A little cut over the head; slightly intoxicated. To cut; to leave a person or company. To cut up well; to die rich.

To Cut. (*Cambridge.*) To renounce acquaintance with any one is to *cut* him. There are several species of the cut. Such as the cut direct, the cut indirect, the cut sublime, the cut infernal, &c. The cut direct, is to start across the street, at the approach of the obnoxious person in order to avoid him. The cut indirect, is to look another way, and pass without appearing to observe him. The cut sublime, is to admire the top of King's College Chapel, or the beauty of the passing clouds, till he is out of sight. The cut infernal, is to analyze the arrangement of your shoe-strings, for the same purpose.

To Cut bene. To speak gently. To cut bene whiddes; to give good words. To cut queer whiddes; to give foul language. To cut a bosh, or a flash; to make a figure. *Cant.*

To Cutty-eye. To look out of the corners of one's eyes, to leer, to look askance. The cull cutty-eyed at us; the fellow looked suspicious at us.

DAM

Dab. An adept; a dab at any feat or exercise. Dab, quoth Dawkins, when he hit his wife on the a-se with a pound of butter.

Dace. Two pence. Tip me a dace; lend me two pence. *Cant.*

Daddles. Hands. Tip us your daddle; give me your hand. *Cant.*

Daddy. Father. Old daddy; a familiar address to an old man. To beat daddy mammy; the first rudiments of drum beating, being the elements of the roll.

Daggers. They are at daggers drawing; i. e. at enmity, ready to fight.

Dairy. A woman's breasts, particularly one that gives suck. She sported her dairy; she pulled out her breast.

Daisy Cutter. A jockey term for a horse that does not lift up his legs sufficiently, or goes too near the ground, and is therefore apt to stumble.

Daisy Kickers. Ostlers at great inns.

Dam. A small Indian coin, mentioned in the Gentoo code of laws: hence etymologists may, if they please, derive the common expression, I do not care a dam, i. e. I do not care half a farthing for it.

Damber. A rascal. See **Dimber.**

Damme Boy. A roaring, mad, blustering fellow, a scourer of the streets, or kicker up of a breeze.

Damned Soul. A clerk in a counting house, whose sole business it is to clear or swear off merchandise at the custom-house; and who, it is said, guards against the crime of perjury, by taking a previous oath, never to swear truly on those occasions.

Damper. A luncheon, or snap before dinner: so called from its damping, or allaying, the appetite; eating and drinking, being, as the proverb wisely observes, apt to take away the appetite.

Dance upon Nothing. To be hanged.

Dancers. Stairs.

Dandy. That's the dandy; i. e. the ton, the clever thing; an expression of similar import to "That's the barber." See **Barber.**

Dandy grey Russet. A dirty brown. His coat's dandy grey russet, the colour of the Devil's nutting bag.

Dandy Prat. An insignificant or trifling fellow.

To Dangle. To follow a woman without asking the question. Also, to be hanged: I shall see you dangle in the sheriff's picture frame; I shall see you hanging on the gallows.

Dangler. One who follows women in general, without any particular attachment.

Dapper Fellow. A smart, well-made, little man.

Darbies. Fetters. *Cant.*

Darby. Ready money. *Cant.*

Dark Cully. A married man that keeps a mistress, whom he visits only at night, for fear of discovery.

Darkee. A dark lanthorn used by housebreakers. Stow the darkee, and bolt, the cove of the crib is fly; hide the dark lanthorn, and run away, the master of the house knows that we are here.

Darkmans. The night. *Cant.*

Darkman's Budge. One that slides into a house in the dark of the evening, and hides himself, in order to let some of the gang in at night to rob it.

Dart. A straight-armed blow in boxing.

Dash. A tavern drawer. To cut a dash: to make a figure.

David Jones. The devil, the spirit of the sea: called Necken in the north countries, such as Norway, Denmark, and Sweden.

David Jones's Locker. The sea.

David's Sow. As drunk as David's sow; a common saying, which took its rise from the following circumstance: One David Lloyd, a Welchman, who kept an alehouse at Hereford, had a living sow with six legs, which was greatly resorted to by the curious; he had also a wife much addicted to drunkenness, for which he used sometimes to give her due correction. One day David's wife having taken a cup too much, and being fearful of the consequences, turned out the sow, and lay down to sleep herself sober in the stye. A company coming in to see the sow, David ushered them into the stye, exclaiming, there is a sow for you! did any of you ever see such another? all the while supposing the sow had really been there; to which some of the company, seeing the state the woman was in, replied, it was the drunkenest sow they had ever beheld; whence the woman was ever after called David's sow.

Davy. I'll take my davy of it; vulgar abbreviation of affidavit.

To Dawb. To bribe. The cull was scragged because he could not dawb; the rogue was hanged because he could not bribe. All bedawbed with lace; all over lace.

Day Lights. Eyes. To darken his day lights, or sow up his sees; to close up a man's eyes in boxing.

Dead Cargo. A term used by thieves, when they are disappointed in the value of their booty.

Dead Horse. To work for the dead horse; to work for wages already paid.

Dead-louse. Vulgar pronunciation of the Dedalus ship of war.

Dead Men. A cant word among journeymen bakers, for loaves falsely charged to their masters' customers; also empty bottles.

Deadly Nevergreen, that bears fruit all the year round. The gallows, or three-legged mare. See Three-legged Mare.

Dear Joys. Irishmen: from their frequently making use of that expression.

Death Hunter. An undertaker, one who furnishes the necessary articles for funerals. See Carrion Hunter.

Death's Head upon a Mop-stick. A poor miserable, emaciated fellow; one quite an otomy. See Otomy.---He looked as pleasant as the pains of death.

Deep-one. A thorough-paced rogue, a sly designing fellow: in opposition to a shallow or foolish one.

Deft Fellow. A neat little man.

Degen, or Dagen. A sword. Nim the degen; steal the sword. Dagen is Dutch for a sword. *Cant.*

Dells. Young buxom wenches, ripe and prone to venery, but who have not lost their virginity, which the *upright man* claims by virtue of his prerogative; after which they become free for any of the fraternity. Also a common strumpet. *Cant.*

Demure. As demure as an old whore at a christening.

Demy-rep. An abbreviation of demy-reputation; a woman of doubtful character.

Derby. To come down with the derbies; to pay the money.

Derrick. The name of the finisher of the law, or hangman about the year 1608.---' For he rides his circuit with ' the Devil, and Derrick must be his host, and Tiburne ' the inne at which he will lighte.' Vide Bellman of London, in art. Priggin Law.—' At the gallows, ' where I leave them, as to the haven at which they must ' all cast anchor, if Derrick's cables do but hold.' Ibid.

Devil. A printer's errand-boy. Also a small thread in the king's ropes and cables, whereby they may be distinguished from all others. The Devil himself; a small streak of blue thread in the king's sails. The Devil may dance in his pocket; i. e. he has no money: the cross on our ancient coins being jocularly supposed to prevent him from visiting that place, for fear, as it is said, of breaking his shins against it. To hold a candle to the Devil; to be civil to any one out of fear: in allusion to the story of the old woman, who set a wax taper before the image of St. Michael, and another before the Devil, whom that saint

saint is commonly represented as trampling under his feet: being reproved for paying such honour to Satan, she answered, as it was uncertain which place she should go to, heaven or hell, she chose to secure a friend in both places. That will be when the Devil is blind, and he has not got sore eyes yet; said of any thing unlikely to happen. It rains whilst the sun shines the Devil is beating his wife with a shoulder of mutton: this phenomenon is also said to denote that cuckolds are going to heaaen; on being informed of this, a loving wife cried out with great vehemence, 'Run, husband, run!'

> The Devil was sick, the Devil a monk would be;
> The Devil was well, the Devil a monk was he.

a proverb signifying that we are apt to forget promises made in time of distress. To pull the Devil by the tail, to be reduced to one's shifts. The Devil go with you and sixpence, and then you will have both money and company.

Devil. The gizzard of a turkey or fowl, scored, peppered, salted and broiled: it derives its appellation from being hot in the mouth.

Devil's Books. Cards.

Devil Catcher, or Devil Driver. A parson. See Snub Devil.

Devil's Daughter. It is said of one who has a termagant for his wife, that he has married the Devil's daughter, and lives with the old folks.

Devil's Daughter's Portion:

> Deal, Dover, and Harwich,
> The Devil gave with his daughter in marriage;
> And, by a codicil to his will,
> He added Helvoet and the Brill;

a saying occasioned by the shameful impositions practised by the inhabitants of those places, on sailors and travellers.

Devil Drawer. A miserable painter.

Devil's Dung. Assafœtida.

Devil's Guts. A surveyor's chain: so called by farmers, who do not like their land should be measured by their landlords.

Devilish. Very: an epithet which in the English vulgar language is made to agree with every quality or thing; as, devilish bad, devilish good; devilish sick, devilish well; devilish sweet, devilish sour; devilish hot, devilish cold, &c. &c.

DEUSEA VILLE. The country. *Cant.*

DEUSEA VILLE STAMPERS. Country carriers. *Cant.*

DEW BEATERS. Feet. *Cant.*

DEWS WINS, or DEUX WINS. Two-pence. *Cant.*

DEWITTED. Torn to pieces by a mob, as that great statesman John de Wit was in Holland, anno 1672.

DIAL PLATE. The face. To alter his dial plate; to disfigure his face.

DICE. The names of false dice:

A bale of bard cinque deuces
A bale of flat cinque deuces
A bale of flat sice aces
A bale of bard cater traes
A bale of flat cater traes
A bale of fulhams
A bale of light graniers
A bale of langrets contrary to the ventage
A bale of gordes, with as many highmen as lowmen, for passage
A bale of demies
A bale of long dice for even and odd
A bale of bristles
A bale of direct contraries.

DICK. That happened in the reign of queen Dick, i. e. never: said of any absurd old story. I am as queer as Dick's hatband; that is, out of spirits, or don't know what ails me.

DICKY. A woman's under-petticoat. It's all Dicky with him; i. e. it's all over with him.

DICKED IN THE NOB. Silly. Crazed.

DICKEY. A sham shirt.

DICKEY. An ass. Roll your dickey; drive your ass. Also a seat for servants to sit behind a carriage, when their master drives.

To DIDDLE. To cheat. To defraud. The cull diddled me out of my dearee; the fellow robbed me of my sweetheart. See Jeremy Diddler in Raising the Wind.

DIDDEYS. A woman's breasts or bubbies.

DIDDLE. Gin.

DIGGERS. Spurs. *Cant.*

DILBERRIES. Small pieces of excrement adhering to the hairs near the fundament.

DILBERRY MAKER. The fundament.

DILDO. [From the Italian *diletto*, q. d. a woman's delight; or from our word *dally*, q. d. a thing to play withal.] Penis succedaneus, called in Lombardy Passo Tempo. *Bailey.*

Diligent. Double diligent, like the Devil's apothecary; said of one affectedly diligent.

Dilly. [An abbreviation of the word *diligence.*] A public voiture or stage, commonly a post chaise, carrying three persons; the name is taken from the public stage vehicles in France and Flanders. The dillies first began to run in England about the year 1779.

Dimber. Pretty. A dimber cove; a pretty fellow. Dimber mort; a pretty wench. *Cant.*

Dimber Damber. A top man, or prince, among the canting crew: also the chief rogue of the gang, or the completest cheat. *Cant.*

Ding. To knock down. To ding it in one's ears; to reproach or tell one something one is not desirous of hearing. Also to throw away or hide: thus a highwayman who throws away or hides any thing with which he robbed, to prevent being known or detected, is, in the canting lingo, styled a Dinger.

Ding Boy. A rogue, a hector, a bully, or sharper. *Cant.*

Ding Dong. Helter skelter, in a hasty disorderly manner.

Dingey Christian. A mulatto; or any one who has, as the West-Indian term is, a lick of the tar-brush, that is, some negro blood in him.

Dining Room Post. A mode of stealing in houses that let lodgings, by rogues pretending to be postmen, who send up sham letters to the lodgers, and, whilst waiting in the entry for the postage, go into the first room they see open, and rob it.

Dip. To dip for a wig. Formerly, in Middle Row, Holborn, wigs of different sorts were, it is said, put into a close-stool box, into which, for three-pence, any one might dip, or thrust in his hand, and take out the first wig he laid hold of; if he was dissatisfied with his prize, he might, on paying three halfpence, return it and dip again.

The Dip. A cook's shop, under Furnival's Inn, where many attornies clerks, and other inferior limbs of the law, take out the wrinkles from their bellies. *Dip* is also a punning name for a tallow-chandler.

Dippers. Anabaptists.

Dipt. Pawned or mortgaged.

Dirty Puzzle. A nasty slut.

Disguised. Drunk.

Disgruntled. Offended, disobliged.

Dished up. He is completely dished up; he is totally ruined. To throw a thing in one's dish; to reproach or twit one with any particular matter.

Dishclout. A dirty, greasy woman. He has made a napkin of his dishclout; a saying of one who has married his cook maid. To pin a dishclout to a man's tail; a punishment often threatened by the female servants in a kitchen, to a man who pries too minutely into the secrets of that place.

Dismal Ditty. The psalm sung by the felons at the gallows, just before they are turned off.

Dispatches. A mittimus, or justice of the peace's warrant, for the commitment of a rogue.

Ditto. A suit of ditto; coat, waistcoat, and breeches, all of one colour.

Dispatchers. Loaded or false dice.

Distracted Division. Husband and wife fighting.

Dive. To dive; to pick a pocket. To dive for a dinner; to go down into a cellar to dinner. A dive, is a thief who stands ready to receive goods thrown out to him by a little boy put in at a window. *Cant.*

Diver. A pickpocket; also one who lives in a cellar.

Divide. To divide the house with one's wife; to give her the outside, and to keep all the inside to one's self, i. e. to turn her into the street.

Do. To do any one; to rob and cheat him. I have done him; I have robbed him. Also to overcome in a boxing match: witness those laconic lines written on the field of battle, by Humphreys to his patron.---'Sir, I have done the Jew.'

To do over. Carries the same meaning, but is not so briefly expressed: the former having received the polish of the present times.

Doash. A cloak. *Cant.*

Dobin Rig. Stealing ribbands from haberdashers early in the morning or late at night; generally practised by women in the disguise of maid servants.

To Dock. To lie with a woman. The cull docked the dell all the darkmans; the fellow laid with the wench all night. Docked smack smooth; one who has suffered an amputation of his penis from a venereal complaint. He must go into dock; a sea phrase, signifying that the person spoken of must undergo a salivation. Docking is also a punishment inflicted by sailors on the prostitutes who have infected them with the venereal disease; it consists in cutting off all their clothes, petticoats, shift and all, close to their stays, and then turning them into the street.

Doctor. Milk and water, with a little rum, and some nutmeg; also the name of a composition used by distillers,

to

to make spirits appear stronger than they really are, or, in their phrase, better proof.

DOCTORS. Loaded dice, that will run but two or three chances. They put the doctors upon him; they cheated him with loaded dice.

DODSEY. A woman: perhaps a corruption of Doxey. *Cant.*

DOG BUFFERS. Dog stealers, who kill those dogs not advertised for, sell their skins, and feed the remaining dogs with their flesh.

DOG IN A DOUBLET. A daring, resolute fellow. In Germany and Flanders the boldest dogs used to hunt the boar. having a kind of buff doublet buttoned on their bodies, Rubens has represented several so equipped, so has Sneyders.

DOG. An old dog at it; expert or accustomed to any thing. Dog in a manger; one who would prevent another from enjoying what he himself does not want: an allusion to the well-known fable. The dogs have not dined; a common saying to any one whose shirt hangs out behind. To dog, or dodge; to follow at a distance. To blush like a blue dog, i. e. not at all. To walk the black dog on any one; a punishment inflicted in the night on a fresh prisoner, by his comrades, in case of his refusal to pay the usual footing or garnish.

DOG LATIN. Barbarous Latin, such as was formerly used by the lawyers in their pleadings.

DOG'S PORTION. A lick and a smell. He comes in for only a dog's portion; a saying of one who is a distant admirer or dangler after women. See DANGLER.

DOG'S RIG. To copulate till you are tired, and then turn tail to it.

DOG'S SOUP. Rain water.

DOG VANE. A cockade. *Sea term.*

DOGGED. Surly.

DOGGESS, DOG'S WIFE OR LADY, PUPPY'S MAMMA. Jocular ways of calling a woman a bitch.

DOLL. Bartholomew doll; a tawdry, over-drest woman, like one of the children's dolls at Bartholomew fair. To mill doll; to beat hemp at Bridewell, or any other house of correction.

DOLLY. A Yorkshire dolly; a contrivance for washing, by means of a kind of wheel fixed in a tub, which being turned about, agitates and cleanses the linen put into it, with soap and water.

DOMINE DO LITTLE. An impotent old fellow.

DOMINEER. To reprove or command in an insolent or haughty

haughty manner. Don't think as how you shall domineer here.

DOMMERER. A beggar pretending that his tongue has been cut out by the Algerines, or cruel and blood-thirsty Turks, or else that he was born deaf and dumb. *Cant.*

DONE, or DONE OVER. Robbed: also, convicted or hanged. *Cant.*—See Do.

DONE UP. Ruined by gaming and extravagances. *Modern term.*

DONKEY, DONKEY DICK. A he, or jack ass: called donkey, perhaps, from the Spanish or don-like gravity of that animal, intitled also the king of Spain's trumpeter.

DOODLE. A silly fellow, or noodle: see NOODLE. Also a child's penis. Doodle doo, or Cock a doodle doo; a childish appellation for a cock, in imitation of its note when crowing.

DOODLE SACK. A bagpipe. *Dutch.*—Also the private parts of a woman.

DOPEY. A beggar's trull.

DOT AND GO ONE. To waddle: generally applied to persons who have one leg shorter than the other, and who, as the sea phrase is, go upon an uneven keel. Also a jeering appellation for an inferior writing-master, or teacher of arithmetic.

DOUBLE. To tip any one the double; to run away in his or her debt.

DOUBLE JUGG. A man's backside. *Cotton's Virgil.*

DOVE-TAIL. A species of regular answer, which fits into the subject, like the contrivance whence it takes its name: Ex. Who owns this? The dovetail is, Not you by your asking.

DOUGLAS. Roby Douglas, with one eye and a stinking breath; the breech. *Sea wit.*

DOWDY. A coarse, vulgar-looking woman.

DOWN HILLS. Dice that run low.

DOWN. Aware of a thing. Knowing it. There is *no down.* A cant phrase used by house-breakers to signify that the persons belonging to any house are not on their guard, or that they are fast asleep, and have not heard any noise to alarm them.

TO DOWSE. To take down: as, Dowse the pendant. Dowse your dog vane; take the cockade out of your hat. Dowse the glim; put out the candle.

DOWSE ON THE CHOPS. A blow in the face.

DOWSER. Vulgar pronunciation of *douceur.*

DOXIES. She beggars, wenches, whores.

DRAP. A nasty, sluttish whore.

DRAG. To go on the drag; to follow a cart or waggon, in order to rob it. *Cant.*

DRAG LAY. Waiting in the streets to rob carts or waggons.

DRAGGLETAIL or DAGGLETAIL. One whose garments are bespattered with dag or dew: generally applied to the female sex, to signify a slattern.

DRAGOONING IT. A man who occupies two branches of one profession, is said to dragoon it; because, like the soldier of that denomination, he serves in a double capacity. Such is a physician who furnishes the medicines, and compounds his own prescriptions.

DRAIN. Gin: so called from the diuretic qualities imputed to that liquor.

DRAM. A glass or small measure of any spirituous liquors, which, being originally sold by apothecaries, were estimated by drams, ounces, &c. Dog's dram; to spit in his mouth, and clap his back.

DRAM-A-TICK. A dram served upon credit.

DRAPER. An ale draper; an alehouse keeper.

DRAUGHT, OR BILL, ON THE PUMP AT ALDGATE. A bad or false bill of exchange. See ALDGATE.

DRAW LATCHES. Robbers of houses whose doors are only fastened with latches. *Cant.*

TO DRAW. To take any thing from a pocket. To draw a swell of a clout. To pick a gentleman's pocket of a handkerchief. To draw the long bow; to tell lies.

DRAWERS. Stockings. *Cant.*

DRAWING THE KING'S PICTURE. Coining. *Cant.*

TO DRESS. To beat. I'll dress his hide neatly; I'll beat him soundly.

DRIBBLE. A method of pouring out, as it were, the dice from the box, gently, by which an old practitioner is enabled to cog one of them with his fore-finger.

DRIPPER. A gleet.

DROMEDARY. A heavy, bungling thief or rogue. A purple dromedary; a bungler in the art and mystery of thieving. *Cant.*

DROMMERARS. See DOMMERER.

DROP. The new drop; a contrivance for executing felons at Newgate, by means of a platform, which drops from under them: this is also called the last drop. See LEAF. See MORNING DROP.

DROP A COG. To let fall, with design, a piece of gold or silver, in order to draw in and cheat the person who sees it picked up; the piece so dropped is called a dropt cog.

Drop in the Eye. Almost drunk.

Dropping Member. A man's yard with a gonorrhœa.

Drop Coves. Persons who practice the fraud of dropping a ring or other article, and picking it up before the person intended to be defrauded, they pretend that the thing is very valuable to induce their gull to lend them money, or to purchase the article. See Fawny Rig, and Money Droppers.

To Drop down. To be dispirited. This expression is used by thieves to signify that their companion did not die game, as the kiddy dropped down when he went to be twisted; the young fellow was very low spirited when he walked out to be hanged.

To Drub. To beat any one with a stick, or rope's end: perhaps a contraction of *dry rub*. It is also used to signify a good beating with any instrument.

Drummer. A jockey term for a horse that throws about his fore legs irregularly: the idea is taken from a kettle drummer, who in beating makes many flourishes with his drumsticks.

Drunk. Drunk as a wheel-barrow. Drunk as David's sow. See David's Sow.

Drury Lane Ague. The venereal disorder.

Drury Lane Vestal. A woman of the town, or prostitute; Drury-lane and its environs were formerly the residence of many of those ladies.

Dry Bob. A smart repartee: also copulation without emission; in law Latin, *siccus robertulus*.

Dry Boots. A sly humorous fellow.

Dub. A picklock, or master-key. *Cant.*

Dub Lay. Robbing houses by picking the locks.

Dub the Jigger. Open the door. *Cant.*

Dub o' th' Hick. A lick on the head.

Dubber. A picker of locks. *Cant.*

Duce. Two-pence.

Duck. A lame duck; an Exchange-alley phrase for a stock-jobber, who either cannot or will not pay his losses, or differences, in which case he is said to *waddle out of the alley*, as he cannot appear there again till his debts are settled and paid; should he attempt it, he would be hustled out by the fraternity.

Ducks and Drakes. To make ducks and drakes: a school-boy's amusement, practised with pieces of tile, oyster-shells, or flattish stones, which being skimmed along the surface of a pond, or still river, rebound many

 times.

times. To make ducks and drakes of one's money; to throw it idly away.

DUCK F-CK-R. The man who has the care of the poultry on board a ship of war.

DUCK LEGS. Short legs.

DUDDERS, or WHISPERING DUDDERS. Cheats who travel the country, pretending to sell smuggled goods: they accost their intended dupes in a whisper. The goods they have for sale are old shop-keepers, or damaged; purchased by them of large manufactories. See DUFFER.

DUDDERING RAKE. A thundering rake, a buck of the first head, one extremely lewd.

DUDGEON. Anger.

DUDS. Clothes.

DUFFERS. Cheats who ply in different parts of the town, particularly about Water-lane, opposite St. Clement's church, in the Strand, and pretend to deal in smuggled goods, stopping all country people, or such as they think they can impose on; which they frequently do, by selling them Spital-fields goods at double their current price.

DUGS. A woman's breasts.

DUKE, or RUM DUKE. A queer unaccountable fellow.

DUKE OF LIMBS. A tall, awkward, ill-made fellow.

DUKE HUMPHREY. To dine with Duke Humphrey; to fast. In old St. Paul's church was an aisle called Duke Humphrey's walk (from a tomb vulgarly called his, but in reality belonging to John of Gaunt), and persons who walked there, while others were at dinner, were said to dine with Duke Humphrey.

DULL SWIFT. A stupid, sluggish fellow, one long going on an errand.

DUMB ARM. A lame arm.

DUMB-FOUNDED. Silenced, also soundly beaten.

DUMB GLUTTON. A woman's privities.

DUMB WATCH. A venereal bubo in the groin.

DUMMEE. A pocket book. A dummee hunter. A pick-pocket, who lurks about to steal pocket books out of gentlemen's pockets. Frisk the dummee of the screens; take all the bank notes out of the pocket book, ding the dummee, and bolt, they sing out beef. Throw away the pocket book, and run off, as they call out "stop thief."

DUMPLIN. A short thick man or woman. Norfolk dumplin; a jeering appellation of a Norfolk man, dumplins being a favourite kind of food in that county.

DUMPS. Down in the dumps; low-spirited, melancholy: jocularly said to be derived from Dumpos, a king of Egypt, who

who died of melancholy. Dumps are also small pieces of lead, cast by schoolboys in the shape of money

DUN. An importunate creditor. Dunny, in the provincial dialect of several counties, signifies *deaf*; to dun, then, perhaps may mean to deafen with importunate demands: some derive it from the word *donnez*, which signifies *give*. But the true original meaning of the word, owes its birth to one Joe Dun, a famous bailiff of the town of Lincoln, so extremely active, and so dexterous in his business, that it became a proverb, when a man refused to pay, Why do not you *Dun* him? that is, Why do not you set Dun to arrest him? Hence it became a cant word, and is now as old as since the days of Henry VII. Dun was also the general name for the hangman, before that of Jack Ketch.

And presently a halter got,
Made of the best strong hempen teer,
And ere a cat could lick her ear,
Had tied it up with as much art,
As DUN himself could do for's heart.

Cotton's Virgil Trav. book iv.

DUNAKER. A stealer of cows and calves.

DUNEGAN. A privy. A water closet.

DUNGHILL. A coward: a cockpit phrase, all but game cocks being styled dunghills. To die dunghill; to repent, or shew any signs of contrition at the gallows. Moving dunghill; a dirty, filthy man or woman. Dung, an abbreviation of dunghill, also means a journeyman taylor who submits to the law for regulating journeymen taylors' wages, therefore deemed by the flints a coward. See FLINTS.

DUNNOCK. A cow. *Cant.*

TO DUP. To open a door: a contraction of *do ope* or *open*. See DUB.

DURHAM MAN. Knocker kneed, he grinds mustard with his knees: Durham is famous for its mustard.

DUST. Money. Down with your dust; deposit the money. To raise or kick up a dust; to make a disturbance or riot: see BREEZE. Dust it away; drink about.

DUSTMAN. A dead man: your father is a dustman.

DUTCH COMFORT. Thank God it is no worse.

DUTCH CONCERT. Where every one plays or signs a different tune.

DUTCH FEAST. Where the entertainer gets drunk before his guest.

DUTCH RECKONING, or ALLE-MAL. A verbal or lump account, without particulars, as brought at spunging or bawdy houses.

DUT-

Dutchess. A woman enjoyed with her pattens on, or by a man in boots, is said to be made a dutchess.

Die hard, or game. To die hard, is to shew no signs of fear or contrition at the gallows; not to whiddle or squeak. This advice is frequently given to felons going to suffer the law, by their old comrades, anxious for the honour of the gang.

Earnest. A deposit in part of payment, to bind a bargain.

Earth Bath. A Grave.

Easy. Make the cull easy or quiet; gag or kill him. As easy as pissing the bed.

Easy Virtue. A lady of easy virtue: an impure or prostitute.

Eat. To eat like a beggar man, and wag his under jaw; a jocular reproach to a proud man. To eat one's words; to retract what one has said.

To Edge. To excite, stimulate, or provoke; or as it is vulgarly called, to egg a man on. Fall back, fall edge; i. e. let what will happen. Some derive to egg on, from the Latin word, *age, age.*

Eight Eyes. I will knock out two of your eight eyes; a common Billingsgate threat from one fish nymph to another: every woman, according to the naturalists of that society, having eight eyes; viz. two seeing eyes, two bub-eyes, a bell-eye, two pope's eyes, and a ***-eye. He has fallen down and trod upon his eye; said of one who has a black eye.

Elbow Grease. Labour. Elbow grease will make an oak table shine.

Elbow Room. Sufficient space to act in. Out at elbows; said of an estate that is mortgaged.

Elbow Shaker. A gamester, one who rattles Saint Hugh's bones, i. e. the dice.

Ellenborough Lodge. The King's Bench Prison. Lord Ellenborough's teeth; the chevaux de frize round the top of the wall of that prison.

Elf. A fairy or hobgoblin, a little man or woman.

Emperor. Drunk as an emperor, i. e. ten times as drunk as a lord.

English Burgundy. Porter.

Ensign Bearer. A drunken man, who looks red in the face, or hoists his colours in his drink.

Equipt. Rich; also, having new clothes. Well equipt; full of money, or well dressed. The cull equipped me with a brace of meggs; the gentleman furnished me with a couple of guineas.

Essex Lion. A calf; Essex being famous for calves, and chiefly supplying the London markets.

Essex Stile. A ditch; a great part of Essex is low marshy ground, in which there are more ditches than stiles.

Eternity Box. A coffin.

Eves. Hen roosts.

Eve's Custom-house, where Adam made his first entry. The monosyllable.

Eves Dropper. One that lurks about to rob hen-roosts; also a listener at doors and windows, to hear private conversation.

Evil. A halter. *Cant.* Also a wife.

Ewe. A white ewe; a beautiful woman. An old ewe, drest lamb fashion; an old woman, drest like a young girl.

Execution Day. Washing day.

Expended. Killed: alluding to the gunner's accounts, wherein the articles consumed are charged under the title of expended. *Sea phrase.*

Eye. It's all my eye and Betty Martin. It's all nonsense, all mere stuff.

Eye-sore. A disagreeable object. It will be an eye-sore as long as she lives, said by a man whose wife was cut for a fistula in ano.

F A G

FACE-MAKING. Begetting children. To face it out; to persist in a falsity. No face but his own: a saying of one who has no money in his pocket or no court cards in his hand.

Facer. A bumper, a glass filled so full as to leave no room for the lip. Also a violent blow on the face.

Fadge. It won't fadge; it won't do. A farthing.

To Fag. To beat. Fag the bloss; beat the wench. *Cant.* A fag also means a boy of an inferior form or class, who acts as a servant to one of a superior, who is said to fag him,

him, he is my fag; whence, perhaps, fagged out, for jaded or tired. To stand a good fag; not to be soon tired.

FAGGER. A little boy put in at a window to rob the house.

FAGGOT. A man hired at a muster to appear as a soldier. To faggot in the canting sense, means to bind: an allusion to the faggots made up by the woodmen, which are all bound. Faggot the culls; bind the men.

FAITHFUL. One of the faithful; a taylor who gives long credit. His faith has made him unwhole; i. e. trusting too much, broke him.

FAIR. A set of subterraneous rooms in the Fleet Prison.

FAKEMENT. A counterfeit signature. A forgery. Tell the macers to mind their fakements; desire the swindlers to be careful not to forge another person's signature.

FALLALLS. Ornaments, chiefly women's, such as ribands, necklaces, &c.

FALLEN AWAY FROM A HORSE LOAD TO A CART LOAD. A saying on one grown fat.

FAMILY MAN. A thief or receiver of stolen goods.

FAM LAY. Going into a goldsmith's shop, under pretence of buying a wedding ring, and palming one or two, by daubing the hand with some viscous matter.

FAMS, OR FAMBLES. Hands. Famble cheats; rings or gloves. *Cant.*

TO FAMGRASP. To shake hands: figuratively, to agree or make up a difference. Famgrasp the cove; shake hands with the fellow. *Cant.*

FAMILY OF LOVE. Lewd women; also, a religious sect.

FANCY MAN. A man kept by a lady for secret services.

TO FAN. To beat any one. I fanned him sweetly; I beat him heartily.

FANTASTICALLY DRESSED, with more rags than ribands.

FART. He has let a brewer's fart, grains and all; said of one who has bewrayed his breeches.

Piss and fart,
Sound at heart.
Mingere cum bumbis,
Res saluberrima est lumbis.

I dare not trust my a-se with a fart: said by a person troubled with a looseness.

FART CATCHER. A valet or footman from his walking behind his master or mistress.

FARTING CRACKERS. Breeches.

FARTLEBERRIES. Excrement hanging about the anus.

FASTNER. A warrant.

FASTNESSES. Bogs.

FAT. The last landed, inned, or stowed, of any sort of merchandise: so called by the water-side porters, carmen, &c. All the fat is in the fire; that is, it is all over with us: a saying used in case of any miscarriage or disappointment in an undertaking; an allusion to overturning the frying pan into the fire. Fat, among printers, means void spaces.

AS FAT AS A HEN IN THE FOREHEAD. A saying of a meagre person.

FAT CULL. A rich fellow.

FAT HEADED. Stupid.

FAULKNER. A tumbler, juggler, or shewer of tricks; perhaps because they lure the people, as a faulconer does his hawks. *Cant.*

FAYTORS, or FATORS. Fortune tellers.

FAWNEY RIG. A common fraud, thus practised: A fellow drops a brass ring, double gilt, which he picks up before the party meant to be cheated, and to whom he disposes of it for less than its supposed, and ten times more than its real, value. See MONEY DROPPER.

FAWNEY. A ring.

FEAGUE. To feague a horse; to put ginger up a horse's fundament, and formerly, as it is said, a live eel, to make him lively and carry his tail well; it is said, a forfeit is incurred by any horse-dealer's servant, who shall shew a horse without first feaguing him. Feague is used, figuratively, for encouraging or spiriting one up.

FEAK. The fundament.

TO FEATHER ONE'S NEST. To enrich one's self.

FEATHER-BED LANE. A rough or stony lane.

FEE, FAW, FUM. Nonsensical words, supposed in childish story-books to be spoken by giants. I am not to be frighted by fee, faw, fum; I am not to be scared by nonsense.

FEEDER. A spoon. To nab the feeder; to steal a spoon.

FEET. To make feet for children's stockings; to beget children. An officer of feet; a jocular title for an officer of infantry.

FEINT. A sham attack on one part, when a real one is meant at another.

FELLOW COMMONER. An empty bottle: so called at the university of Cambridge, where fellow commoners are not in general considered as over full of learning. At Oxford an empty bottle is called a gentleman commoner for the same reason. They pay at Cambridge 250l. a year for the privilege of wearing a gold or silver tassel to their caps. The younger branches of the nobility have the pri-

privilege of wearing a hat, and from thence are denominated HAT FELLOW COMMONERS.

FEN. A bawd, or common prostitute. *Cant.*

TO FENCE. To pawn or sell to a receiver of stolen goods. The kiddey fenced his thimble for three quids; the young fellow pawned his watch for three guineas. To fence invariably means to pawn or sell goods to a receiver.

FENCING KEN. The magazine, or warehouse, where stolen goods are secreted.

FERME. A hole. *Cant.*

FERMERDY BEGGARS. All those who have not the sham sores or clymes.

FERRARA. Andrea Ferrara; the name of a famous sword-cutler: most of the Highland broad-swords are marked with his name; whence an Andrea Ferrara has become the common name for the glaymore or Highland broad-sword. See GLAYMORE.

FERRET. A tradesman who sells goods to young unthrift heirs, at excessive rates, and then continually duns them for the debt. To ferret; to search out or expel any one from his hiding-place, as a ferret drives out rabbits; also to cheat. Ferret-eyed; red-eyed: ferrets have red eyes.

FETCH. A trick, wheedle, or invention to deceive.

FEUTERER A dog-keeper: from the French *vautrier*, or *vaultrier*, one that leads a lime hound for the chase.

TO FIB. To beat. Fib the cove's quarron in the rumpad for the lour in his bung; beat the fellow in the highway for the money in his purse. *Cant.*--A fib is also a tiny lie.

FICE, or FOYSE. A small windy escape backwards, more obvious to the nose than ears; frequently by old ladies charged on their lap-dogs. See FIZZLE.

FID OF TOBACCO. A quid, from the small pieces of tow with which the vent or touch hole of a cannon is stopped. *Sea term.*

FIDDLE FADDLE. Trifling discourse, nonsense. A mere fiddle faddle fellow; a trifler.

FIDDLESTICK'S END. Nothing; the end of the ancient fiddlesticks ending in a point; hence metaphorically used to express a thing terminating in nothing.

FIDGETS. He has got the fidgets; said of one that cannot sit long in a place.

FIDLAM BEN. General thieves; called also St. Peter's sons, having every finger a fish-hook. *Cant.*

FIDDLERS MONEY. All sixpences: sixpence being the usual sum paid by each couple, for music at country wakes and hops. Fiddler's fare; meat, drink, and money. Fiddler's pay; thanks and wine.

FIELD LANE DUCK. A baked sheep's head.

FIERI FACIAS. A red-faced man is said to have been served with a writ of fieri facias.

FIGDEAN. To kill.

FIGGER. A little boy put in at a window to hand out goods to the diver. See DIVER.

FIGGING LAW. The art of picking pockets. *Cant.*

FIGURE DANCER. One who alters figures on bank notes, converting tens to hundreds.

FILCH, or FILEL. A beggar's staff, with an iron hook at the end, to pluck clothes from an hedge, or any thing out of a casement. Filcher; the same as angler. Filching cove; a man thief. Filching mort; a woman thief

FILE, FILE CLOY, or BUNGNIPPER. A pick pocket. To file; to rob or cheat. The file, or bungnipper goes generally in company with two assistants, the adam tiler, and another called the bulk or bulker, whose business it is to jostle the person they intend to rob, and push him against the wall, while the file picks his pocket, and gives the booty to the adam tiler, who scours off with it. *Cant.*

FIN. An arm. A one finned fellow; a man who has lost an arm. *Sea phrase.*

FINE. Fine as five pence. Fine as a cow-t—d stuck with primroses.

FINE. A man imprisoned for any offence. A fine of eighty-four months; a transportation for seven years.

FINGER IN EYE. To put finger in eye; to weep: commonly applied to women. The more you cry the less you'll p-ss; a consolatory speech used by sailors to their doxies. It is as great a pity to see a woman cry, as to see a goose walk barefoot; another of the same kind.

FINGER POST. A parson: so called, because he points out a way to others which he never goes himself. Like the finger post, he points out a way he has never been, and probably will never go, i. e. the way to heaven.

FINISH. The finish; a small coffee-house in Covent-Garden market, opposite Russel-street, open very early in the morning, and therefore resorted to by debauchees shut out of every other house· it is also called Carpenter's coffee-house.

FIRING A GUN. Introducing a story by head and shoulders. A man wanting to tell a particular story, said to the company, Hark! did you not hear a gun?—but now we are talking of a gun, I will tell you the story of one.

TO FIRE A SLUG. To drink a dram.

FIRE PRIGGERS. Villains who rob at fires, under pretence of assisting in removing the goods.

FIRE SHIP. A wench who has the venereal disease.

FIRE SHOVEL. He or she when young, was fed with a fire shovel; a saying of persons with wide mouths.

FISH. A seaman. A scaly fish; a rough, blunt tar. To have other fish to fry; to have other matters to mind, something else to do.

FIT. Suitable. It won't fit; It will not suit or do.

FIVE SHILLINGS. The sign of five shillings, i. e. the crown. Fifteen shillings; the sign of the three crowns.

FIZZLE. An escape backward.

FLABAGASTED. Confounded.

FLABBY. Relaxed, flaccid, not firm or solid.

FLAG. A groat. *Cant.*—The flag of defiance, or bloody flag is out; signifying the man is drunk, and alluding to the redness of his face. *Sea phrase.*

FLAM. A lie, or sham story: also a single stroke on a drum. To flam; to hum, to amuse, to deceive. Flim flams; idle stories.

FLAP DRAGON. A clap, or pox.

TO FLARE. To blaze, shine or glare.

FLASH. Knowing. Understanding another's meaning. The swell was flash, so I could not draw his fogle. The gentleman saw what I was about, and therefore I could not pick his pocket of his silk handkerchief. To patter flash, to speak the slang language. See PATTER.

FLASH PANNEYS. Houses to which thieves and prostitutes resort.

> Next for his favourite *mot* (1) the *kiddey* (2) looks about,
> And if she's in a *flash panney* (3) he swears he'll have her out;
> So he *fences* (4) all his *togs* (5) to buy her *duds*, (6) anh then
> He *frisks* (7) his master's *lob* (8) to take her from the bawdy *ken* (9).
>
> FLASH SONG.

FLASH. A periwig. Rum flash; a fine long wig. Queer flash; a miserable weather-beaten caxon.

TO FLASH. To shew ostentatiously. To flash one's ivory; to laugh and shew one's teeth. Don't flash your ivory, but shut your potatoe trap, and keep your guts warm; the Devil loves hot tripes.

TO FLASH THE HASH. To vomit. *Cant.*

FLASH KEN. A house that harbours thieves.

FLASH LINGO. The canting or slang language.

FLASH MAN. A bully to a bawdy house. A whore's bully.

FLAT. A bubble, gull, or silly fellow.

FLAT COCK. A female.

FLAWD. Drunk.

(1) Girl. (2) Youth. (3) Brothel. (4) Pawns. (5) Cloaths. (6) Wearing Apparel. (7) Robs. (8) Till. (9) House.

FLAYBOTTOMIST. A bum-brusher, or schoolmaster.

To FLAY, or FLEA, THE FOX. To vomit.

FLEA BITE. A trifling injury. To send any one away with a flea in his ear; to give any one a hearty scolding.

To FLEECE. To rob, cheat, or plunder.

FLEMISH ACCOUNT. A losing, or bad account.

FLESH BROKER. A match-maker, a bawd.

FLICKER. A drinking glass. *Cant.*

FLICKERING. Grinning or laughing in a man's face.

FLICKING. Cutting. Flick me some panam and caffan; cut me some bread and cheese. Flick the peter; cut off the cloak-bag, or portmanteau.

To FLING. To trick or cheat. He flung me fairly out of it: he cheated me out of it.

FLINTS. Journeymen taylors, who on a late occasion refused to work for the wages settled by law. Those who submitted, were by the mutineers styled dungs, i. e. dunghills.

FLIP. Small beer, brandy, and sugar: this mixture, with the addition of a lemon, was by sailors, formerly called Sir Cloudsly, in memory of Sir Cloudsly Shovel, who used frequently to regale himself with it.

FLOATING ACADEMY. See CAMPBELL'S ACADEMY.

FLOATING HELL. The hulks.

To FLOG. To whip.

FLOGGER. A horsewhip. *Cant.*

FLOGGING CULLY. A debilitated lecher, commonly an old one.

FLOGGING COVE. The beadle, or whipper, in Bridewell.

FLOGGING STAKE. The whipping-post.

To FLOOR. To knock down. Floor the pig; knock down the officer.

FLOURISH. To take a flourish; to enjoy a woman in a hasty manner, to take a flyer. See FLYER.

To FLOUT. To jeer, to ridicule.

FLUMMERY. Oatmeal and water boiled to a jelly; also compliments, neither of which are over-nourishing.

FLUSH IN THE POCKET. Full of money. The cull is flush in the fob. The fellow is full of money.

FLUSTERED. Drunk.

FLUTE. The recorder of a corporation; a recorder was an antient musical instrument.

To FLUX. To cheat, cozen, or over-reach; also to salivate. To flux a wig; to put it up in curl, and bake it.

FLY. Knowing. Acquainted with another's meaning or proceeding. The rattling cove is fly; the coachman knows what we are about.

Fly. A waggon. *Cant.*

Fly-by-Night. You old fly-by-night; an ancient term of reproach to an old woman, signifying that she was a witch, and alluding to the nocturnal excursions attributed to witches, who were supposed to fly abroad to their meetings, mounted on brooms.

Fly Slicers. Life-guard men, from their sitting on horseback, under an arch, where they are frequently observed to drive away flies with their swords.

Flyer. To take a flyer; to enjoy a woman with her clothes on, or without going to bed.

Flyers. Shoes.

Fly-flapped. Whipt in the stocks, or at the cart's tail.

Flying Camps. Beggars plying in a body at funerals.

Flying Giggers. Turnpike gates.

Flying Horse. A lock in wrestling, by which he who uses it throws his adversary over his head.

Flying Pasty. Sirreverence wrapped in paper and thrown over a neighbour's wall.

Flying Porters. Cheats who obtain money by pretending to persons who have been lately robbed, that they may come from a place or party where, and from whom, they may receive information respecting the goods stolen from them, and demand payment as porters.

Flying Stationers. Ballad-singers and hawkers of penny histories.

Flymsey. A bank note.

Fob. A cheat, trick, or contrivance. I will not be fobbed off so; I will not be thus deceived with false pretences. The fob is also a small breeches pocket for holding a watch.

Fog. Smoke. *Cant.*

Fogey. Old Fogey. A nick name for an invalid soldier: derived from the French word *fougeux*, fierce or fiery.

Fogle. A silk handkerchief.

Fogram. An old fogram; a fusty old fellow.

Fogus. Tobacco. Tip me a gage of fogus; give me a pipe of tobacco. *Cant.*

Fool. A fool at the end of a stick; a fool at one end, and a maggot at the other; gibes on an angler.

Fool Finder. A bailiff.

Foolish. An expression among impures, signifying the cully who pays, in opposition to a flash man. Is he foolish or flash?

Foot Pads, or Low Pads. Rogues who rob on foot.

Foot Wabbler. A contemptuous appellation for a foot soldier, commonly used by the cavalry.

Foot-

Footman's Mawnd. An artificial sore made with unslaked lime, soap, and the rust of old iron, on the back of a beggar's hand, as if hurt by the bite or kick of a hórse.

Footy Despicable. A footy fellow, a despicable fellow; from the French *foutüe.*

Fore Foot, or Paw. Give us your fore foot; give us your hand.

Foreman of the Jury. One who engrosses all the talk to himself, or speaks for the rest of the company.

Fork. A pickpocket. Let us fork him; let us pick his pocket.—'The newest and most dexterous way, which is, 'to thrust the fingers strait, stiff, open, and very quick, 'into the pocket, and so closing them, hook what can 'be held between them.' *N. B.* This was taken from a book written many years ago: doubtless the art of picking pockets, like all others, must have been much improved since that time.

Forlorn Hope. A gamester's last stake.

Fortune Hunters. Indigent men, seeking to enrich themselves by marrying a woman of fortune.

Fortune Teller, or Cunning Man. A judge, who tells every prisoner his fortune, lot or doom. To go before the fortune teller, lambskin men, or conjuror; to be tried at an assize. See **Lambskin Men.**

Foul. To foul a plate with a man, to take a dinner with him.

Foul-mouthed. Abusive.

Foundling. A child dropped in the streets, and found, and educated at the parish expence.

Fousil. The name of a public house, where the Eccentrics assemble in May's Buildings, St. Martin's Lane.

Fox. A sharp, cunning fellow. Also an old term for a sword, probably a rusty one, or else from its being dyed red with blood; some say this name alluded to certain swords of remarkable good temper, or metal, marked with the figure of a fox, probably the sign, or rebus, of the maker.

Fox's Paw. The vulgar pronunciation of the French words *faux pâs.* He made a confounded fox's paw.

Foxed. Intoxicated.

Foxey. Rank. Stinking.

Foxing a Boot. Mending the foot by capping it.

Foyst. A pickpocket, cheat, or rogue. See **Wotton's Gang.**

To Foyst. To pick a pocket.

Foysted in. Words or passages surreptitiously interpolated or inserted into a book or writing.

Fraters. Vagabonds who beg with sham patents, or briefs, for hospitals, fires, inundations, &c.

Free. Free of fumblers hall; a saying of one who cannot get his wife with child.

FREE AND EASY JOHNS. A society which meet at the Hole in the Wall, Fleet-street, to tipple porter, and sing bawdry.

FREE BOOTERS. Lawless robbers and plunderers: originally soldiers who served without pay, for the privilege of plundering the enemy.

FREEHOLDER. He whose wife accompanies him to the alehouse.

FREEMAN'S QUAY. Free of expence. To lush at Freeman's Quay; to drink at another's cost.

FREEZE. A thin, small, hard cider, much used by vintners and coopers in parting their wines, to lower the price of them, and to advance their gain. A freezing vintner: a vintner who balderdashes his wine.

FRENCH CREAM. Brandy; so called by the old tabbies and dowagers when drank in their tea.

FRENCH DISEASE. The venereal disease, said to have been imported from France. French gout; the same. He suffered by a blow over the snout with a French faggot-stick; i. e. he lost his nose by the pox.

FRENCH LEAVE. To take French leave; to go off without taking leave of the company: a saying frequently applied to persons who have run away from their creditors.

FRENCHIFIED. Infected with the venereal disease. The mort is Frenchified: the wench is infected.

FRESH MILK. Cambridge new comers to the university.

FRESHMAN. One just entered a member of the university.

FRIBBLE. An effeminate fop; a name borrowed from a celebrated character of that kind, in the farce of Miss in her Teens, written by Mr. Garrick.

FRIDAY-FACE. A dismal countenance. Before, and even long after the Reformation, Friday was a day of abstinence, or *jour maigre*. Immediately after the restoration of king Charles II. a proclamation was issued, prohibiting all publicans from dressing any suppers on a Friday.

To FRIG. Figuratively used for trifling.

FRIG PIG. A trifling, fiddle-faddle fellow.

FRIGATE. A well-rigged frigate; a well-dressed wench.

FRISK. To dance the Paddington frisk; to be hanged.

To FRISK. Used by thieves to signify searching a person whom they have robbed. Blast his eyes! frisk him.

FROE, or VROE. A woman, wife, or mistress. Brush to your froe, or bloss, and wheedle for crop; run to your mistress, and sooth and coax her out of some money. *Dutch.*

FROGLANDER. A Dutchman.

FROSTY

Frosty Face. One pitted with the small pox.

Frog's Wine. Gin.

Fruitful Vine. A woman's private parts, i. e. that has *flowers* every month, and bears fruit in nine months.

Frummagemmed. Choaked, strangled, suffocated, or hanged. *Cant.*

Fubsey. Plump. A fubsey wench; a plump, healthy wench.

Fuddle. Drunk. This is rum fuddle; this is excellent tipple, or drink. Fuddle; drunk. Fuddle cap; a drunkard.

Fudge. Nonsense.

Fulhams. Loaded dice are called high and lowmen, or high and low fulhams, by Ben Jonson and other writers of his time; either because they were made at Fulham, or from that place being the resort of sharpers.

Full of Emptiness. Jocular term for empty.

Full March. The Scotch greys are in full march by the crown office; the lice are crawling down his head.

Fumbler. An old or impotent man. To fumble, also means to go awkwardly about any work, or manual operation.

Fun. A cheat, or trick. Do you think to fun me out of it? Do you think to cheat me?---Also the breech, perhaps from being the abbreviation of fundament. I'll kick your fun. *Cant.*

To Funk. To use an unfair mot on of the hand in plumping at taw. *Schoolboy's term.*

Funk. To smoke; figuratively, to smoke or stink through fear. I was in a cursed funk. To funk the cobler; a schoolboy's trick, performed with assafœtida and cotton, which are stuffed into a pipe: the cotton being lighted, and the bowl of the pipe covered with a coarse handkerchief, the smoke is blown out at the small end, through the crannies of a cobler's stall.

Furmen. Aldermen.

Furmity, or Fromenty. Wheat boiled up to a jelly. To simper like a furmity kettle: to smile, or look merry about the gills.

Fuss. A confusion, a hurry, an unnecessary to do about trifles.

Fussock. A lazy fat woman. An old fussock; a frowsy old woman.

Fustian. Bombast language. Red fustian; port wine.

Fusty Luggs. A beastly, sluttish woman.

To Fuzz. To shuffle cards minutely: also, to change the pack.

GAB, or Gob. The mouth. Gift of the gab; a facility of speech, nimble tongued eloquence. To blow the gab; to confess, or peach.

Gab, or Gob, String. A bridle.

Gabey. A foolish fellow.

Gad-so. An exclamation said to be derived from the Italian word *cazzo*.

Gaff. A fair. The drop coves maced the joskins at the gaff; the ring-droppers cheated the countryman at the fair.

To Gaff. To game by tossing up halfpence.

Gag. An instrument used chiefly by housebreakers and thieves, for propping open the mouth of a person robbed, thereby to prevent his calling out for assistance.

Gage. A quart pot, or a pint; also a pipe. *Cant.*

Gage, or Fogus. A pipe of tobacco.

Gaggers. High and Low. Cheats, who by sham pretences, and wonderful stories of their sufferings, impose on the credulity of well meaning people. See Rum Gagger.

Galimaufrey. A hodgepodge made up of the remnants and scraps of the larder.

Gall. His gall is not yet broken; a saying used in prisons of a man just brought in, who appears dejected.

Galley. Building the galley; a game formerly used at sea, in order to put a trick upon a landsman, or fresh-water sailor. It being agreed to play at that game, one sailor personates the builder, and another the merchant or contractor: the builder first begins by laying the keel, which consists of a number of men laid all along on their backs, one after another, that is, head to foot; he next puts in the ribs or knees, by making a number of men sit feet to feet, at right angles to, and on each side of, the keel: he now fixing on the person intended to be the object of the joke, observes he is a fierce-looking fellow, and fit for the lion; he accordingly places him at the head, his arms being held or locked in by the two persons next to him, representing the ribs. After several other dispositions, the builder delivers over the galley to the contractor as complete: but he, among other faults and objections,

tions, observes the lion is not gilt, on which the builder or one of his assistants, runs to the head, and dipping a mop in the excrement, thrusts it into the face of the lion.

GALLEY FOIST. A city barge, used formerly on the lord mayor's day, when he was sworn in at Westminster.

GALLIED. Hurried, vexed, over-fatigued, perhaps like a galley slave.

GALLIGASKINS. Breeches.

GALLIPOT. A nick name for an apothecary,

GALLORE, or GOLORE. Plenty.

GALLOPER. A blood horse. A hunter. The toby gill clapped his bleeders to his galloper and tipped the straps the double. The highwayman spurred his horse and got away from the officers.

GALLOWS BIRD. A thief, or pickpocket: also one that associates with them.

GAMBS. Thin, ill-shaped legs: a corruption of the French word *jambes*. Farcy gambs; sore or swelled legs.

GAMBADOES. Leathern cases of stiff leather, used in Devonshire instead of boots; they are fastened to the saddle, and admit the leg, shoe and all: the name was at first jocularly given.

GAMBLER. A sharper, or tricking gamester.

GAME. Any mode of robbing. The toby is now a queer game; to rob on the highway is now a bad mode of acting. This observation is frequently made by thieves; the roads being now so well guarded by the horse patrole; and gentlemen travel with little cash in their pockets.

GAME. Bubbles or pigeons drawn in to be cheated. Also, at bawdy-houses, lewd women. Mother have you any game; mother, have you any girls? To die game; to suffer at the gallows without shewing any signs of fear or repentance. Game pullet; a young whore, or forward girl in the way of becoming one.

GAMON. To humbug. To deceive. To tell lies. What rum gamon the old file pitched to the flat; how finely the knowing old fellow humbugged the fool.

GAMON AND PATTER. Common place talk of any profession; as the gamon and patter of a horse-dealer, sailor, &c.

GAN. The mouth or lips. *Cant.*

GANDER MONTH. That month in which a man's wife lies in: wherefore, during that time, husbands plead a sort of indulgence in matters of gallantry.

GANG. A company of men, a body of sailors, a knot of

thieves, pickpockets, &c. A gang of sheep trotters; the four feet of a sheep.

GAOLER'S COACH. A hurdle: traitors being usually conveyed from the gaol, to the place of execution, on a hurdle or sledge.

GAP STOPPER. A whoremaster.

GAPESEED. Sights; any thing to feed the eye. I am come abroad for a little gapeseed.

GARNISH. An entrance fee demanded by the old prisoners of one just committed to gaol.

GARRET, or UPPER STORY. The head. His garret, or upper story, is empty, or unfurnished; i. e. he has no brains, he is a fool.

GARRET ELECTION. A ludicrous ceremony, practised every new parliament: it consists of a mock election of two members to represent the borough of Garret (a few straggling cottages near Wandsworth in Surry); the qualification of a voter is, having enjoyed a woman in the open air within that district: the candidates are commonly fellows of low humour, who dress themselves up in a ridiculous manner. As this brings a prodigious concourse of people to Wandsworth, the publicans of that place jointly contribute to the expence, which is sometimes considerable.

GAWKEY. A tall, thin, awkward young man or woman.

GAYING INSTRUMENT. The penis.

GAZEBO. An elevated observatory or summer-house.

GEE. It won't gee; it won't hit or do, it does not suit or fit.

GELDING. An eunuch.

GELT. Money, *German.*—Also, castrated.

GENTLE CRAFT. The art of shoemaking. One of the gentle craft: a shoemaker: so called because once practised by St. Crispin.

GENTLEMAN COMMONER. An empty bottle; an university joke, gentlemen commoners not being deemed over full of learning.

GENTLEMAN'S COMPANION. A louse.

GENTLEMAN'S MASTER. A highway robber, because he makes a gentleman obey his commands, i. e. stand and deliver.

GENTLEMAN OF THREE INS. In debt, in gaol, and in danger of remaining there for life: or, in gaol, indicted, and in danger of being hanged in chains.

GENTLEMAN OF THREE OUTS. That is, without money, without wit, and without manners: some add another out, i. e. without credit.

GENTRY COVE. A gentleman. *Cant.*

GENTRY COVE KEN. A gentleman's house. *Cant.*

GENTRY MORT. A gentlewoman.

GEORGE. Yellow George; a guinea. Brown George: an ammunition loaf.

GERMAN DUCK. Half a sheep's head boiled with onions.

GET. One of his get; one of his offspring, or begetting.

GIB CAT. A northern name for a he cat, there commonly called Gilbert. As melancholy as a gib cat; as melancholy as a he cat who has been caterwauling, whence they always return scratched, hungry, and out of spirits. Aristotle says, *Omne animal post coitum est triste*; to which an anonymous author has given the following exception, *preter gallum gallinaceum, et sacerdotem gratis fornicantem.*

GIBBERISH. The cant language of thieves and gypsies, called Pedlars' French, and St. Giles's Greek: see ST. GILES'S GREEK. Also the mystic language of Geber, used by chymists. Gibberish likewise means a sort of disguised language, formed by inserting any consonant between each syllable of an English word; in which case it is called the gibberish of the letter inserted: if F, it is the F gibberish; if G, the G gibberish; as in the sentence How do you do? Howg dog youg dog.

GIBBE. A horse that shrinks from the collar and will not draw.

GIBLETS. To join giblets; said of a man and woman who cohabit as husband and wife, without being married; also to copulate.

GIBSON, or SIR JOHN GIBSON. A two-legged stool, used to support the body of a coach whilst finishing.

GIFTS. Small white specks under the finger nails, said to portend gifts or presents. A stingy man is said to be as full of gifts as a brazen horse of his farts.

GIFT OF THE GAB. A facility of speech.

GIGG. A nose. Snitchel his gigg; fillip his nose. Grunter's gigg; a hog's snout. Gigg is also a high one-horse chaise, and a woman's privities. To gigg a Smithfield hank; to hamstring an over-drove ox, vulgarly called a mad bullock.

GIGGER. A latch, or door. Dub the gigger; open the door. Gigger dubber; the turnkey of a jaol.

TO GIGGLE. To suppress a laugh. Gigglers; wanton women.

GILES'S OR ST. GILES'S BREED. Fat, ragged, and saucy; Newton and Dyot streets, the grand head-quarters of most of the thieves and pickpockets about London, are in St.

Giles's

Giles's parish. St. Giles's Greek; the cant language, called also Slang, Pedlars' French, and Flash.

GILFLURT. A proud minks, a vain capricious woman.

GILL. The abbreviation of Gillian, figuratively used for woman. Every jack has his gill; i. e. every jack has his gillian, or female mate.

GILLS. The cheeks. To look rosy about the gills; to have a fresh complexion. To look merry about the gills; to appear cheerful.

GILLY GAUPUS. A Scotch term for a tall awkward fellow.

GILT, or RUM DUBBER. A thief who picks locks, so called from the gilt or picklock key: many of them are so expert, that, from the lock of a church door to that of the smallest cabinet, they will find means to open it; these go into reputable public houses, where, pretending business, they contrive to get into private rooms, up stairs, where they open any bureaus or trunks they happen to find there.

GIMBLET-EYED. Squinting, either in man or woman.

GIMCRACK, or JIMCRACK. A spruce wench; a gimcrack also means a person who has a turn for mechanical contrivances.

GIN SPINNER. A distiller.

GINGAMBOBS. Toys, bawbles; also a man's privities. See THINGAMBOBS.

GINGER-PATED, or GINGER-HACKLED. Red haired: a term borrowed from the cockpit, where red cocks are called gingers.

GINGERBREAD. A cake made of treacle, flour, and grated ginger; also money. He has the gingerbread; he is rich.

GINGERBREAD WORK. Gilding and carving: these terms are particularly applied by seamen on board Newcastle colliers, to the decorations of the sterns and quarters of West-Indiamen, which they have the greatest joy in defacing.

GINGERLY. Softly, gently, tenderly. To go gingerly to work; to attempt a thing gently, or cautiously.

GINNY. An instrument to lift up a great, in order to steal what is in the window. *Cant.*

GIP from γυπς, a *wolf*. A servant at college.

GIRDS. Quips, taunts, severe or biting reflections.

GIZZARD. To grumble in the gizzard; to be secretly displeased,

Glass Eyes. A nick name for one wearing spectacles.

Glaymore. A Highland broad-sword; from the Erse *glay*, or *glaive*, a sword; and *more*, great.

Glaze. A window.

Glazier. One who breaks windows and shew-glasses, to steal goods exposed for sale. Glaziers; eyes. *Cant.*— Is your father a glazier; a question asked of a lad or young man, who stands between the speaker and the candle, or fire. If it is answered in the negative, the rejoinder is— I wish he was, that he might make a window through your body, to enable us to see the fire or light.

Glib. Smooth, slippery. Glib tongued; talkative.

Glim. A candle, or dark lantern, used in housebreaking; also fire. To glim; to burn in the hand. *Cant.*

Glimfenders. Andirons. *Cant.*

Glimflashy. Angry, or in a passion. *Cant.*

Glimjack. A link-boy. *Cant.*

Glimmer. Fire. *Cant.*

Glimmerers. Persons begging with sham licences, pretending losses by fire.

Glimms. Eyes.

Glimstick. A candlestick. *Cant.*

Globe. Pewter. *Cant.*

Gloves. To give any one a pair of gloves; to make them a present or bribe. To win a pair of gloves; to kiss a man whilst he sleeps: for this a pair of gloves is due to any lady who will thus earn them.

Gluepot. A parson: from joining men and women together in matrimony.

Glum. Sullen.

Glutton. A term used by bruisers to signify a man who will bear a great deal of beating.

Gnarler. A little dog that by his barking alarms the family when any person is breaking into the house.

Go, The. The dash. The mode. He is quite the go, he is quite varment, he is prime, he is bang up, are synonimous expressions.

Glybe. A writing. *Cant.*

Go Between. A pimp or bawd.

Go by the Ground. A little short person, man or woman.

Go Shop. The Queen's Head in Duke's court, Bow street, Covent Garden; frequented by the under players: where gin and water was sold in three-halfpenny bowls, called Goes; the gin was called Arrack. The go, the fashion; as, large hats are all the go.

GOADS. Those who wheedle in chapmen for horse-dealers.

GOAT. A lascivious person. Goatsjigg; making the beast with two backs, copulation.

GOB. The mouth; also a bit or morsel: whence gobbets. Gift of the gob; wide-mouthed, or one who speaks fluently, or sings well.

GOB STRING. A bridle.

GOBBLER. A turkey cock.

GODFATHER. He who pays the reckoning, or answers for the rest of the company: as, Will you stand godfather, and we will take care of the brat; i. e. repay you another time. Jurymen are also called godfathers, because they name the crime the prisoner before them has been guilty of, whether felony, petit larceny, &c.

GOG. All-a-gog; impatient, anxious, or desirous of a thing.

GOG AND MAGOG. Two giants, whose effigies stand on each side of the clock in Guildhall, London; of whom there is a tradition, that, when they hear the clock strike one, on the first of April, they will walk down from their places.

GOGGLES. Eyes: see OGLES. Goggle eyes; large prominent eyes. To goggle; to stare.

GOING UPON THE DUB. Going out to break open, or pick the locks of, houses.

GOLD DROPPERS. Sharpers who drop a piece of gold, which they pick up in the presence of some unexperienced person, for whom the trap is laid, this they pretend to have found, and, as he saw them pick it up, they invite him to a public house to partake of it: when there, two or three of their comrades drop in, as if by accident, and propose cards, or some other game, when they seldom fail of stripping their prey.

GOLD FINDER. One whose employment is to empty necessary houses; called also a tom-turd-man, and night-man: the latter, from that business being always performed in the night.

GOLDFINCH. One who has commonly a purse full of gold. Goldfinches; guineas.

GOLGOTHA OR THE PLACE OF SCULLS. Part of the Theatre at Oxford, where the heads of houses sit; those gentlemen being by the wits of the university called sculls.

GOLLUMPUS. A large, clumsy fellow.

GOLOSHES, i. e. Goliah's shoes. Large leathern clogs, worn by invalids over their ordinary shoes.

GOOD MAN. A word of various imports, according to the place where it is spoken: in the city it means a rich man; at at Hockley in the Hole, or St. Giles's, an expert boxer; at a bagnio in Covent Garden, a vigorous fornicator; at an alehouse or tavern, one who loves his pot or bottle; and sometimes, though but rarely, a virtuous man

GOOD WOMAN. A nondescript, represented on a famous sign in St. Giles's, in the form of a common woman, but without a head.

GOODYER'S PIG. Like Goodyer's pig; never well but when in mischief.

GOOSE. A taylor's goose; a smoothing iron used to press down the seams, for which purpose it must be heated: hence it is a jocular saying, that a taylor, be he ever so poor, is always sure to have a goose at his fire. He cannot say boh to a goose; a saying of a bashful or sheepish fellow.

GOOSE RIDING. A goose, whose neck is greased, being suspended by the legs to a cord tied to two trees or high posts, a number of men on horseback, riding full speed, attempt to pull off the head: which if they effect, the goose is their prize. This has been practised in Derbyshire within the memory of persons now living.

GOOSEBERRY. He played up old gooseberry among them; said of a person who, by force or threats, suddenly puts an end to a riot or disturbance.

GOOSEBERRY-EYED. One with dull grey eyes, like boiled gooseberries.

GOOSEBERRY WIG. A large frizzled wig: perhaps from a supposed likeness to a gooseberry bush.

GOOSECAP. A silly fellow or woman.

GORGER. A gentleman. A well dressed man. Mung kiddey. Mung the gorger; beg child beg, of the gentleman.

GOSPEL SHOP. A church.

GOREE. Money, chiefly gold: perhaps from the traffic carried on at that place, which is chiefly for gold dust. *Cant.*

GORMAGON. A monster with six eyes, three mouths, four arms, eight legs, five on one side and three on the other, three arses, two tarses, and a *** upon its back; a man on horseback, with a woman behind him.

GOTCH-GUTTED. Pot bellied: a gotch in Norfolk signifying a pitcher, or large round jug.

To GOUGE. To squeeze out a man's eye with the thumb: a cruel practice used by the Bostonians in America.

To GRABBLE. To seize. To grabble the bit; to seize any one's money. *Cant.*

GRAFTED. Cuckolded, i. e. having horns grafted on his head.

TO GRAB. To seize a man. The pigs grabbed the kiddey for a crack: the officers seized the youth for a burglary.

GRANNAM. Corn.

GRANNUM'S GOLD. Hoarded money: supposed to have belonged to the grandmother of the possessor.

GRANNY. An abbreviation of grandmother; also the name of an idiot, famous for licking her eye, who died Nov. 14, 1719. Go teach your granny to suck eggs; said to such as would instruct any one in a matter he knows better than themselves.

GRAPPLE THE RAILS. A cant name used in Ireland for whiskey.

GRAPPLING IRONS. Handcuffs.

GRAVE DIGGER. Like a grave digger; up to the a-se in business, and don't know which way to turn.

GRAVY-EYED. Blear-eyed, one whose eyes have a running humour.

TO GREASE. To bribe. To grease a man in the fist; to bribe him. To grease a fat sow in the a-se; to give to a rich man. Greasy chin; a treat given to parish officers in part of commutation for a bastard: called also, Eating a child.

GREAT INTIMATE. As great as shirt and shitten a-se.

GREAT JOSEPH. A surtout. *Cant.*

GREEDY GUTS. A covetous or voracious person.

GREEK. St. Giles's Greek; the slang lingo, cant, or gibberish.

GREEN. Doctor Green; i. e. grass: a physician, or rather medicine, found very successful in curing most disorders to which horses are liable. My horse is not well, I shall send him to Doctor Green.

GREEN. Young, inexperienced, unacquainted, ignorant. How green the cull was not to stag how the old file planted the books. How ignorant the booby was not to perceive how the old sharper placed the cards in such a manner as to insure the game.

GREEN BAG. An attorney: those gentlemen carry their clients' deeds in a green bag; and, it is said, when they have no deeds to carry, frequently fill them with an old pair of breeches, or any other trumpery, to give themselves the appearance of business.

GREEN GOWN. To give a girl a green gown; to tumble her on the grass.

Green Sickness. The disease of maids occasioned by celibacy.

Greenhead. An inexperienced young man.

Greenhorn. A novice on the town, an undebauched young fellow, just initiated into the society of bucks and bloods.

Greenwich Barbers. Retailers of sand from the pits at and about Greenwich, in Kent: perhaps they are styled barbers, from their constant shaving the sand-banks.

Greenwich Goose. A pensioner of Greenwich Hospital.

Gregorian Tree. The gallows: so named from Gregory Brandon, a famous finisher of the law; to whom Sir William Segar, garter king of arms (being imposed on by Brooke, a herald), granted a coat of arms.

Grey Beard. Earthen jugs formerly used in public house for drawing ale: they had the figure of a man with a large beard stamped on them; whence probably they took the name: see *Ben Jonson's Plays, Bartholomew Fair, &c. &c.* Dutch earthen jugs, used for smuggling gin on the coasts of Essex and Suffolk, are at this time called grey beards.

Grey Mare. The grey mare is the better horse; said of a woman who governs her husband.

Grey Parson. A farmer who rents the tithes of the rector or vicar.

Grig. A farthing. A merry grig; a fellow as merry as a grig: an allusion to the apparent liveliness of a grig, or young eel.

Grim. Old Mr. Grim; death.

Grimalkin. A cat: mawkin signifies a hare in Scotland.

Grin. To grin in a glass case; to be anatomized for murder: the skeletons of many criminals are preserved in glass cases, at Surgeons' hall.

Grinagog, the Cat's Uncle. A foolish grinning fellow, one who grins without reason.

Grinders. Teeth. Gooseberry grinder; the breech. Ask bogey, the gooseberry grinder; ask mine a-se.

To Grind. To have carnal knowledge of a woman.

Groats. To save his groats; to come off handsomely: at the universities, nine groats are deposited in the hands of an academic officer, by every person standing for a degree; which if the depositor obtains with honour, the groats are returned to him.

Grog. Rum and water. Grog was first introduced into the navy about the year 1740, by Admiral Vernon, to prevent the sailors intoxicating themselves with their allowance of rum or spirits. Groggy, or groggified; drunk.

Grog-blossom. A carbuncle, or pimple in the face, caused by drinking.

Grogged. A grogged horse; a foundered horse.

Grogham. A horse. *Cant.*

Gropers. Blind men; also midwives.

Ground Sweat. A grave.

Ground Squirrel. A hog, or pig. *Sea term.*

Grub. Victuals. To grub; to dine.

Grub Street. A street near Moorfields, formerly the supposed habitation of many persons who wrote for the booksellers: hence a Grub-street writer means a hackney author, who manufactures books for the booksellers.

Grub Street News. Lying intelligence.

To Grubshite. To make foul or dirty.

Grumble. To grumble in the gizzard; to murmur or repine. He grumbled like a bear with a sore head.

Grumbletonian. A discontented person; one who is always railing at the times or ministry.

Grunter. A hog; to grunt; to groan, or complain of sickness.

Grunter's Gig. A smoaked hog s face.

Grunting Peck. Pork, bacon, or any kind of hog's flesh.

Gruts. Tea.

Gudgeon. One easily imposed on. To gudgeon; to swallow the bait, or fall into a trap: from the fish of that name, which is easily taken.

Gull. A simple credulous fellow, easily cheated.

Gulled. Deceived, cheated, imposed on.

Gullgropers. Usurers who lend money to the gamesters.

Gum. Abusive language. Come, let us have no more of your gum.

Gummy. Clumsy: particularly applied to the ancles of men or women, and the legs of horses.

Gumption, or Rum Gumption. Docility, comprehension, capacity.

Gun. He is in the gun; he is drunk: perhaps from an allusion to a vessel called a gun, used for ale in the universities.

Gundiguts. A fat, pursy fellow.

Gunner's Daughter. To kiss the gunner's daughter; to be tied to a gun and flogged on the posteriors; a mode of punishing boys on board a ship of war.

Gunpowder. An old woman. *Cant.*

Guts. My great guts are ready to eat my little ones; my guts begin to think my throat's cut; my guts curse my teeth: all expressions signifying the party is extremely hungry.

Guts and Garbage. A very fat man or woman. More guts than brains; a silly fellow. He has plenty of guts, but no bowels: said of a hard, merciless, unfeeling person.

Gutfoundered. Exceeding hungry.

Gut Scraper, or Tormentor of Catgut. A fiddler.

Gutter Lane. The throat, the swallow, the red lane. See Red Lane.

Gutting a Quart Pot. Taking out the lining of it: i. e. drinking it off. Gutting an oyster; eating it. Gutting a house; clearing it of its furniture. See Poulterer.

Guy. A dark lanthorn: an allusion to Guy Faux, the principal actor in the gunpowder plot. Stow the guy: conceal the lanthorn.

Guzzle. Liquor. To guzzle; to drink greedily.

Guzzle Guts. One greedy of liquor.

Gybe, or Jybe. Any writing or pass with a seal.

Gybing. Jeering or ridiculing.

Gyles, or Giles. Hopping Giles; a nick name for a lame person: St. Giles was the tutelar saint of cripples.

Gyp. A college runner or errand-boy at Cambridge, called at Oxford a scout. See Scout.

Gypsies. A set of vagrants, who, to the great disgrace of our police, are suffered to wander about the country. They pretend that they derive their origin from the ancient Egyptians, who were famous for their knowledge in astronomy and other sciences; and, under the pretence of fortune-telling, find means to rob or defraud the ignorant and superstitious. To colour their impostures, they artificially discolour their faces, and speak a kind of gibberish peculiar to themselves. They rove up and down the country in large companies, to the great terror of the farmers, from whose geese, turkeys, and fowls, they take very considerable contributions.

When a fresh recruit is admitted into the fraternity, he is to take the following oath, administered by the principal maunder, after going through the annexed forms:

First, a new name is given him by which he is ever after to be called; then standing up in the middle of the assembly, and directing his face to the dimber damber, or principal man of the gang, he repeats the following oath, which is dictated to him by some experienced member of the fraternity:

I, Crank Cuffin, do swear to be a true brother, and that I will in all things obey the commands of the great tawney prince, and keep his counsel and not divulge the secrets of my brethren.

I will never leave nor forsake the company, but observe and keep all the times of appointment, either by day or by night, in every place whatever.

I will not teach any one to cant, nor will I disclose any of our mysteries to them.

I will take my prince's part against all that shall oppose him, or any of us, according to the utmost of my ability; nor will I suffer him, or any one belonging to us, to be abused by any strange abrams, rufflers, hookers, pailliards, swaddlers, Irish toyles, swigmen, whip jacks, jarkmen, bawdy baskets, dommerars, clapper dogeons, patricoes, or curtals; but will defend him, or them, as much as I can, against all other outliers whatever. I will not conceal aught I win out of libkins or from the ruffmans, but will preserve it for the use of the company. Lastly, I will cleave to my doxy wap stiffly, and will bring her duds, marjery praters, goblers, grunting cheats, or tibs of the buttery, or any thing else I can come at, as winnings for her weppings.

The canters have, it seems, a tradition, that from the three first articles of this oath, the first founders of a certain boastful, worshipful fraternity (who pretend to derive their origin from the earliest times) borrowed both the hint and form of their establishment; and that their pretended derivation from the first *Adam* is a forgery, it being only from the first *Adam Tiler*: see ADAM TILER. At the admission of a new brother, a general stock is raised for booze, or drink, to make themselves merry on the occasion. As for peckage or eatables, they can procure without money; for while some are sent to break the ruffmans, or woods and bushes, for firing, others are detached to filch geese, chickens, hens, ducks (or mallards), and pigs. Their morts are their butchers, who presently make bloody work with what living things are brought them; and having made holes in the ground under some remote hedge in an obscure place, they make a fire and boil or broil their food; and when it is enough, fall to work tooth and nail: and having eaten more like beasts than men, they drink more like swine than human creatures, entertaining one another all the time with songs in the canting dialect.

As they live, so they lie, together promiscuously, and know not how to claim a property either in their goods or children: and this general interest ties them more firmly together than if all their rags were twisted into ropes, to bind them indissolubly from a separation; which detestable union is farther consolidated by the above oath.

They

They stroll up and down all summer-time in droves, and dexterously pick pockets, while they are telling of fortunes; and the money, rings, silver thimbles, &c. which they get, are instantly conveyed from one hand to another, till the remotest person of the gang (who is not suspected because they come not near the person robbed) gets possession of it; so that, in the strictest search, it is impossible to recover it; while the wretches with imprecations, oaths, and protestations, disclaim the thievery.

That by which they are said to get the most money, is, when young gentlewomen of good families and reputation have happened to be with child before marriage, a round sum is often bestowed among the gypsies, for some one mort to take the child; and as that is never heard of more by the true mother and family, so the disgrace is kept concealed from the world; and, if the child lives, it never knows its parents.

HAN

HABERDASHER OF PRONOUNS. A schoolmaster, or usher.

HACKNEY WRITER. One who writes for attornies or booksellers.

HACKUM. Captain Hackum; a bravo, a slasher.

HAD'EM. He has been at Had'em, and came home by Clapham; said of one who has caught the venereal disease.

HAIR SPLITTER. A man's yard.

HALBERT. A weapon carried by a serjeant of foot. To get a halbert; to be appointed a serjeant. To be brought to the halberts; to be flogged *a la militaire*: soldiers of the infantry, when flogged, being commonly tied to three halberts, set up in a triangle, with a fourth fastened across them. He carries the halbert in his face; a saying of one promoted from a serjeant to a commission officer.

HALF A HOG. Sixpence.

HALF SEAS OVER. Almost drunk.

HAMLET. A high constable. *Cant.*

HAMS, or HAMCASES. Breeches.

HAND. A sailor. We lost a hand; we lost a sailor. Bear a hand; make haste. Hand to fist; opposite: the same as tête-à-tête, or cheek by joul.

HAND AND POCKET SHOP. An eating house, where ready money is paid for what is called for.

Hand Basket Portion. A woman whose husband receives frequent presents from her father, or family, is said to have a hand-basket portion.

Handle. To know how to handle one's fists; to be skilful in the art of boxing. The cove flashes a rare handle to his physog; the fellow has a large nose.

Handsome. He is a handsome-bodied man in the face; a jeering commendation of an ugly fellow. Handsome is that handsome does: a proverb frequently cited by ugly women.

Handsome Reward. This, in advertisements, means a horse-whipping.

To Hang an arse. To hang back, to hesitate.

Hang Gallows Look. A thievish, or villainous appearance.

Hang in Chains. A vile, desperate fellow. Persons guilty of murder, or other atrocious crimes, are frequently, after execution, hanged on a gibbet, to which they are fastened by iron bandages; the gibbet is commonly placed on or near the place where the crime was committed.

Hang it up. Score it up: speaking of a reckoning.

Hang out. The traps scavey where we hang out; the officers know where we live.

Hanger on. A dependant.

Hangman's Wages. Thirteen pence halfpenny; which, according to the vulgar tradition, was thus allotted: one shilling for the executioner, and three halfpence for the rope, ---N. B. This refers to former times; the hangmen of the present day having, like other artificers, raised their prices. The true state of this matter is, that a Scottish mark was the fee allowed for an execution, and the value of that piece was settled by a proclamation of James I. at thirteen pence halfpenny.

Hank. He has a hank on him; i. e. an ascendancy over him, or a hold upon him. A Smithfield hank; an ox, rendered furious by overdriving and barbarous treatment. See Bull Hank.

Hanker. To hanker after any thing; to have a longing after or for it.

Hans in Kelder. Jack in the cellar, i. e. the child in the womb: a health frequently drank to breeding women or their husbands.

Hard. Stale beer, nearly sour, is said to be hard. Hard also means severe: as, hard fate, a hard master.

Hard at his A-se. Close after him.

Hare. He has swallowed a hare; he is drunk; more probably a *hair*, which requires washing down.

Hark-ye-ing. Whispering on one side to borrow money.

Harman. A constable. *Cant.*

Harman Beck. A beadle. *Cant.*

Harmans. The stocks. *Cant.*

Harp. To harp upon; to dwell upon a subject. Have among you, my blind harpers; an expression used in throwing or shooting at random among the crowd. Harp is also the Irish expression for woman, or tail, used in tossing up in Ireland: from Hibernia, being represented with a harp on the reverse of the copper coins of that country; for which it is, in hoisting the copper, i. e. tossing up, sometimes likewise called music.

Harridan. A hagged old woman; a miserable, scraggy, worn-out harlot, fit to take her bawd's degree: derived from the French word *haridelle*, a worn-out jade of a horse or mare.

Harry. A country fellow. *Cant.*—Old Harry; the Devil.

Harum scarum. He was running harum scarum; said of any one running or walking hastily, and in a hurry, after they know not what.

Hash. To flash the hash; to vomit. *Cant.*

Hasty. Precipitate, passionate. He is none of the Hastings sort; a saying of a slow, loitering fellow: an allusion to the Hastings pea, which is the first in season.

Hasty Pudding. Oatmeal and milk boiled to a moderate thickness, and eaten with sugar and butter. Figuratively, a wet, muddy road: as, The way through Wandsworth is quite a hasty pudding. To eat hot hasty pudding for a laced hat, or some other prize, is a common feat at wakes and fairs.

Hat. Old hat; a woman's privities: because frequently felt.

Hatches. Under the hatches; in trouble, distress, or debt.

Hatchet Face. A long thin face.

Havil. A sheep. *Cant.*

Havy Cavy. Wavering, doubtful, shilly shally.

Hawk. Ware hawk; the word to look sharp, a bye-word when a bailiff passes. Hawk also signifies a sharper, in opposition to pigeon. See Pigeon. See Ware Hawk.

Hawkers. Licensed itinerant retailers of different commodities, called also pedlars; likewise the sellers of news-papers. Hawking; an effort to spit up the thick phlegm, called *oysters*: whence it is wit upon record, to ask the person so doing whether he has a licence; a punning allusion to the Act of hawkers and pedlars.

To Hazel Gild. To beat any one with a hazel stick.

H HEAD

Head Cully of the Pass, or Passage Bank. The top tilter of that gang throughout the whole army, who demands and receives contribution from all the pass banks in the camp.

Head Rails. Teeth. *Sea phrase.*

Hearing Cheats. Ears. *Cant.*

Heart's Ease. Gin.

Hearty Choak. He will have a hearty choak and caper sauce for breakfast; i. e. he will be hanged.

Heathen Philosopher. One whose breech may be seen through his pocket-hole: this saying arose from the old philosophers, many of whom depised the vanity of dress to such a point, as often to fall into the opposite extreme.

To Heave. To rob. To heave a case; to rob a house. To heave a bough; to rob a booth. *Cant.*

Heaver. The breast. *Cant.*

Heavers. Thieves who make it their business to steal tradesmen's shop-books. *Cant.*

Hector. A bully, a swaggering coward. To hector; to bully, probably from such persons affecting the valour of Hector, the Trojan hero.

Hedge. To make a hedge; to secure a bet, or wager, laid on one side, by taking the odds on the other, so that, let what will happen, a certain gain is secured, or hedged in, by the person who takes this precaution; who is then said to be on velvet.

Hedge Alehouse. A small obscure alehouse.

Hedge Creeper. A robber of hedges.

Hedge Priest. An illiterate unbeneficed curate, a patrico.

Hedge Whore. An itinerant harlot, who bilks the bagnios and bawdy-houses, by disposing of her favours on the wayside, under a hedge; a low beggarly prostitute.

Heels. To be laid by the heels; to be confined, or put in prison. Out at heels; worn, or diminished: his estate or affairs are out at heels. To turn up his heels; to turn up the knave of trumps at the game of all-fours.

Heel Tap. A peg in the heel of a shoe, taken out when it is finished. A person leaving any liquor in his glass, is frequently called upon by the toast-master to take off his heel-tap.

Hell. A taylor's repository for his stolen goods, called cabbage: see Cabbage. Little hell; a small dark covered passage, leading from London-wall to Bell-alley.

Hell-born Babe. A lewd graceless youth, one naturally of a wicked disposition.

Hell Cat. A termagant, a vixen, a furious scolding woman. See Termagant and Vixen.

HELL HOUND. A wicked abandoned fellow.

HELL FIRE DICK. The Cambridge driver of the Telegraph. The favorite companion of the University fashionables, and the only tutor to whose precepts they attend.

HELTER SKELTER. To run helter skelter, hand over head, in defiance of order.

HEMP. Young hemp; an appellation for a graceless boy.

HEMPEN FEVER. A man who was hanged is said to have died of a hempen fever; and, in Dorsetshire, to have been stabbed with a Bridport dagger; Bridport being a place famous for manufacturing hemp into cords.

HEMPEN WIDOW. One whose husband was hanged.

HEN-HEARTED. Cowardly.

HEN HOUSE. A house where the woman rules; called also a *she house*, and *hen frigate*: the latter a sea phrase, originally applied to a ship, the captain of which had his wife on board, supposed to command him.

HENPECKED. A husband governed by his wife, is said to be henpecked.

HEN. A woman. A cock and hen club; a club composed of men and women.

HERE AND THEREIAN. One who has no settled place of residence.

HERRING. The devil a barrel the better herring; all equally bad.

HERRING GUTTED. Thin, as a shotten hering.

HERRING POND. The sea. To cross the herring pond at the king's expence; to be transported.

HERTFORDSHIRE KINDNESS. Drinking twice to the same person.

HICK. A country hick; an ignorant clown. *Cant.*

HICKENBOTHOM. Mr. Hickenbothom; a ludicrous name for an unknown person, similar to that of Mr. Thingambob. Hickenbothom, i. e. a corruption of the German word *ickenbaum*, i. e. oak tree.

HICKEY. Tipsey; quasi, hickupping.

HIDE AND SEEK. A childish game. He plays at hide and seek; a saying of one who is in fear of being arrested for debt, or apprehended for some crime, and therefore does not chuse to appear in public, but secretly skulks up and down. See SKULK.

HIDEBOUND. Stingy, hard of delivery: a poet poor in invention, is said to have a hidebound muse.

HIGGLEDY PIGGLEDY. Confusedly mixed.

HIGH EATING. To eat skylarks in a garret.

HIGH FLYERS. Tories, Jacobites.

HIGH JINKS. A gambler at dice, who, having a strong head, drinks to intoxicate his adversary, or pigeon.

HIGH LIVING. To lodge in a garret, or cockloft.

HIGH PAD. A highwayman. *Cant.*

HIGH ROPES. To be on the high ropes; to be in a passion.

HIGH SHOON, or CLOUTED SHOON. A country clown.

HIGH WATER. It is high water with him; he is full of money.

HIGHGATE. Sworn at Highgate---a ridiculous custom formerly prevailed at the public houses in Highgate, to administer a ludicrous oath to all travellers of the middling rank who stopped there. The party was sworn on a pair of horns, fastened on a stick: the substance of the oath was, never to kiss the maid when he could kiss the mistress, never to drink small beer when he could get strong, with many other injunctions of the like kind; to all which was added the saving cause of "unless you like it best." The person administering the oath was always to be called father by the juror; and he, in return, was to style him son, under the penalty of a bottle.

HIKE. To hike off; to run away. *Cant.*

HIND-LEG. To kick out a hind leg; to make a rustic bow.

HINNEY, MY HONEY. A north country hinney, particularly a Northumbrian: in that county, hinney is the general term of endearment.

HISTORY OF THE FOUR KINGS, or CHILD'S BEST GUIDE TO THE GALLOWS. A pack of cards. He studies the history of the four kings assiduously; he plays much at cards.

HOAXING. Bantering, ridiculing. Hoaxing a quiz; joking an odd fellow. *University wit.*

HOB, or HOBBINOL, a clown.

HOB OR NOB. Will you hob or nob with me? a question formerly in fashion at polite tables, signifying a request or challenge to drink a glass of wine with the proposer: if the party challenged answered Nob, they were to chuse whether white or red. This foolish custom is said to have originated in the days of good queen Bess, thus: when great chimnies were in fashion, there was at each corner of the hearth, or grate, a small elevated projection, called the hob; and behind it a seat. In winter time the beer was placed on the hob to warm: and the cold beer was set on a small table, said to have been called the nob; so that the question, Will you have hob or nob? seems only to have meant, Will you have warm or cold beer? i.e. beer from the hob, or beer from the nob.

HOBBERDEHOY. Half a man and half a boy; a lad between both.

HOBBLED. Impeded, interrupted, puzzled. To hobble; to walk lamely.

HOBBLEDYGEE. A pace between a walk and a run, a dog-trot.

HOBBY. Sir Posthumous's hobby; one nice or whimsical in his clothes.

HOBBY HORSE. A man's favourite amusement, or study, is called his hobby horse. It also means a particular kind of small Irish horse: and also a wooden one, such as is given to children.

HOBBY HORSICAL. A man who is a great keeper or rider of hobby horses; one that is apt to be strongly attached to his systems of amusement.

HOBNAIL. A country clodhopper: from the shoes of country farmers and ploughmen being commonly stuck full of hob-nails, and even often clouted, or tipped with iron. The Devil ran over his face with hobnails in his shoes; said of one pitted with the small pox.

HOBSON'S CHOICE. That or none; from old Hobson, a famous carrier of Cambridge, who used to let horses to the students; but never permitted them to chuse, always allotting each man the horse he thought properest for his manner of riding and treatment.

HOCKS. A vulgar appellation for the feet. You have left the marks of your dirty hocks on my clean stairs; a frequent complaint from a mop squeezer to a footman.

HOCKEY. Drunk with strong stale beer, called old hock. See HICKEY.

HOCKING, or HOUGHING. A piece of cruelty practised by the butchers of Dublin, on soldiers, by cutting the tendon of Achilles; this has been by law made felony.

HOCUS POCUS. Nonsensical words used by jugglers, previous to their deceptions, as a kind of charm, or incantation. A celebrated writer supposes it to be a ludicrous corruption of the words *hoc est corpus*, used by the popish priests in consecrating the host. Also Hell Hocus is used to express drunkenness: as, he is quite hocus; he is quite drunk.

HOD. Brother Hod; a familiar name for a bricklayer's labourer: from the hod which is used for carrying bricks and mortar.

HODDY DODDY, ALL A-SE AND NO BODY. A short clumsy person, either male or female.

HODGE. An abbreviation of Roger: a general name for a country booby.

HODGE PODGE. An irregular mixture of numerous things.

HODMANDODS. Snails in their shells.

HOG. A shilling. To drive one's hogs; to snore: the noise made

made by some persons in snoring, being not much unlike the notes of that animal. He has brought his hogs to a fine market; a saying of any one who has been remarkably successful in his affairs, and is spoken ironically to signify the contrary. A hog in armour; an awkward or mean looking man or woman, finely dressed, is said to look like a hog in armour. To hog a horse's mane; to cut it short, so that the ends of the hair stick up like hog's bristles. Jonian hogs; an appellation given to the members of St. John's College, Cambridge.

HOG GRUBBER. A mean stingy fellow.

HOGGISH. Rude, unmannerly, filthy.

HOGO. Corruption of *haut goust*, high taste, or flavour; commonly said of flesh somewhat tainted. It has a confounded hogo; it stinks confoundedly.

HOIST. To go upon the hoist; to get into windows accidentally left open: this is done by the assistance of a confederate, called the hoist, who leans his head against the wall, making his back a kind of step or ascent.

HOISTING. A ludicrous ceremony formerly performed on every soldier, the first time he appeared in the field after being married; it was thus managed: As soon as the regiment, or company, had grounded their arms to rest a while, three or four men of the same company to which the bridegroom belonged, seized upon him, and putting a couple of bayonets out of the two corners of his hat, to represent horns, it was placed on his head, the back part foremost. He was then hoisted on the shoulders of two strong fellows, and carried round the arms, a drum and fife beating and playing the pioneers call, named Round Heads and Cuckolds, but on this occasion styled the Cuckold's March; in passing the colours, he was to take off his hat: this, in some regiments, was practised by the officers on their brethren. Hoisting, among pickpockets, is, setting a man on his head, that his money, watch, &c. may fall out of his pockets; these they pick up, and hold to be no robbery. See REVERSED.

HOITY-TOITY. A hoity-toity wench; a giddy, thoughtless, romping girl.

HOLBORN HILL. To ride backwards up Holborn hill; to go to the gallows: the way to Tyburn, the place of execution for criminals condemned in London, was up that hill. Criminals going to suffer, always ride backwards, as some conceive to increase the ignominy, but more probably to prevent them being shocked with a distant view of the gallows; as, in amputations, surgeons conceal the instruments with which they are going to operate. The last execution at Tyburn, and cons quently of this procession, was in the year 1784, since which the criminals have been executed near Newgate.

HOLIDAY. A holiday bowler; a bad bowler. Blind man's holiday; darkness, night. A holiday is any part of a ship's bottom, left uncovered in paying it. *Sea term.* It is all holiday; See ALL HOLIDAY.

HOLY FATHER. A butcher's boy of St. Patrick's Market, Dublin, or other Irish blackguard; among whom the exclamation, or oath, by the Holy Father (meaning the Pope), is common.

HOLY LAMB. A thorough-paced villain. *Irish.*

HOLY WATER. He loves him as the Devil loves holy water, i. e. hates him mortally. Holy water, according to the Roman Catholics, having the virtue to chase away the Devil and his imps.

HOLLOW. It was quite a hollow thing; i. e. a certainty, or decided business.

HONEST MAN. A term frequently used by superiors to inferiors. As honest a man as any in the cards when all the kings are out; i. e. a knave. I dare not call thee rogue for fear of the law, said a quaker to an attorney; but I will give thee five pounds, if thou canst find any creditable person who wilt say thou art an honest man.

HONEST WOMAN. To marry a woman with whom one has cohabited as a mistress, is termed, making an honest woman of her.

HONEY MOON. The first month after marriage. A poor honey; a harmless, foolish, goodnatured fellow. It is all honey or all t---d with them; said of persons who are either in the extremity of friendship or enmity, either kissing or fighting.

HOOD-WINKED Blindfolded by a handkerchief, or other ligature, bound over the eyes.

HOOF. To beat the hoof; to travel on foot. He hoofed it or beat the hoof, every step of the way from Chester to London.

HOOK AND SNIVEY, WITH NIX THE BUFFER. This rig consists in feeding a man and a dog for nothing, and is carried on thus: Three men, one of whom pretends to be sick and unable to eat, go to a public house; the two well men make a bargain with the landlord for their dinner, and when he is out of sight, feed their pretended sick companion and dog gratis.

HOOKEE WALKER. An expression signifying that the story is not true, or that the thing will not occur. HOOK-

HOOKED. Over-reached, tricked, caught: a simile taken from fishing. **** hooks; fingers.

HOOKERS. See ANGLERS.

HOOP. To run the hoop; an ancient marine custom. Four or more boys having their left hands tied fast to an iron hoop, and each of them a rope, called a nettle, in their right, being naked to the waist, wait the signal to begin: this being made by a stroke with a cat of nine tails, given by the boatswain to one of the boys, he strikes the boy before him, and every one does the same: at first the blows are but gently administered; but each irritated by the strokes from the boy behind him, at length lays it on in earnest. This was anciently practised when a ship was wind-bound.

To HOOP. To beat. I'll well hoop his or her barrel. I'll beat him or her soundly.

To HOP THE TWIG. To run away. *Cant.*

HOP MERCHANT. A dancing master. See CAPER MERCHANT.

HOP-O-MY-THUMB. A diminutive person, man or woman. She was such a-hop-o-my thumb, that a pigeon, sitting on her shoulder, might pick a pea out of her a-se.

HOPKINS. Mr. Hopkins; a ludicrous address to a lame or limping man, being a pun on the word *hop*.

HOPPING GILES. A jeering appellation given to any person who limps, or is lame: St. Giles was the patron of cripples, lepers, &c. Churches dedicated to that saint commonly stand out of town, many of them having been chapels to hospitals. See GYLES.

HOPPER-ARSED. Having large projecting buttocks: from their resemblance to a small basket, called a hopper or hoppet, worn by husbandmen for containing seed corn, when they sow the land.

HORNS. To draw in one's horns; to retract an assertion through fear: metaphor borrowed from a snail, who on the apprehension of danger, draws in his horns, and retires to his shell.

HORN COLIC. A temporary priapism.

HORN FAIR. An annual fair held at Charlton, in Kent, on St. Luke's day, the 18th of October. It consists of a riotous mob, who after a printed summons dispersed through the adjacent towns, meet at Cuckold's Point, near Deptford, and march from thence in procession, through that town and Greenwich, to Charlton, with horns of different kinds upon their heads; and at the fair there are sold rams horns, and every sort of toy made of horn; even the gingerbread figures have horns. The vulgar tradition gives the follow-

following history of the origin of this fair; King John, or some other of our ancient kings, being at the palace of Eltham, in this neighbourhood, and having been out a hunting one day, rambled from his company to this place, then a mean hamlet; when entering a cottage to inquire his way, he was struck with the beauty of the mistress, whom he found alone; and having prevailed over her modesty, the husband returning suddenly, surprised them together; and threatening to kill them both, the king was obliged to discover himself, and to compound for his safety by a purse of gold, and a grant of the land from this place to Cuckold's Point, besides making the husband master of the hamlet. It is added that, in memory of this grant, and the occasion of it, this fair was established, for the sale of horns, and all sorts of goods made with that material. A sermon is preached at Charlton church on the fair day.

Horn Mad. A person extremely jealous of his wife, is said to be horn mad. Also a cuckold, who does not cut or breed his horns easily.

Horn Work. Cuckold-making.

Hornified. Cuckolded.

Horse Buss. A kiss with a loud smack; also a bite.

Horse Coser. A dealer in horses: vulgarly and corruptly pronounced *horse courser*. The verb *to cose* was used by the Scots, in the sense of bartering or exchanging.

Horse Godmother. A large masculine woman, a gentlemanlike kind of a lady.

Horse Ladder. A piece of Wiltshire wit, which consists in sending some raw lad, or simpleton, to a neighbouring farm house, to borrow a horse ladder, in order to get up the horses, to finish a hay-mow.

Horse's Meal. A meal without drinking.

Hosteler, i. e. oat stealer. Hosteler was originally the name for an inn-keeper; inns being in old English styled hostels, from the French signifying the same.

Hot Pot. Ale and brandy made hot.

Hot Stomach. He has so hot a stomach, that he burns all the clothes off his back; said of one who pawns his clothes to purchase liquor.

House, or Tenement, to Let. A widow's weeds; also an atchievement marking the death of a husband, set up on the outside of a mansion: both supposed to indicate that the dolorous widow wants a male comforter.

Hoydon. A romping girl.

Hubble-bubble. Confusion. A hubble-bubble fellow; a man

a man of confused ideas, or one thick of speech, whose words sound like water bubbling out of a bottle. Also an instrument used for smoaking through water in the East Indies, called likewise a caloon, and hooker.

HUBBLE DE SHUFF. Confusedly. To fire hubble de shuff, to fire quick and irregularly. *Old military term.*

HUBBUB. A noise, riot, or disturbance.

HUCKLE MY BUFF. Beer, egg, and brandy, made hot.

HUCKSTERS. Itinerant retailers of provisions. He is in hucksters hands; he is in a bad way.

To HUE. To lash. The cove was hued in the naskin; the rogue was soundly lashed in bridewell. *Cant.*

To HUFF. To reprove, or scold at any one; also to bluster, bounce, ding, or swagger. A captain huff; a noted bully. To stand the huff; to be answerable for the reckoning in a public house.

HUG. To hug brown bess; to carry a firelock, or serve as a private soldier. He hugs it as the Devil hugs a witch: said of one who holds any thing as if he was afraid of losing it.

HUGGER MUGGER. By stealth, privately, without making an appearance. They spent their money in a hugger mugger way.

HUGOTONTHEONBIQUIFFINARIANS. A society existing in 1748.

HULKY, or HULKING. A great hulky fellow; an over-grown clumsy lout, or fellow.

HULVER-HEADED. Having a hard impenetrable head; hulver, in the Norfolk dialect, signifying holly, a hard and solid wood.

To HUM, or HUMBUG. To deceive, or impose on one by some story or device. A humbug; a jocular imposition, or deception. To hum and haw; to hesitate in speech, also to delay, or be with difficulty brought to consent to any matter or business.

HUMS. Persons at church. There is a great number of hums in the autem; there is a great congregation in the church.

HUM BOX. A pulpit.

HUM CAP. Very old and strong beer, called also stingo. See STINGO.

HUM DRUM. A hum drum fellow; a dull tedious narrator, a bore; also a set of gentlemen, who (Bailey says) used to meet near the Charter House, or at the King's Head in St. John's-street, who had more of pleasantry, and less of mystery, than the free masons.

HUM DURGEON. An imaginary illness. He has got the hum

dur-

durgeon, the thickest part of his thigh is nearest his a-se; i. e. nothing ails him except low spirits.

HUMBUGS. The brethren of the venerable society of humbugs was held at brother Hallam's, in Goodman's Fields.

HUMMER. A great lye, a rapper. See RAPPER.

HUMMING LIQUOR. Double ale, stout pharaoh. See PHARAOH.

HUMMUMS. A bagnio, or bathing house.

HUM TRUM. A musical instrument made of a mopstick, a bladder, and some packthread, thence also called a bladder and string, and hurdy gurdy; it is played on like a violin, which is sometimes ludicrously called a humstrum; sometimes, instead of a bladder, a tin canister is used.

HUMP. To hump; once a fashionable word for copulation.

HUMPTY DUMPTY. A little humpty dumpty man or woman; a short clumsy person of either sex: also ale boiled with brandy.

TO HUNCH. To jostle, or thrust.

HUNCH-BACKED. Hump-backed.

HUNG BEEF. A dried bull's pizzle. How the dubber served the cull with hung beef; how the turnkey beat the fellow with a bull's pizzle.

HUNKS. A covetous miserable fellow, a miser; also the name of a famous bear mentioned by Ben Jonson.

HUNT'S DOG. He is like Hunt's dog, will neither go to church nor stay at home. One Hunt, a labouring man at a small town in Shropshire, kept a mastiff, who on being shut up on Sundays, whilst his master went to church, howled so terribly as to disturb the whole village; wherefore his master resolved to take him to church with him: but when he came to the church door, the dog having perhaps formerly been whipped out by the sexton, refused to enter; whereupon Hunt exclaimed loudly against his dog's obstinacy, who would neither go to church nor stay at home. This shortly became a bye-word for discontented and whimsical persons.

HUNTING. Drawing in unwary persons to play or game. *Cant.*

HUNTING THE SQUIRREL. An amusement practised by postboys and stage-coachmen, which consists in following a one-horse chaise, and driving it before them, passing close to it, so as to brush the wheel, and by other means terrifying any woman or person that may be in it. A man whose turn comes for him to drink, before he has emptied his former glass, is said to be hunted.

HUNTSUP. The reveillier of huntsmen, sounded on the French horn, or other instrument.

Hurdy Gurdy. A kind of fiddle, originally made perhaps out of a gourd. See Humstrum.

Hurly Burly. A rout, riot, bustle or confusion.

Hush. Hush the cull; murder the fellow.

Hush Money. Money given to hush up or conceal a robbery, theft, or any other offence, or to take off the evidence from appearing against a criminal.

Huskylour. A guinea, or job. *Cant.*

Hussy. An abbreviation of housewife, but now always used as a term of reproach; as, How now, hussy? or, She is a light hussy.

Huzza. Said to have been originally the cry of the huzzars or Hungarian light horse; but now the national shout of the English, both civil and military, in the sea phrase termed a cheer; to give three cheers being to huzza thrice.

Hyp, or Hip. A mode of calling to one passing by. Hip, Michael, your head's on fire; a piece of vulgar wit to a red haired man.

Hyp. The hypochondriac: low spirits. He is hypped; he has got the blue devils, &c.

Jabber. To talk thick and fast, as great praters usually do, to chatter like a magpye; also to speak a foreign language. He jabbered to me in his damned outlandish parlez vous, but I could not understand him; he chattered to me in French, or some other foreign language, but I could not understand him.

Jack. A farthing, a small bowl serving as the mark for bowlers. An instrument for pulling off boots.

Jack Adams. A fool. Jack Adams's parish; Clerkenwell.

Jack at a Pinch. A poor hackney parson.

Jack in a Box. A sharper, or cheat. A child in the mother's womb.

Jack in an Office. An insolent fellow in authority.

Jack Ketch. The hangman; vide Derrick and Ketch.

Jack Nasty Face. A sea term, signifying a common sailor.

Jack of Legs. A tall long-legged man; also a giant, said to be buried in Weston church, near Baldock, in Hertfordshire, where there are two stones fourteen feet distant,

tant, said to be the head and feet stones of his grave. This giant, says Salmon, as fame goes, lived in a wood here, and was a great robber, but a generous one; for he plundered the rich to feed the poor: he frequently took bread for this purpose from the Baldock bakers, who catching him at an advantage, put out his eyes, and afterwards hanged him upon a knoll in Baldock field. At his death he made one request, which was, that he might have his bow and arrow put into his hand, and on shooting it off, where the arrow fell, they would bury him; which being granted the arrow fell in Weston churchyard. Above seventy years ago, a very large thigh bone was taken out of the church chest, where it had lain many years for a show, and was sold by the clerk to Sir John Tradescant, who, it is said, put it among the rarities of Oxford.

JACK PUDDING. The merry andrew, zany, or jester to a mountebank.

JACK ROBINSON. Before one could say Jack Robinson; a saying to express a very short time, originating from a very volatile gentleman of that appellation, who would call on his neighbours, and be gone before his name could be announced.

JACK SPRAT. A dwarf, or diminutive fellow.

JACK TAR. A sailor.

JACK WEIGHT. A fat man.

JACK WHORE. A large masculine overgrown wench.

JACKANAPES. An ape; a pert, ugly, little fellow.

JACKED. Spavined. A jacked horse.

JACKMEN. See JARKMEN.

JACKEY. Gin.

JACOB. A soft fellow. A fool.

JACOB. A ladder: perhaps from Jacob's dream. *Cant.* Also the common name for a jay, jays being usually taught to say, Poor Jacob! a cup of sack for Jacob.

JACOBITES. Sham or collar shirts. Also partizans for the Stuart family: from the name of the abdicated king, i. e. James or Jacobus. It is said by the whigs, that God changed Jacob's name to Israel, lest the descendants of that patriarch should be called Jacobites.

JADE. A term of reproach to women.

JAGUE. A ditch: perhaps from jakes.

JAIL BIRDS. Prisoners.

JAKES. A house of office, a cacatorium.

JAMMED. Hanged. *Cant.*

JANIZARIES. The mob, sometimes so called; also bailiffs, their setters, and followers.

Japanned. Ordained. To be japanned; to enter into holy orders, to become a clergyman, to put on the black cloth: from the colour of the japan ware, which is black.

Jark. A seal.

Jarkmen. Those who fabricate counterfeit passes, licences, and certificates for beggars.

Jarvis. A hackney coachman.

Jason's Fleece. A citizen cheated of his gold.

Jaw. Speech, discourse. Give us none of your jaw; let us have none of your discourse. A jaw-me-dead; a talkative fellow. Jaw work; a cry used in fairs by the sellers of nuts.

Jazey. A bob wig.

Idea Pot. The knowledge box, the head. See Knowledge Box.

Jeffy. It will be done in a jeffy; it will be none in a short space of time, in an instant.

Jehu. To drive jehu-like; to drive furiously: from a king of Israel of that name, who was a famous charioteer, and mentioned as such in the Bible.

Jem. A gold ring. *Cant.*

Jemmy Fellow. A smart spruce fellow.

Jemmy. A crow. This instrument is much used by housebreakers. Sometimes called Jemmy Rook.

Jenny. An instrument for lifting up the grate or top of a show-glass, in order to rob it. *Cant.*

Jerrycummumble. To shake, towzle, or tumble about.

Jerry Sneak. A henpecked husband: from a celebrated character in one of Mr. Foote's plays, representing a man governed by his wife.

Jessamy. A smart jemmy fellow, a fopling.

Jesuit. See To Box the Jesuit.

Jesuitical. Sly, evasive, equivocal. A jesuitical answer; an equivocal answer.

Jet. A lawyer. Autem jet; a parson.

Jew. An over-reaching dealer, or hard, sharp fellow; an extortioner: the brokers formerly behind St. Clement's church in the Strand were called Jews by their brethren the taylors.

Jew. A tradesman who has no faith, i. e. will not give credit.

Jew Bail. Insufficient bail: commonly Jews, who for a sum of money will bail any action whatsoever, and justify, that is, swear to their sufficiency; but, when called on, are not to be found.

Jew's Eye. That's worth a Jew's eye; a pleasant or agreeable sight: a saying taken from Shakespeare.

Jibber the Kibber. A method of deceiving seamen, by fixing a candle and lanthorn round the neck of a horse, one of whose fore feet is tied up; this at night has the appearance of a ship's light. Ships bearing towards it, run on shore, and being wrecked, are plundered by the inhabitants. This diabolical device is, it is said, practised by the inhabitants of our western coasts.

Jig. A trick. A pleasant jig; a witty arch trick. Also a lock or door. The feather-bed jig; copulation.

Jigger. A whipping-post. *Cant.*

Jilt. A tricking woman, who encourages the addresses of a man whom she means to deceive and adandon.

Jilted. Rejected by a woman who has encouraged one's advances.

Jingle Boxes. Leathern jacks tipped with silver, and hung with bells, formerly in use among fuddle caps. *Cant.*

Jingle Brains. A wild, thoughtless, rattling fellow.

Jinglers. Horse cosers, frequenting country fairs.

Impost takers. Usurers who attend the gam'ing-tables, and lend money at great premiums.

Impudent Stealing. Cutting out the backs of coaches, and robbing the seats.

Impure. A modern term for a lady of easy virtue.

Inching. Encroaching.

Indies. Black Indies; Newcastle.

India Wipe. A silk handkerchief.

Indorser. A sodomite. To indorse with a cudgel; to drub or beat a man over the back with a stick, to lay *cane* upon Abel.

Inexpressibles. Breeches.

Inkle Weavers. Supposed to be a very brotherly set of people; ' as great as two inkle weavers' being a proverbial saying.

Inlaid. Well inlaid; in easy circumstances, rich or well to pass.

Innocents. One of the innocents; a weak or simple person, man or woman.

Inside and Outside. The inside of a **** and the outside of a gaol.

Job. A guinea.

Job's Comfort. Reproof instead of consolation.

Job's Comforter. One who brings news of some additional misfortune.

Job's Dock. He is laid up in Job's dock; i. e. in a salivation.

The

The apartments for the foul or venereal patients in St. Bartholomew's hospital, are called Job's ward.

JOBATION. A reproof.

JOBBERNOLE. The head.

To JOB. To reprove or reprehend. *Cambridge term.*

JOB. Any robbery. To do a job; to commit some kind of robbery.

JOCK, or CROWDY-HEADED JOCK. A jeering appellation for a north country seaman, particularly a collier; Jock being a common name, and crowdy the chief food, of the lower order of the people in Northumberland.

To JOCK, or JOCKUM CLOY. To enjoy a woman.

JOCKUM GAGE. A chamber-pot, jordan, looking-glass, or member-mug. *Cant.*

JOGG-TROT. To keep on a jogg-trot; to get on with a slow but regular pace.

JOHNNY BUM. A he or jack ass: so called by a lady that affected to be extremely polite and modest, who would not say Jack because it was vulgar, nor ass because it was indecent.

JOINT. To hit a joint in carving, the operator must think of a cuckold. To put one's nose out of joint; to rival one in the favour of a patron or mistress.

JOLLY, or JOLLY NOB. The head. I'll lump your jolly nob for you; I'll give you a knock on the head.

JOLLY DOG. A merry facetious fellow; a *bon vivant*, who never flinches from his glass, nor cries to go home to bed.

JOLTER HEAD. A large head; metaphorically a stupid fellow.

JORDAIN. A great blow, or staff. I'll tip him a jordain if I transnear; i. e. I'll give him a blow with my staff, if I come near him. *Cant.*

JORDAN. A chamber-pot.

JORUM. A jugg, or large pitcher.

JOSEPH. A woman's great coat. Also, a sheepish bashful young fellow: an allusion to Joseph who fled from Potiphar's wife. You are Josephus rex; you are jo-king, i. e. joking.

JOSKIN. A countryman. The dropcove maced the Joskin of twenty quid; The ring dropper cheated the countryman of twenty guineas.

JOWL. The cheek. Cheek by jowl; close together, or cheek to cheek. My eyes how the cull sucked the blowen's jowl; he kissed the wench handsomely.

IRISH APRICOTS. Potatoes. It is a common joke against the Irish vessels, to say they are loaded with fruit and timber, that is, potatoes and broomsticks. Irish assurance; a bold forward behaviour: as being dipt in the river Styx was formerly supposed to render persons invulnerable, so it is said that a dipping in the river Shannon totally annihilates bashfulness; whence arises the saying of an impudent Irishman, that he has been dipt in the Shannon.

IRISH BEAUTY. A woman with two black eyes.

IRISH EVIDENCE. A false witness.

IRISH LEGS. Thick legs, jocularly styled the Irish arms. It is said of the Irish women, that they have a dispensation from the pope to wear the thick end of their legs downwards.

IRISH TOYLES. Thieves who carry about pins, laces, and other pedlars wares, and under the pretence of offering their goods to sale, rob houses, or pilfer any thing they can lay hold of.

IRON. Money in general. To polish the king's iron with one's eyebrows; to look out of grated or prison windows, or, as the Irishman expresses them, the iron glass windows. Iron doublet; a prison. See STONE DOUBLET.

IRONMONGER'S SHOP. To keep an ironmonger's shop by the side of a common, where the sheriff sets one up; to be hanged in chains. Iron-bound; laced. An iron-bound hat; a silver-laced hat.

ISLAND. He drank out of the bottle till he saw the island; the island is the rising bottom of a wine bottle, which appears like an island in the centre, before the bottle is quite empty.

IVORIES. Teeth. How the swell flashed his ivories; how the gentleman shewed his teeth.

ITCHLAND, or SCRATCHLAND. Scotland.

JUG. See DOUBLE JUG.

JUGGLER'S BOX. The engine for burning culprits in the hand. *Cant.*

JUKRUM. A licence.

JUMBLEGUT LANE. A rough road or lane.

JUMP. The jump, or dining-room jump; a species of robbery effected by ascending a ladder placed by a sham lamplighter, against the house intended to be robbed. It is so called, because, should the lamp-lighter be put to flight, the thief who ascended the ladder has no means of escaping but that of jumping down.

JUMPERS. Persons who rob houses by getting in at the windows. Also a set of Methodists established in South Wales.

Juniper Lecture. A round scolding bout.

Jury Leg. A wooden leg: allusion to a jury mast, which is a temporary substitute for a mast carried away by a storm, or any other accident. *Sea phrase.*

Jury Mast. A *journiere* mast; i. e. a mast for the day or occasion.

Just-ass. A punning appellation for a justice.

Ivy Bush. Like an owl in an ivy bush; a simile for a meagre or weasel-faced man, with a large wig, or very bushy hair.

Kate. A picklock. 'Tis a rum kate; it is a clever picklock. *Cant.*

Keel Bullies. Men employed to load and unload the coal vessels.

Keelhauling. A punishment in use among the Dutch seamen, in which, for certain offences, the delinquent is drawn once, or oftener, under the ship's keel: ludicrously defined, undergoing a great hard-ship.

To Keep. To inhabit. Lord, where do you keep? i. e. where are your rooms? *Academical phrase.* Mother, your tit won't keep; your daughter will not preserve her virginity.

To Keep it up. To prolong a debauch. We kept it up finely last night; metaphor drawn from the game of shuttlecock.

Keeping Cully. One who keeps a mistress, as he supposes, for his own use, but really for that of the public.

Keffel. A horse. *Welsh.*

Kelter. Condition, order. Out of kelter; out of order.

Kelter. Money.

Kemp's Morris. William Kemp, said to have been the original Dogberry in Much ado about Nothing, danced a morris from London to Norwich in nine days: of which he printed the account, A. D. 1600, intitled, Kemp's Nine Days Wonder, &c.

Kemp's Shoes. Would I had Kemp's shoes to throw after you. *Ben Jonson.* Perhaps Kemp was a man remarkable for his good luck or fortune; throwing an old shoe, or shoes, after any one going on an important business, being by the vulgar deemed lucky.

Ken. A house. A bob ken, or a bowman ken; a well-furnished

nished house, also a house that harbours thieves. Biting the ken; robbing the house. *Cant.*

KEN MILLER, or KEN CRACKER. A housebreaker. *Cant.*

KENT-STREET EJECTMENT. To take away the street door: a method practised by the landlords in Kent-street, Southwark, when their tenants are above a fortnight's rent in arrear.

KERRY SECURITY. Bond, pledge, oath, and keep the money.

KETCH. Jack Ketch; a general name for the finishers of the law, or hangmen, ever since the year 1682, when the office was filled by a famous practitioner of that name, of whom his wife said, that any bungler might put a man to death, but only her husband knew how to make a gentleman die sweetly. This officer is mentioned in Butler's Ghost, page 54, published about the year 1682, in the following lines:

Till Ketch observing he was chous'd,
And in his profits much abus'd.
In open hall the tribute dunn'd,
To do his office, or refund.

Mr. Ketch had not long been elevoted to his office, for the name of his predecessor Dun occurs in the former part of this poem, page 29:

For you yourself to act squire Dun,
Such ignominy ne'er saw the sun.

The addition of 'squire,' with which Mr. Dun is here dignified, is a mark that he had beheaded some state criminal for high treason; an operation which, according to custom for time out of mind, has always entitled the operator to that distinction. The predecessor of Dun was Gregory Brandon, from whom the gallows was called the Gregorian tree, by which name it is mentioned in the prologue to Mercurius Pragmaticus, tragi-comedy acted at Paris, &c. 1641:

This trembles under the black rod, and he
Doth fear his fate from the Gregorian tree.

Gregory Brandon succeeded Derrick. See DERRICK.

KETTLE DRUMS. Cupid's kettle drums; a woman's breasts, called by sailors chest and bedding.

KETTLE OF FISH. When a person has perplexed his affairs in general, or any particular business, he is said to have made a fine kettle of fish of it.

KICKS. Breeches. A high kick; the top of the fashion. It is all the kick; it is the present mode. Tip us your kicks, we'll have them as well as your lour; pull off your breeches, for we must have them as well as your money. A kick;

 six-

sixpence. Two and a kick; half-a-crown. A kick in the guts; a dram of gin, or any other spirituous liquor. A kick up; a disturbance, also a hop or dance. An odd kick in one's gallop; a strange whim or peculiarity.

To Kick the Bucket. To die. He kicked the bucket one day: he died one day. To kick the clouds before the hotel door; i. e. to be hanged.

Kickerapoo. Dead. *Negro word.*

Kickseys. Breeches.

Kickshaws. French dishes: corruption of *quelque chose.*

Kid. A little dapper fellow. A child. The blowen has napped the kid. The girl is with child.

To Kid. To coax or wheedle. To inveigle. To amuse a man or divert his attention while another robs him. The sneaksman kidded the cove of the ken, while his pall frisked the panney; the thief amused the master of the house, while his companion robbed the house.

Kid Lay. Rogues who make it their business to defraud young apprentices, or errand-boys, of goods committed to their charge, by prevailing on them to execute some trifling message, pretending to take care of their parcels till they come back; these are, in cant terms, said to be on the kid lay.

Kidder. A forestaller: see Crocker. Kidders are also persons employed by the gardeners to gather peas.

Kiddeys. Young thieves.

Kiddy Nippers. Taylors out of work, who cut off the waistcoat pockets of their brethren, when cross-legged on their board, thereby grabbling their bit. *Cant.*

Kidnapper. Originally one who stole or decoyed children or apprentices from their parents or masters, to send them to the colonies; called also spiriting: but now used for all recruiting crimps for the king's troops, or those of the East India company, and agents for indenting servants for the plantations, &c.

Kidney. Disposition, principles, humour. Of a strange kidney; of an odd or unaccountable humour. A man of a different kidney; a man of different principles.

Kilkenny. An old frize coat.

Kill Care Club. The members of this club, styled also the Sons of Sound Sense and Satisfaction, met at their fortress, the Castle-tavern, in Paternoster-row.

Kill Devil. New still-burnt rum.

Kill Priest. Port wine.

To Kimbaw. To trick, cheat or cozen; also to beat or to bully. Let's kimbaw the cull; let's bully the fellow,

To set one's arms a-kimbaw, vulgarly pronounced a-kimbo, is to rest one's hands on the hips, keeping the elbows square, and sticking out from the body; an insolent bullying attitude. *Cant.*

KINCHIN. A little child. Kinchin coes; orphan beggar boys, educated in thieving. Kinchin morts; young girls under the like circumstances and training. Kinchin morts, or coes in slates; beggars' children carried at their mother's backs in sheets. Kinchin cove; a little man. *Cant.*

KING'S PLATE. Fetters.

KING'S WOOD LION. An Ass. Kingswood is famous for the great number of asses kept by the colliers who inhabit that place.

KING'S BAD BARGAIN. One of the king's bad bargains; a malingeror, or soldier who shirks his duty.

KING'S HEAD INN, OR CHEQUER INN, IN NEWGATE STREET. The prison of Newgate.

KING JOHN'S MEN. He is one of king John's men, eight score to the hundred: a saying of a little undersized man.

KING OF THE GYPSIES. The captain, chief, or ringleader of the gang of misrule: in the cant language called also the upright man.

KING'S PICTURES. Coin, money.

KINGDOM COME. He is gone to kingdom come, he is dead.

KIP. The skin of a large calf, in the language of the Excise-office.

KISS MINE A-SE. An offer, as Fielding observes, very frequently made, but never, as he could learn, literally accepted. A kiss mine a-se fellow; a sycophant.

KISSING CRUST. That part where the loaves have touched the oven.

KIT. A dancing-master, so called from his kit or cittern, a small fiddle, which dancing-masters always carry about with them, to play to their scholars. The kit is likewise the whole of a soldier's necessaries, the contents of his knapsack: and is used also to express the whole of different commodities: as, Here, take the whole kit; i. e. take all.

KIT-CAT CLUB. A society of gentlemen, eminent for wit and learning, who in the reign of queen Anne and George I. met at a house kept by one Christopher Cat. The portraits of most of the members of this society were painted by Sir Godfrey Kneller, of one size; thence still called the kit-cat size.

KITCHEN PHYSIC. Food, good meat roasted or boiled. A little kitchen physic will set him up; he has more need of a cook than a doctor.

Kittle Pitchering. A jocular method of hobbling or bothering a troublesome teller of long stories: this is done by contradicting some very immaterial circumstance at the beginning of the narration, the objections to which being settled, others are immediately started to some new particular of like consequence; thus impeding, or rather not suffering him to enter into, the main story. Kittle pitchering is often practised in confederacy, one relieving the other, by which the design is rendered less obvious.

Kittys. Effects, furniture; stock in trade. To seize one's kittys; to take his sticks.

Knack Shop. A toy-shop, a nick-nack-atory.

Knappers Poll. A sheep's head. *Cant.*

Knave in Grain. A knave of the first rate: a phrase borrowed from the dyehouse, where certain colours are said to be in grain, to denote their superiority, as being dyed with cochineal, called grain. Knave in grain is likewise a pun applied to a cornfactor or miller.

Knight of the Blade. A bully.

Knight of the Post. A false evidence, one that is ready to swear any thing for hire.

Knight of the Rainbow. A footman: from the variety of colours in the liveries and trimming of gentlemen of that cloth.

Knight of the Road. A highwayman.

Knight of the Sheers. A taylor.

Knight of the Thimble, or Needle. A taylor or staymaker.

Knight of the Whip. A coachman.

Knight of the Trencher. A great eater.

Knight and Barrow Pig, more hog than gentleman. A saying of any low pretender to precedency.

Knob. The head. See Nob.

Knock. To knock a woman; to have carnal knowledge of her. To knock off; to conclude: phrase borrowed from the blacksmith. To knock under; to submit.

Knock me Down. Strong ale or beer, stingo.

Knot. A crew, gang, or fraternity. He has tied a knot with his tongue, that he cannot untie with his teeth: i. e. he is married.

Knowing Ones. Sportsmen on the turf, who from experience and an acquaintance with the jockies, are supposed to be in the secret, that is, to know the true merits or powers of each horse; notwithstanding which it often happens that the knowing ones are taken in.

Knowledge Box. The head.

Knuckles. Pickpockets who attend the avenues to public places to steal pocket-books, watches, &c. a superior kind of pickpockets. To knuckle to, to submit.

To Knuckle one's Wipe. To steal his handkerchief.

Knuckle-dabs, or Knuckle-confounders. Ruffles.

Konoblin Rig. Stealing large pieces of coal from coal sheds.

Laced Mutton. A prostitute.

Lacing. Beating. I'll lace your jacket handsomely.

Ladder. To go up the ladder to rest; to be hanged.

Lady. A crooked or hump-backed woman.

Lady of Easy Virtue. A woman of the town, an impure, a prostitute.

Ladybirds. Light or lewd women.

Lady Dacre's Wine. Gin.

Lag. A man transported. The cove was lagged for a drag. The man was transported for stealing something out of a waggon.

Lag Fever. A term of ridicule applied to men who being under sentence of transportation, pretend illness, to avoid being sent from gaol to the hulks.

To Lag. To drop behind, to keep back. Lag last; the last of a company.

Lage. Water. *Cant.*

Lage of Duds. A buck of linen.

Laid on the Shelf, or Laid up in Lavender. Pawned.

To Lamb, or Lambaste. To beat. Lamb pye; a beating: from *lambo.*

Lamb's Wool. Apples roasted and put into strong ale.

Lambskin Men. The judges: from their robes lined and bordered with ermine.

Lamp. An eye. The cove has a queer lamp. The man has a blind or squinting eye.

Land. How lies the land? How stands the reckoning? Who has any land in Appleby? a question asked the man at whose door the glass stands long, or who does not circulate it in due time.

Land Lopers, or Land Lubbers. Vagabonds lurking about the country who subsist by pilfering.

Land Pirates. Highwaymen.

Lank Sleeve. The empty sleeve of a one armed man. A fellow with a lank sleeve; a man who has lost an arm.

Lansprisado. One who has only two-pence in his pocket. Also a lance, or deputy corporal; that is, one doing the duty without the pay of a corporal. Formerly a lancier, or horseman, who being dismounted by the death of his horse, served in the foot, by the title of lansprisado, or *lancepesato*, a broken lance.

Lanthorn-jawed. Thin-visaged: from their cheeks being almost transparent. Or else, lenten jawed; i. e. having the jaws of one emaciated by a too rigid observation of Lent. Dark lanthorn; a servant or agent at court, who receives a bribe for his principal or master.

Lap. Butter-milk or whey. *Cant.*

Lark. A boat.

Lark. A piece of merriment. People playing together jocosely.

Larry Dugan's Eye Water. Blacking: Larry Dugan was a famous shoe-black at Dublin.

Latch. Let in.

Lathy. Thin, slender. A lathy wench; a girl almost as slender as a lath.

Latitat. A nick-name for an attorney; from the name of a writ.

Lavender. Laid up in lavender; pawned.

Laugh. To laugh on the wrong side of the mouth; to cry. I'll make him laugh on the wrong (or t'other) side of his mouth.

Launch. The delivery, or labour, of a pregnant woman; a crying out or groaning.

Law. To give law to a hare; a sporting term, signifying to give the animal a chance of escaping, by not setting on the dogs till the hare is at some distance; it is also more figuratively used for giving any one a chance of succeeding in a scheme or project.

Lawful Blanket. A wife.

Lay. Enterprize, pursuit, or attempt: to be sick of the lay. It also means a hazard or chance: he stands a queer lay; i. e. he is in danger. *Cant.*

Laystall. A dunghill about London, on which the soil brought from necessary houses is emptied; or, in more technical terms, where the old gold collected at weddings by the Tom t—d man, is stored.

Lazy. As lazy as Ludman's dog, who leaned against the wall to bark. As lazy as the tinker, who laid down his budget to f--t.

Lazy Man's Load. Lazy people frequently take up more than they can safely carry, to save the trouble of coming a second time.

Lazybones. An instrument like a pair of tongs, for old or very fat people to take any thing from the ground without stooping.

Leaf. To go off with the fall of the leaf; to be hanged: criminals in Dublin being turned off from the outside of the prison by the falling of a board, propped up, and moving on a hinge, like the leaf of a table. *Irish term.*

To Leak. To make water.

Leaky. Apt to blab; one who cannot keep a secret is said to be leaky.

Leaping over the Sword. An ancient ceremonial said to constitute a military marriage. A sword being laid down on the ground, the parties to be married joined hands, when the corporal or serjeant of the company repeated these words:

Leap rogue, and jump whore,
And then you are married for evermore.

Whereupon the happy couple jumped hand in hand over the sword, the drum beating a ruffle; and the parties were ever after considered as man and wife.

Least in Sight. To play least in-sight; to hide, keep out of the way, or make one's self scarce.

Leather. To lose leather; to be galled with riding on horseback, or, as the Scotch express it, to be saddle sick. To leather also meant to beat, perhaps originally with a strap: I'll leather you to your heart's content. Leather-headed; stupid. Leathern conveniency; term used by quakers for a stage-coach.

Leery. On one's guard. See Peery.

Left-handed Wife. A concubine; an allusion to an ancient German custom, according to which, when a man married his concubine, or a woman greatly his inferior, he gave her his left hand.

Leg. To make a leg; to bow. To give leg-bail and land security; to run away. To fight at the leg; to take unfair advantages: it being held unfair by back-sword players to strike at the leg. To break a leg; a woman who has had a bastard, is said to have broken a leg.

Leggers. Sham leggers; cheats who pretend to sell smuggled goods, but in reality only deal in old shop-keepers or damaged goods.

Lenten Fare. Spare diet.

Letch. A whim of the amorous kind, out of the common way.

Levite. A priest or parson.

To Lib. To lie together. *Cant.*

Libbege. A bed. *Cant.*

Libben. A private dwelling-house. *Cant.*

Libken. A house to lie in. *Cant.*

To Lick. To beat; also to wash, or to paint slightly over. I'll give you a good lick o' the chops; I'll give you a good stroke or blow on the face. Jack tumbled into a cow t--d, and nastied his best clothes, for which his father stept up, and licked him neatly.—I'll lick you! the dovetail to which is, If you lick me all over, you won't miss ———.

Lick spittle. A parasite, or talebearer.

Lift. To give one a lift; to assist. A good hand at a dead lift; a good hand upon an emergency. To lift one's hand to one's head; to drink to excess, or to drink drams. To lift or raise one's elbow; the same.

Lift. See Shoplifter, &c.

Lifter. A crutch.

Lig. A bed. See Lib.

Light Bob. A soldier of the light infantry company.

Light-fingered. Thievish, apt to pilfer.

Light-heeled. Swift in running. A light-heeled wench; one who is apt, by the flying up of her heels, to fall flat on her back, a willing wench.

Light House. A man with a red fiery nose.

Light Troops. Lice; the light troops are in full march; the lice are crawling about.

Lightmans. The day. *Cant.*

Lightning. Gin. A flash of lightning; a glass of gin.

Likeness. A phrase used by thieves when the officers or turnkeys are examining their countenance. As the traps are taking our likeness; the officers are attentively observing us.

Lilipution. A diminutive man or woman: from Gulliver's Travels, written by Dean Swift, where an imaginary kingdom of dwarfs of that name is described.

Lily White. A chimney-sweeper.

Lily Shallow. (*Whip slang*) A white driving hat.

Limbs. Duke of limbs; a tall awkward fellow.

Limb of the Law. An inferior or pettyfogging attorney.

Limbo. A prison, confinement.

To Line. A term for the act of coition between dog and bitch.

Line of the Old Author. A dram of brandy.

Line. To get a man into a line, i. e. to divert his attention by a ridiculous or absurd story. To humbug.

Lingo. Language. An outlandish lingo; a foreign tongue. The parlezvous lingo; the French language.

Linen Armourers. Taylors.

Lion. To tip the lion; to squeeze the nose of the party tipped, flat to his face with the thumb. To shew the lions and tombs; to point out the particular curiosities of any place, to act the ciceroni: an allusion to Westminster Abbey, and the Tower, where the tombs and lions are shewn. A lion is also a name given by the gownsmen of Oxford to an inhabitant or visitor. It is a standing joke among the city wits to send boys and country folks, on the first of April, to the Tower-ditch, to see the lions washed.

Liquor. To liquor one's boots; to drink before a journey: among Roman Catholics, to administer the extreme unction.

Little Barbary. Wapping.

Little Breeches. A familiar appellation used to a little boy.

Little Clergyman. A young chimney-sweeper.

Little Ease. A small dark cell in Guildhall, London, where disorderly apprentices are confined by the city chamberlain: it is called Little Ease from its being so low that a lad cannot stand upright in it.

Little Snakesman. A little boy who gets into a house through the sink-hole, and then opens the door for his accomplices: he is so called, from writhing and twisting like a snake, in order to work himself through the narrow passage.

Live Lumber. A term used by sailors, to signify all landsmen on board their ships.

Live Stock. Lice or fleas.

Loaf. To be in bad loaf, to be in a disagreeable situation, or in trouble.

Lob. A till in a tradesman's shop. To frisk a lob; to rob a till. See Flash Panney.

Lob. Going on the lob; going into a shop to get change for gold, and secreting some of the change.

Lob's Pound. A prison. Dr. Grey, in his notes on Hudibras, explains it to allude to one Doctor Lob, a dissenting preacher, who used to hold forth when conventicles were prohibited, and had made himself a retreat by means of a trap door at the bottom of his pulpit. Once being pursued by the officers of justice, they followed him through divers subterraneous passages, till they got into a dark cell, from whence they could not find their way out, but calling to some of their companions, swore they had got into Lob's Pound.

Lobcock. A large relaxed penis: also a dull inanimate fellow.

Lobkin. A house to lie in: also a lodging.

Loblolley Boy. A nick name for the surgeon's servant on board a man of war, sometimes for the surgeon himself: from the water gruel prescribed to the sick, which is called loblolley.

Lobonian Society. A society which met at Lob Hall, at the King and Queen, Norton Falgate, by order of Lob the great.

Lobscouse. A dish much eaten at sea, composed of salt beef, biscuit and onions, well peppered, and stewed together.

Lobster. A nick name for a soldier, from the colour of his clothes. To boil one's lobster, for a churchman to become a soldier: lobsters, which are of a bluish black, being made red by boiling. I will not make a lobster kettle of my ****, a reply frequently made by the nymphs of the Point at Portsmouth, when requested by a soldier to grant him a favour.

Lock. A scheme, a mode. I must fight that lock; I must try that scheme.

Lock. Character. He stood a queer lock; he bore but an indifferent character. A lock is also a buyer of stolen goods, as well as the receptacle for them.

Lock Hospital. An hospital for venereal patients.

Lock up House. A spunging house; a public house kept by sheriff's officers, to which they convey the persons they have arrested, where they practise every species of imposition and extortion with impunity. Also houses kept by agents or crimps, who enlist, or rather trepan, men to serve the East India or African company as soldiers.

Lockeram-J wed. Thin-faced, or lanthorn-jawed. See Lanthorn Jawed.

Locksmith's Daughter. A key.

Loggerhead. A blockhead, or stupid fellow. We three loggerheads be: a sentence frequently written under two heads, and the reader by repeating it makes himself the third. A loggerhead is also a double-headed, or bar shot of iron. To go to loggerheads; to fall to fighting.

Loll. Mother's loll; a favourite child, the mother's darling.

Loll Tongue. He has been playing a game at loll tongue; he has been salivated.

Lollipops. Sweet lozenges purchased by children.

To Lollop. To lean with one's elbows on a table.

Lollpoop. A lazy, idle drone.

Lombard Fever. Sick of the lombard fever; i. e. of the idles.

Long one. A hare; a term used by poachers.

Long. Great. A long price; a great price.

Long Gallery. Throwing, or rather trundling, the dice the whole length of the board.

Long Meg. A jeering name for a very tall woman: from one famous in story, called Long Meg of Westminster.

Long Shanks. A long-legged person.

Long Stomach. A voracious appetite.

Long Tongued. Loquacious, not able to keep a secret. He is as long-tongued as Granny: Granny was an idiot who could lick her own eye. See Granny.

Long-winded. A long-winded parson; one who preached long, tedious sermons. A long-winded paymaster; one who takes long credit.

Loo. For the good of the loo; for the benefit of the company or community.

Looby. An awkward, ignorant fellow.

Looking as if one could not help it. Looking like a simpleton, or as if one could not say boh! to a goose.

Looking-glass. A chamber pot, jordan, or member mug.

Loon, or Lout. A country bumkin, or clown.

Loonslate. Thirteen pence halfpenny.

Loophole. An opening, or means of escape. To find a loophole in an act of parliament; i. e. a method of evading it.

Lop-sided. Uneven, having one side larger or heavier than the other: boys' paper kites are often said to be lop-sided.

To Lope. To leap, to run away. He loped down the dancers; he ran down stairs.

Lord. A crooked or hump-backed man. These unhappy people afford great scope for vulgar raillery; such as, 'Did 'you come straight from home? if so, you have got con- 'foundedly bent by the way.' 'Don't abuse the gemman,' adds a by-stander, 'he has been grossly insulted already; 'don't you see his back's up?' Or some one asks him if the show is behind; 'because I see,' adds he, 'you have the 'drum at your back.' Another piece of vulgar wit is let loose on a deformed person: If met by a party of soldiers on their march, one of them observes that that gentleman is on his march too, for he has got his knapsack at his back. It is said in the British Apollo, that the title of lord was first given to deformed persons in the reign of Richard III. from several persons labouring under that misfortune being created peers by him; but it is more probably derived from the Greek word λορδος, *crooked.*

Louse. A gentleman's companion. He will never louse a grey head of his own; he will never live to be old.

Love Begotten Child. A bastard.

Lounge. A loitering place, or gossiping shop.

Louse Bag. A black bag worn to the hair or wig.

Louse House. The round house, cage, or any other place of confinement.

Louse Ladder. A stitch fallen in a stocking.

Louse Land. Scotland.

Louse Trap. A small toothed comb.

Lout. A clumsy stupid fellow.

Lowing Rig. Stealing oxen or cows.

Low Pad. A footpad.

Low Tide, or Low Water. When there is no money in a man's pocket.

Lowre. Money. *Cant.*

Lubber. An awkward fellow: a name given by sailors to landsmen.

Luck, or Good Luck. To tread in a surreverence, to be bewrayed: an allusion to the proverb, Sh-tt-n luck is good luck.

Lud's Bulwark. Ludgate prison.

Lugs. Ears or wattles. See Wattles.

Lullaby Cheat. An infant. *Cant.*

Lullies. Wet linen. *Cant.*

Lully Priggers. Thieves who steal wet linen. *Cant.*

Lumb. Too much.

Lumber. Live lumber; soldiers or passengers on board a ship are so called by the sailors.

Lumber Troop. A club or society of citizens of London.

Lumber House. A house appropriated by thieves for the reception of their stolen property.

To Lump. To beat; also to include a number of articles under one head.

To Lump the Lighter. To be transported.

Lumpers. Persons who contract to unload ships; also thieves who lurk about wharfs to pilfer goods from ships, lighters, &c.

Lumping. Great. A lumping pennyworth; a great quantity for the money, a bargain. He has got a lumping pennyworth; frequently said of a man who marries a fat woman.

Lun. Harlequin.

Lurch. To be left in the lurch; to be abandoned by one's confederates or party, to be left in a scrape.

Lurched. Those who lose a game of whist, without scoring five, are said to be lurched.

Lurcher. A lurcher of the law; a bum bailiff, or his setter.

Lurries. Money, watches, rings, or other moveables.

Lush.

Lush. Strong beer.

To **Lush.** To drink.

Lushey. Drunk. The rolling kiddeys had a spree, and got bloody lushey; the dashing lads went on a party of pleasure, and got very drunk.

Lye. Chamber lye; urine.

Maccaroni. An Italian paste made of flour and eggs. Also a fop: which name arose from a club, called the Maccaroni Club, instituted by some of the most dressy travelled gentlemen about town, who led the fashions; whence a man foppishly dressed, was supposed a member of that club, and by contraction styled a Maccaroni.

Mace Cove. A swindler, a sharper, a cheat. On the mace; to live by swindling.

Machines. Mrs. Phillips's ware. See **Cundum.**

Mackerel. A bawd: from the French *maquerel.* Mackerel-backed; long-backed.

Mad Tom, or Tom of Bedlam, otherwise an Abram Man. A rogue that counterfeits madness. *Cant.*

Madam. A kept madam; a kept mistress.

Madam Ran. A whore. *Cant.*

Made. Stolen. *Cant.*

Madge. The private parts of a woman.

Madge Culls. Sodomites. *Cant.*

Magg. A halfpenny.

Maggot Boiler. A tallow-chandler.

Maggotty. Whimsical, capricious.

Magnum Bonum. A bottle containing two quarts of wine. See **Scotch Pint.**

Mahometan Gruel. Coffee: because formerly used chiefly by the Turks.

Maiden Sessions. A sessions where none of the prisoners are capitally convicted.

Make. A halfpenny. *Cant.*

Make Weight. A small candle: a term applied to a little slender man.

Malingeror. A military term for one who, under pretence of sickness, evades his duty.

Malkin, or Maulkin. A general name for a cat; also a parcel of rags fastened to the end of a stick, to clean an oven; also a figure set up in a garden to scare the birds; likewise an awkward woman. The cove's so scaly, he'd

spice

spice a malkin of his jazey : the fellow is so mean, that he would rob a scare-crow of his old wig.

MALKINTRASH. One in a dismal garb.

MALMSEY NOSE. A red pimpled snout, rich in carbuncles and rubies.

MAN OF THE TOWN. A rake, a debauchee.

MAN OF THE TURF. A horse racer, or jockey.

MANOEUVRING THE APOSTLES. Robbing Peter to pay Paul, i. e. borrowing of one man to pay another.

MAN TRAP. A woman's commodity.

MAN OF THE WORLD. A knowing man.

MAN, (*Cambridge.*) Any undergraduate from fifteen to thirty. As a man of Emanuel---a young member of Emanuel.

MANUFACTURE. Liquors prepared from materials of English growth.

MARE'S NEST. He has found a mare's nest, and is laughing at the eggs; said of one who laughs without any apparent cause.

MARGERY PRATER. A hen. *Cant.*

MARINE OFFICER. An empty bottle: marine officers being held useless by the seamen. *Sea wit.*

MARPLOT. A spoil sport.

MARRIAGE MUSIC. The squalling and crying of children.

MARRIED. Persons chained or handcuffed together, in order to be conveyed to gaol, or on board the lighters for transportation, are in the cant language said to be married together.

MARROW BONES. The knees. To bring any one down on his marrow bones; to make him beg pardon on his knees: some derive this from Mary's bones, i. e. the bones bent in honour of the Virgin Mary; but this seems rather far-fetched. Marrow bones and cleavers; principal instruments in the band of rough music: these are generally performed on by butchers, on marriages, elections, riding skimmington, and other public or joyous occasions.

MARTINET. A military term for a strict disciplinarian: from the name of a French general, famous for restoring military discipline to the French army. He first disciplined the French infantry, and regulated their method of encampment: he was killed at the siege of Doesbourg in the year 1672.

MASON'S MAUND. A sham sore above the elbow, to counterfeit a broken arm by a fall from a scaffold.

MASTER OF THE MINT. A gardener.

MASTER OF THE ROLLS. A baker.

MASTER OF THE WARDROBE. One who pawns his clothes to purchase liquor.

MATRI-

Matrimonial Peace-maker. The sugar-stick, or arbor vitæ.

Maudlin Drunk. Crying drunk: perhaps from Mary Magdalene, called Maudlin, who is always painted in tears.

Mauled. Extremely drunk, or soundly beaten.

Maundering Broth. Scolding.

Maunding. Asking or begging. *Cant.*

Mawkes. A vulgar slattern.

Mawley. A hand. Tip us your mawley; shake hands with me. Fam the mawley; shake hands.

Maw-wallop. A filthy composition, sufficient to provoke vomiting.

Max. Gin.

May Bees. May bees don't fly all the year long; an answer to any one who prefaces a proposition with, It may be.

Mealy-mouthed. Over-modest or backward in speech.

Medlar. A fruit, vulgarly called an open a-se; of which it is more truly than delicately said, that it is never ripe till it is as rotten as a t--d, and then it is not worth a f--t.

Mellow. Almost drunk.

Melting Moments. A fat man and woman in the amorous congress.

To Melt. To spend. Will you melt a borde? will you spend a shilling? The cull melted a couple of decusses upon us; the gentleman spent a couple of crowns upon us. *Cant.*

Member Mug. A chamber pot.

Men of Straw. Hired bail, so called from having straw stuck in their shoes to distinguish them.

Men of Kent. Men born east of the river Medway, who are said to have met the Conqueror in a body, each carrying a green bough in his hand, the whole appearing like a moving wood; and thereby obtaining a confirmation of their ancient privileges. The inhabitants of Kent are divided into Kentish men and men of Kent. Also a society held at the Fountain Tavern, Bartholomew Lane, A. D. 1743.

Merkin. Counterfeit hair for women's privy parts. See *Bailey's Dict.*

Merry Andrew, or Mr. Merryman. The jack pudding, jester, or zany of a mountebank, usually dressed in a party-coloured coat.

Merry A–se Christian. A whore.

Merry-begotten. A bastard.

Man of the World. A knowing man.

Mess John. A Scotch presbyterian teacher or parson.

Messmate. One who eats at the same mess, companion or comrade.

Mettle. The semen. To fetch mettle; the act of self pollution. Mettle is also figuratively used for courage.

Mettlesome. Bold, courageous.

Michael. Hip, Michael, your head's on fire. See Hyp.

Midshipman's Watch and Chain. A sheep's heart and pluck.

Milch Cow. One who is easily tricked out of his property; a term used by gaolers, for prisoners who have money and bleed freely.

Milk and Water. Both ends of the busk.

To Milk the Pigeon. To endeavour at impossibilities.

Milling Cove. A boxer. How the milling cove served the cull out; how the boxer beat the fellow.

Mill. A chisel.

To Mill. To rob; also to break, beat out, or kill. I'll mill your glaze; I'll beat out your eye. To mill a bleating cheat; to kill a sheep. To mill a ken; to rob a house. To mill doll; to beat hemp in bridewell. *Cant.*

Mill Lay. To force open the doors of houses in order to rob them.

Miller. A murderer.

Mine A-se on a Bandbox. An answer to the offer of any thing inadequate to the purpose for which it is wanted, just as a bandbox would be if used for a seat.

Mine Uncle's. A pawnbroker's shop; also a necessary house. Carried to my uncle's; pawned. New-married men are also said to go to their uncle's, when they leave their wives soon after the honey moon.

Minikin. A little man or woman: also the smallest sort of pin.

Minor Clergy. Young chimney sweepers.

Mint. Gold. A mint of money; common phrase for a large sum.

Mischief. A man loaded with mischief, i. e. a man with his wife on his back.

Mish. A shirt, smock, or sheet. *Cant.*

Mish Topper. A coat, or petticoat.

Miss. A miss or kept mistress; a harlot.

Miss Laycock. The monosyllable.

Mite. A nick name for a cheesemonger: from the small insect of that name found in cheese.

Mix Metal. A silversmith.

Moabites. Bailiffs, or Philistines.

Mob, or Mab. A wench, or harlot.

Mobility. The mob: a sort of opposite to nobility.

Mohair. A man in the civil line, a townsman, or tradesman: a military term, from the mohair buttons worn by persons of those descriptions, or any others not in the army, the buttons of military men being always of metal: this is generally used as a term of contempt, meaning a bourgeois, tradesman, or mechanic.

Moiety. Half, but vulgarly used to signify a share or portion: as, He will come in for a small moiety.

Moll. A whore.

Moll Peatly's Gig. A rogering bout.

Moll Thompson's Mark. M. T. i. e. empty: as, Take away this bottle, it has Moll Thompson's mark upon it.

Molly. A Miss Molly; an effeminate fellow, a sodomite.

Monday. Saint Monday. See Saint.

Money. A girl's private parts, commonly applied to little children: as, Take care, Miss, or you will shew your money.

Money Droppers. Cheats who drop money, which they pretend to find just before some country lad; and by way of giving him a share of their good luck, entice him into a public house, where they and their confederates cheat or rob him of what money he has about him.

Mongrel. A hanger on among cheats, a spunger; also a child whose father and mother are of different countries.

Monks and Friars. Terms used by printers: monks are sheets where the letters are blotted, or printed too black; friars, those letters where the ink has failed touching the type, which are therefore white or faint.

Monkey. To suck the monkey; to suck or draw wine, or any other liquor, privately out of a cask, by means of a straw, or small tube. Monkey's allowance; more kicks than halfpence. Who put that monkey on horseback without tying his legs? vulgar wit on a bad horseman.

Monosyllable. A woman's commodity.

Moon Curser. A link-boy: link-boys are said to curse the moon, because it renders their assistance unnecessary; these gentry frequently, under colour of lighting passengers over kennels, or through dark passages, assist in robbing them. *Cant.*

Moon-eyed Hen. A squinting wench.

Moon Men. Gypsies.

Moon Rakers. Wiltshire men: because it is said that some men of that county, seeing the reflection of the moon in a pond, endeavoured to pull it out with a rake.

Moonshine. A matter or mouthful of moonshine; a trifle, nothing.

nothing. The white brandy smuggled on the coasts of Kent and Sussex, and the gin in the north of Yorkshire, are also called moonshine.

MOP. A kind of annual fair in the west of England, where farmers usually hire their servants.

To MOP UP. To drink up. To empty a glass or pot.

MOPED. Stupid, melancholy for want of society.

MOPSEY. A dowdy, or homely woman.

MOPSQUEEZER. A maid servant, particularly a housemaid.

MOPUSSES. Money.

MORGLAG. A brown bill, or kind of halbert, formerly carried by watchmen ; corruption of *more*, great or broad, and *glave*, blade.

MORNING DROP. The gallows. He napped the king's pardon and escaped the morning drop ; he was pardoned, and was not hanged.

MORRIS. Come, morris off ; dance off, or get you gone . allusion to morris, i. e. *morisco*, or Moorish dancing.

MORT. A woman or wench ; also a yeoman's daughter. To be taken all-a mort ; to be confounded, surprised, or motionless through fear.

MOSES. To stand Moses : a man is said to stand Moses when he has another man's bastard child fathered upon him, and he is obliged by the parish to maintain it.

MOSS. A cant term for lead, because both are found on the tops of buildings.

MOSSY FACE. The mother of all saints.

MOT. A girl, or wench. See MORT.

MOTHER, or THE MOTHER. A bawd. Mother abbess ; the same. Mother midnight ; a midwife. Mother in law's bit ; a small piece, mothers in law being supposed not apt to overload the stomachs of their husband's children.

MOTHER OF ALL SAINTS. The Monosyllable.

MOTHER OF ALL SOULS. The same. *Irish.*

MOTHER OF ST. PATRICK. The same. *Irish.*

MOTHER OF THE MAIDS. A bawd.

MOUCHETS. Small patches worn by ladies : from the French word *mouches*.

MOVEABLES. Rings, watches, or any toys of value.

MOUSE. To speak like a mouse in a cheese ; i. e. faintly or indistinctly.

MOUSETRAP. The parson's mousetrap ; the state of matrimony.

MOUTH. A noisy fellow. Mouth half cocked ; one gaping and staring at every thing he sees. To make any one laugh

laugh on the wrong, or t'other side of his mouth; to make him cry or grieve.

MOUTH. A silly fellow. A dupe. To stand mouth; i. e. to be duped.

To MOW. A Scotch word for the act of copulation.

MOW HEATER. A drover: from their frequent sleeping on hay mows. *Cant.*

MOWER. A cow.

MUCK. Money; also dung.

MUCKWORM. A miser.

MUCKINDER. A child's handkerchief tied to the side.

MUD. A fool, or thick-sculled fellow; also, among printers the same as dung among journeymen taylors. See DUNG.

MUD LARK. A fellow who goes about by the water side picking up coals, nails, or other articles in the mud. Also a duck.

MUFF. The private parts of a woman. To the well wearing of your muff, mort; to the happy consummation of your marriage, girl; a health.

MUFFLING CHEAT. A napkin.

MUGGLETONIANS. The sect or disciples of Lodowick Muggleton.

MULLIGRUBS. Sick of the mulligrubs with eating chopped hay: low-spirited, having an imaginary sickness.

MUM. An interjection directing silence. Mum for that; I shall be silent as to that. As mute as Mumchance, who was hanged for saying nothing; a friendly reproach to any one who seems low-spirited and silent.

MUMCHANCE. An ancient game like hazard, played with dice: probably so named from the silence observed in playing at it.

MUM GLASS. The monument erected on Fish-street Hill, London, in memory of the great fire in 1666.

MUMBLE A SPARROW. A cruel sport practised at wakes and fairs, in the following manner: A cock sparrow whose wings are clipped, is put into the crown of a hat; a man having his arms tied behind him, attempts to bite off the sparrow's head, but is generally obliged to desist, by the many pecks and pinches he receives from the enraged bird.

MUMMER. The mouth.

MUMPERS. Originally beggars of the genteel kind, but since used for beggars in general.

MUMPERS HALL. An alehouse where beggars are harboured.

Mundungus. Bad or rank tobacco: from *mondongo*, a Spanish word signifying tripes, or the uncleaned entrails of a beast, full of filth.

Mung. To beg.

Muns. The face, or rather the mouth: from the German word *mund*, the mouth. Toute his muns; look at his face.

Munster Plums. Potatoes. *Irish.*

Munster Heifer. An Irish woman. A woman with thick legs is said to be like a Munster heifer; i. e. beef to the heels.

Murder. He looked like God's revenge against murder; he looked angrily.

Murphies. Potatoes.

Mushroom. A person or family suddenly raised to riches and eminence: an allusion to that fungus, which starts up in a night.

Music. The watch-word among highwaymen, signifying the person is a friend, and must pass unmolested. Music is also an Irish term, in tossing up, to express the harp side, or reverse, of a farthing or halfpenny, opposed to the head.

Mute. An undertaker's servant, who stands at the door of a person lying in state: so named from being supposed mute with grief.

Mutton-headed. Stupid.

Mutton Monger. A man addicted to wenching.

Mutton. In her mutton, i. e. having carnal knowledge of a woman.

Muzzle. A beard.

Muzzler. A violent blow on the mouth. The milling cove tipped the cull a muzzler; the boxer gave the fellow a blow on the mouth.

Mynt. See Mint.

Myrmidons. The constable's assistants, watchmen, &c.

NAB

Nab, or Nab Cheat. A hat. Penthouse nab; a large hat.

To Nab. To seize, or catch unawares. To nab the teaze; to be privately whipped. To nab the stoop; to stand in the pillory. To nab the rust; a jockey term for a horse that becomes restive. To nab the snow: to steal linen left out to bleach or dry. *Cant.*

To NAB GIRDER, or NOB GIRDER. A bridle.

NACK. To have a nack; to be ready at any thing, to have a turn for it.

NACKY. Ingenious.

NAILED. Secured, fixed. He offered me a decus, and I nailed him; he offered me a crown, and I struck or fixed him.

NANNY HOUSE. A brothel.

To NAP. To cheat at dice by securing one chance. Also to catch the venereal disease. You've napt it; you are infected.

NAPPING. To take any one napping; i. e. to come upon him unexpectedly, to find him asleep: as, He caught him napping, as Morse caught his mare.

NAPPER. The head; also a cheat or thief.

NAPPER OF NAPS. A sheep stealer. *Cant.*

NAPPY ALE. Strong ale.

NASK, or NASKIN. A prison or bridewell. The new nask; Clerkenwell bridewell. Tothil-fields nask; the bridewell at Tothil-fields. *Cant.*

NATION. An abbreviation of damnation: a vulgar term used in Kent, Sussex, and the adjacent counties, for very. Nation good; very good. A nation long way; a very long way.

NATTY LADS. Young thieves or pickpockets. *Cant.*

NATURAL. A mistress, a child; also an idiot. A natural son or daughter; a love or merry-begotten child, a bastard.

NAVY OFFICE, The Fleet prison. Commander of the Fleet; the warden of the Fleet prison.

NAY WORD. A bye-word, proverb.

NAZARENE FORETOP. The foretop of a wig made in imitation of Christ's head of hair, as represented by the painters and sculptors.

NAZY. Drunken. Nazy cove or mort; a drunken rogue or harlot. Nazy nabs; drunken coxcombs.

NEB, or NIB. The bill of a bird, and the slit of a pen. Figuratively, the face and mouth of a woman; as, She holds up her neb; she holds up her mouth to be kissed.

NECK STAMPER. The boy who collects the pots belonging to an alehouse, sent out with beer to private houses.

NECK VERSE. Formerly the persons claiming the benefit of clergy were obliged to read a verse in a Latin manuscript

script psalter: this saving them from the gallows, was termed their neck verse: it was the first verse of the fifty-first psalm, *Miserere mei*, &c.

NECK WEED. Hemp.

NEEDLE POINT. A sharper.

NEGLIGEE. A woman's undressed gown, vulgarly termed a neggledigee.

NEGROE. A black-a-moor: figuratively used for a slave. I'll be no man's negro; I will be no man's slave.

NEGROE'S HEADS. Brown loaves delivered to the ships in ordinary.

NESCIO. He sports a Nescio; he pretends not to understand any thing. After the senate house examination for degrees, the students proceed to the schools, to be questioned by the proctor. According to custom immemorial the answers *must* be *Nescio*. The following is a translated specimen:

Qües. What is your name?—*Ans.* I do not know.

Ques. What is the name of this university?—*Ans.* I do not know.

Ques. Who was your father?—*Ans.* I do not know.

This last is probably the only true answer of the three!

NETTLED. Teized, provoked, out of temper. He or she has pissed on a nettle; said of one who is peevish or out of temper.

NEW COLLEGE STUDENTS. Golden scholars, silver bachelors, and leaden masters.

NEW DROP. The scaffold used at Newgate for hanging criminals; which dropping down, leaves them suspended. By this improvement, the use of that vulgar vehicle, a cart, is entirely left off.

NEW LIGHT. One of the new light; a methodist.

NEWGATE BIRD. A thief or sharper, frequently caged in Newgate.

NEWGATE SOLICITOR. A petty fogging and roguish attorney, who attends the gaols to assist villains in evading justice.

NEWMAN'S LIFT. The gallows.

NEWMAN'S TEA GARDENS. Newgate.

NEWMAN'S HOTEL. Newgate.

TO NICK. To win at dice, to hit the mark just in the nick of time, or at the critical moment.

NICK. Old nick; the Devil.

NICK NAME. A name given in ridicule or contempt: from the French *nom de nique*. *Nique* is a movement of the head to mark a contempt for any person or thing.

NICK NINNY. A simpleton.

NICKIN, NIKEY or NIZEY. A soft simple fellow; also a diminutive of Isaac.

NICKNACKS. Toys, baubles, or curiosities.

NICKNACKATORY. A toyshop.

NICKUMPOOP, or NINCUMPOOP. A foolish fellow; also one who never saw his wife's ****.

NIFFYNAFFY FELLOW. A trifler.

NIG. The clippings of money. Nigging; clipping. Nigler, a clipper. *Cant.*

NIGGLING. Cutting awkwardly, trifling; also accompanying with a woman.

NIGHT MAGISTRATE. A constable.

NIGHTINGALE. A soldier who, as the term is, sings out at the halberts. It is a point of honour in some regiments, among the grenadiers, never to cry out, or become nightingales, whilst under the discipline of the cat of nine tails: to avoid which, they chew a bullet.

NIGHTMAN. One whose business it is to empty necessary houses in London, which is always done in the night; the operation is called a wedding. See WEDDING.

NIGMENOG. A very silly fellow.

TO NIM. To steal or pilfer: from the German *nemen*, to take. Nim a togeman; steal a cloak.

NIMGIMMER. A physician or surgeon, particularly those who cure the venereal disease.

NINE LIVES. Cats are said to have nine lives, and women ten cats lives.

NINNY, or NINNYHAMMER. A simpleton.

NIP. A cheat. Bung nipper; a cutpurse.

NIP CHEESE. A nick name for the purser of a ship: from those gentlemen being supposed sometimes to nip, or diminish, the allowance of the seamen, in that and every other article. It is also applied to stingy persons in general.

NIPPERKIN. A small measure.

NIPPS. The sheers used in clipping money.

NIT SQUEEGER, i. e. SQUEEZER. A hair-dresser.

NIX. Nothing.

NO CATCHY NO HAVY. If I am not caught, I cannot be hurt. *Negro saying.*

NOB. A king. A man of rank.

NOB. The head.

NOB THATCHER. A peruke-maker.

NOCK. The breech; from *nock*, a notch.

NOCKY BOY. A dull simple fellow.

NOD. He is gone to the land of nod; he is asleep.

NODDLE. The head.

Noddy. A simpleton or fool. Also a kind of low cart, with a seat before it for the driver, used in and about Dublin, in the manner of a hackney coach: the fare is just half that of a coach, for the same distance; so that for sixpence one may have a set down, as it is called, of a mile and half, and frequently a tumble down into the bargain: it is called a noddy from the nutation of its head. Knave noddy; the old-fashioned name for the knave of trumps.

Noisy Dog Racket. Stealing brass knockers from doors.

Nokes. A ninny, or fool. John-a-Nokes and Tom-a-Stiles; two honest peaceable gentlemen, repeatedly set together by the ears by lawyers of different denominations: two fictitious names formerly used in law proceedings, but now very seldom, having for several years past been supplanted by two other honest peaceable gentlemen, namely, John Doe and Richard Roe.

Noll. Old Noll; Oliver Cromwell.

Non-con. A nonconformist, presbyterian, or any other dissenter.

None-Such. One that is unequalled: frequently applied ironically.

Nonsense. Melting butter in a wig.

Noozed. Married, hanged.

Nope. A blow: as, I took him a nope on the costard.

Norfolk Capon. A red herring.

Norfolk Dumpling. A nick name, or term of jocular reproach to a Norfolk man; dumplings being a favourite food in that county.

North Allertons. Spurs; that place, like Rippon, being famous for making them.

Northumberland. Lord Northumberland's arms; a black eye: so called in the last century.

Norway Neckcloth. The pillory, usually made of Norway fir.

Nose. As plain as the nose on your face; evidently to be seen. He is led by the nose; he is governed. To follow one's nose; to go strait forward. To put one's nose out of joint; to rival one in the favour of any person. To make a bridge of any one's nose; to pass by him in drinking. To nose a stink; to smell it. He cut off his nose to be revenged of his face; said of one who, to be revenged on his neighbour, has materially injured himself.

Nose. A man who informs or turns king's evidence.

To Nose. To give evidence. To inform. His pall nosed and he was twisted for a crack; his confederate turned king's evidence, and he was hanged for burglary.

To Nose. To bully.

Nose Bag. A bag fastened to the horse's head, in which the soldiers of the cavalry put the oats given to their horses: whence the saying, I see the nose bag in his face; i. e. he has been a private man, or rode private.

Nose Gent. A nun.

Nostrum. A medicine prepared by particular persons only, a quack medicine.

Notch. The private parts of a woman.

Note. He changed his note; he told another sort of a story.

Nous-Box. The head.

Nozzle. The nose of a man or woman.

Nub. The neck; also coition.

Nubbing. Hanging. Nubbing cheat: the gallows. Nubbing cove; the hangman. Nubbing ken; the sessions house.

Nug. An endearing word: as, My dear nug; my dear love.

Nugging Dress. An out-of-the-way old-fashioned dress, or rather a loose kind of dress, denoting a courtesan.

Nugging House. A brothel.

To Null. To beat: as, He nulled him heartily.

Numbers. To consult the book of numbers: a term used in the House of Commons, when, instead of answering or confuting a pressing argument, the minister calls for a division, i. e. puts the matter to the vote.

Numbscull. A stupid fellow.

Numms. A sham collar, to be worn over a dirty shirt.

Nunnery. A bawdy house.

To Nurse. To cheat: as, they nursed him out of it. An estate in the hands of trustees, for the payment of debts, is said to be at nurse.

Nuts. It was nuts for them; i. e. it was very agreeable to them.

Nuts. Fond; pleased. She's nuts upon her cull; she's pleased with her cully. The cove's nutting the blowen; the man is trying to please the girl.

Nutcrackers. The pillory: as, The cull peeped through the nutcrackers.

Nutmegs. Testicles.

Nyp, or Nip. A half pint, a nip of ale: whence the nipperkin, a small vessel.

Nyp Shop. The Peacock in Gray's Inn Lane, where Burton ale is sold in nyps.

Nypper. A cut-purse: so called by one Wotton, who in the year 1585 kept an academy for the education and perfection of pickpockets and cut-purses: his school was near Billingsgate, London. As in the dress of ancient times

times many people wore their purses at their girdles, cutting them was a branch of the light-fingered art, which is now lost, though the name remains. Maitland, from Stow, gives the following account of this Wotton: This man was a gentleman born, and sometime a merchant of good credit, but fallen by time into decay: he kept an alehouse near Smart's Key, near Billingsgate, afterwards for some misdemeanor put down. He reared up a new trade of life, and in the same house he procured all the cut-purses about the city, to repair to his house; there was a school-house set up to learn young boys to cut purses: two devices were hung up; one was a pocket, and another was a purse; the pocket had in it certain counters, and was hung about with hawks bells, and over the top did hang a little sacring bell. The purse had silver in it; and he that could take out a counter, without noise of any of the bells, was adjudged a judicial *nypper*: according to their terms of art, a *foyster* was a pick-pocket; a *nypper* was a pick purse, or cut-purse.

OBS

O BE JOYFUL. I'll make you sing O be joyful on the other side of your mouth; a threat, implying the party threatened will be made to cry. To sing O be easy; to appear contented when one has cause to complain, and dare not.

OAF. A silly fellow.

OAFISH. Simple.

OAK. A rich man, a man of good substance and credit. To sport oak; to shut the outward door of a student's room at college. An oaken towel; an oaken cudgel. To rub a man down with an oaken towel; to beat him.

OATS. He has sowed his wild oats; he is staid, or sober, having left off his wild tricks.

OATHS. The favourite oaths of the thieves of the present day are, "God strike me blind!" "I wish my bloody eyes may drop out if it is not true!" "So help me God!" "Bloody end to me!"

OAR. To put in one's oar; to intermeddle, or give an opinion unasked: as, To be sure, you must put in your oar!

OBSTROPULOUS. Vulgar misnomer of *obstreperous*: as, I was

was going my rounds, and found this here gemman very obstropulous, whereof I comprehended him as an auspicious parson.

OCCUPY. To occupy a woman; to have carnal knowledge of her.

ODD FELLOWS. A convivial society; the introduction to the most noble grand, arrayed in royal robes, is well worth seeing at the price of becoming a member.

ODDS PLUT AND HER NAILS. A Welch oath, frequently mentioned in a jocular manner by persons, it is hoped, ignorant of its meaning; which is, By God's blood, and the nails with which he was nailed to the cross.

ODD-COME-SHORTLYS. I'll do it one of these odd-come-shortly's; I will do it some time or another.

OFFICE. To give the office; to give information, or make signs to the officers to take a thief.

OGLES. Eyes. Rum ogles; fine eyes.

OIL OF BARLEY, or BARLEY BROTH. Strong beer.

OIL OF GLADNESS. I will anoint you with the oil of gladness; ironically spoken for, I will beat you.

OIL OF STIRRUP. A dose the cobler gives his wife whenever she is obstropulous.

ΟΙ ΠΟΛΛΟΙ. (*Cambridge.*) The many; the multitude; who take degrees without being entitled for an honor. All that is *required*, are three books of Euclid, and as far as Quadratic Equations in Algebra. See PLUCKED.

OLD. Ugly. *Cant.*

OLD DOG AT IT. Expert, accustomed.

OLD HAND. Knowing or expert in any business.

OLD HARRY. A composition used by vintners to adulterate their wines; also the nick-name for the devil.

OLD DING. See OLD HAT.

OLD MR. GORY. A piece of gold.

OLD NICK. The Devil: from *Neken*, the evil spirit of the north.

OLD ONE. The Devil. Likewise an expression of quizzical familiarity, as "how d'ye do, OLD ONE?"

OLD PEGG. Poor Yorkshire cheese, made of skimmed milk.

OLD POGER. The Devil.

OLD STAGER. One accustomed to business, one who knows mankind.

OLD TOAST. A brisk old fellow. *Cant.*

OLD DOSS. Bridewell.

OLIVER'S SCULL. A chamber pot.

OLLI COMPOLLI. The name of one of the principal rogues of the canting crew. *Cant.*

Omnium Gatherum. The whole together: jocular imitation of law Latin.

One in ten. A parson: an allusion to his tithes.

One of us, or one of my Cousins. A woman of the town, a harlot.

Onion. A seal. Onion hunters, a class of young thieves who are on the look out for gentlemen who wear their seals suspended on a ribbon, which they cut, and thus secure the seals or other trinkets suspended to the watch.

Open Arse. A medlar. See Medlar.

Optime. The senior and junior optimes are the second and last classes of Cambridge honors conferred on taking a degree. That of wranglers is the first. The last junior optime is called the Wooden Spoon.

Organ. A pipe. Will you cock your organ? will you smoke your pipe?

Orthodoxy and Heterodoxy. Somebody explained these terms by saying, the first was a man who had a doxy of his own, the second a person who made use of the doxy of another man.

Oschives. Bone-handled knives. *Cant.*

Ostler. Oatstealer.

Ottomy. The vulgar word for a skeleton.

Ottomised. To be ottomised; to be dissected. You'll be scragged, ottomised, and grin in a glass case: you'll be hanged, anatomised, and your skeleton kept in a glass case at Surgeons' Hall.

Oven. A great mouth; the old woman would never have looked for her daughter in the oven, had she not been there herself.

Overseer. A man standing in the pillory, is, from his elevated situation, said to be made an overseer.

Out at Heels, or Out at Elbows. In declining circumstances.

Outrun the Constable. A man who has lived above his means, or income, is said to have outrun the constable.

Outs. A gentleman of three outs. See Gentleman.

Owl. To catch the; a trick practised upon ignorant country boobies, who are decoyed into a barn under pretence of catching an owl, where, after divers preliminaries, the joke ends in their having a pail of water poured upon their heads.

Owl in an Ivy Bush. He looks like an owl in an ivy bush; frequently said of a person with a large frizzled wig, or a woman whose hair is dressed a-la-blowze.

Owlers. Those who smuggle wool over to France.

Ox House. He must go through the ox house to bed; a saying of an old fellow who marries a young girl.

Oyes. Corruption of oyez, proclaimed by the crier of all courts of justice.

Oyster. A gob of thick phlegm, spit by a consumptive man; in law Latin. *unum viridum gobbum.*

P'S. To mind one's P's and Q's; to be attentive to the main chance.

P.P.C. An inscription on the visiting cards of our modern fine gentleman, signifying that they have called *pour prendre conge*, i.e. ' to take leave,' This has of late been ridiculed by cards inscribed D.I.O. i.e. ' Damme, I'm off.'

Packet. A false report.

Packthread. To talk packthread; to use indecent language well wrapt up.

Pad. The highway, or a robber thereon; also a bed. Footpads; foot robbers. To go out upon the pad; to go out in order to commit a robbery.

Pad Borrowers. Horse stealers.

To Pad the Hoof. See To Beat the Hoof.

Paddington Fair Day. An execution day, Tyburn being in the parish or neighbourhood of Paddington. To dance the Paddington frisk; to be hanged.

Paddy. The general name for an Irishman: being the abbreviation of Patrick, the name of the tutelar saint of that island.

Painter. I'll cut your painter for you; I'll send you off; the painter being the rope that holds the boat fast to the ship. *Sea term.*

Pair of Wings. Oars. *Cant.*

To Palaver. To flatter: originally an African word for a treaty, talk, or conference.

Palliards. Those whose fathers were clapperdogens, or beggars born, and who themselves follow the same trade: the female sort beg with a number of children, borrowing them, if they have not a sufficient number of their own, and making them cry by pinching in order to excite charity; the males make artificial sores on different parts of their bodies, to move compassion.

Pall. A companion. One who generally accompanies another, or who commit robberies together.

Pam. The knave of clubs.

Pannam. Bread.

Pannier Man. A servant belonging to the Temple and Gray's Inn, whose office is to announce the dinner. This in the Temple, is done by blowing a horn; and in Gray's Inn proclaiming the word Manger, Manger, Manger, in each of the three courts.

Panny. A house. To do a panny: to rob a house. See the Sessions Papers. Probably, panny originally meant the butler's pantry, where the knives and forks, spoons, &c. are usually kept. The pigs frisked my panney, and nailed my screws; the officers searched my house, and seized my picklock keys. *Cant.*

Panter. A hart: that animal is, in the Psalms, said to pant after the fresh water-brooks. Also the human heart, which frequently pants in time of danger. *Cant.*

Pantile Shop. A presbyterian, or other dissenting meeting house, frequently covered with pantiles: called also a cock-pit.

Pantler. A butler.

Pap. Bread sauce; also the food of infants. His mouth is full of pap; he is still a baby.

Paper Scull. A thin-scull'd foolish fellow.

Papler. Milk pottage.

Parell. Whites of eggs, bay salt, milk, and pump water, beat together, and poured into a vessel of wine to prevent its fretting.

Parenthesis. To put a man's nose into a parenthesis; to pull it, the fingers and thumb answering the hooks or crochets. A wooden parenthesis; the pillory. An iron parenthesis; a prison.

Parings. The chippings of money. *Cant.*

Parish Bull. A parson.

Parish. His stockings are of two parishes; i. e. they are not fellows.

Parish Soldier. A jeering name for a militia man: from substitutes being frequently hired by the parish from which one of its inhabitants is drawn.

Park Pailing. Teeth.

Parson. A guide post, hand or finger post by the road side for directing travellers: compared to a parson, because, like him, it sets people in the right way. See Guide Post. He that would have luck in horse-flesh, must kiss a parson's wife.

Parson's Journeyman. A curate.

Parson Palmer. A jocular name, or term of reproach, to one who stops the circulation of the glass by preaching over his liquor; as it is said was done by a parson of that name whose cellar was under his pulpit.

PARTIAL. Inclining more to one side than the other, crooked, all o' one hugh.

PASS BANK. The place for playing at passage, cut into the ground almost like a cock-pit. Also the stock or fund.

PASSAGE. A camp game with three dice: doublets, making up ten or more, to pass or win; any other chances lose.

PAT. Apposite, or to the purpose.

PATE. The head. Carroty-pated; red-haired.

PATRICO, or PATER-COVE. The fifteenth rank of the canting tribe; strolling priests that marry people under a hedge, without gospel or common prayer book: the couple standing on each side of a dead beast, are bid to live together till death them does part; so shaking hands, the wedding is ended. Also any minister or parson.

PATTERING. The maundering or pert replies of servants; also talk or palaver in order to amuse one intended to be cheated. Pattering of prayers; the confused sound of a number of persons praying together.

To PATTER. To talk. To patter flash; to speak flash, or the language used by thieves. How the blowen lushes jackey, and patters flash; how the wench drinks gin, and talks flash.

PAVIOUR'S WORKSHOP. The street.

To PAUM. To conceal in the hand. To paum a die: to hide a die in the palm of the hand. He paums; he cheats. Don't pretend to paum that upon me.

PAUNCH. The belly. Some think paunch was the original name of that facetious prince of puppets, now called Mr. Punch, as he is always represented with a very prominent belly: though the common opinion is, that both the name and character were taken from a celebrated Italian comedian, called Polichenello.

PAW. A hand or foot; look at his dirty paws. Fore paw; the hand. Hind paw; the foot. To paw; to touch or handle clumsily.

PAW PAW TRICKS. Naughty tricks: an expression used by nurses, &c. to children.

To PAY. To smear over. To pay the bottom of a ship or boat; to smear it over with pitch: The devil to pay, and no pitch hot or ready. *Sea term.*---Also to beat: as, I will pay you as Paul paid the Ephesians, over the face and eyes, and all your d---d jaws. To pay away; to fight manfully, also to eat voraciously. To pay through the nose: to pay an extravagant price.

To Peach. To impeach: called also to blow the gab, squeak, or turn stag.

Peak. Any kind of lace.

Peal. To ring a peal in a man's ears; to scold at him: his wife rang him such a peal!

Pear Making. Taking bounties from several regiments and immediately deserting. The cove was fined in the steel for pear making; the fellow was imprisoned in the house of correction for taking bounties from different regiments.

Peccavi. To cry peccavi; to acknowledge one's self in an error, to own a fault: from the Latin *peccavi*, I have sinned.

Peck. Victuals. Peck and booze; victuals and drink.

Peckish. Hungry.

Peculiar. A mistress.

Ped. A basket. *Cant.*

Pedlar's French. The cant language. Pedlar's pony; a walking-stick.

To Peel. To strip: allusion to the taking off the coat or rind of an orange or apple.

Peeper. A spying glass; also a looking-glass. Track up the dancers, and pike with the peeper; whip up stairs, and run off with the looking-glass. *Cant.*

Peepers. Eyes. Single peeper, a one-eyed man.

Peeping Tom. A nick name for a curious prying fellow: derived from an old legendary tale, told of a taylor of Coventry, who, when Godiva countess of Chester rode at noon quite naked through that town, in order to procure certain immunities for the inhabitants, (notwithstanding the rest of the people shut up their houses) slily peeped out of his window, for which he was miraculously struck blind. His figure, peeping out of a window, is still kept up in remembrance of the transaction.

Peepy. Drowsy.

To Peer. To look about, to be circumspect.

Peery. Inquisitive, suspicious. The cull's peery; that fellow suspects something. There's a peery, tis snitch; we are observed, there's nothing to be done.

Peg. Old Peg; poor hard Suffolk or Yorkshire cheese. A peg is also a blow with a straight arm: a term used by the professors of gymnastic arts. A peg in the day-light, the victualling office, or the haltering-place; a blow in the eye, stomach, or under the ear.

Peg Trantum's. Gone to Peg Trantum's; dead.

Pego. The penis of man or beast.

Pell-mell. Tumultuously, helter skelter, jumbled together.

PELT. A heat, chafe, or passion, as, What a pelt he was in! Pelt is also the skin of several beasts.

PENANCE BOARD. The pillory.

PENNY WISE AND POUND FOOLISH. Saving in small matters, and extravagant in great.

PENNYWORTH. An equivalent. A good pennyworth; cheap bargain.

PENTHOUSE NAB. A broad brimmed hat.

PEPPERED. Infected with the venereal disease.

PEPPERY. Warm, passionate.

PERKIN. Water cyder.

PERRIWINKLE. A wig.

PERSUADERS. Spurs. The kiddey clapped his persuaders to his prad, but the traps boned him; the highwayman spurred his horse hard, but the officers seized him.

PET. In a pet; in a passion or miff.

PETER. A portmanteau or cloke-bag. Biter of peters; one that makes it a trade to steal boxes and trunks from behind stage coaches or out of waggons. To rob Peter to pay Paul; to borrow of one man to pay another: styled also manœuvring the apostles.

PETER GUNNER, will kill all the birds that died last summer. A piece of wit commonly thrown out at a person walking through a street or village near London, with a gun in his hand.

PETER LAY. The department of stealing portmanteaus, trunks, &c.

PETER LUG. Who is Peter Lug? who lets the glass stand at his door, or before him.

PETTICOAT HOLD. One who has an estate during his wife's life, called the apron-string hold.

PETTICOAT PENSIONER. One kept by a woman for secret services.

PETTISH. Passionate.

PETTY FOGGER. A little dirty attorney, ready to undertake any litigious or bad cause: it is derived from the French words *petit vogue*, of small credit, or little reputation.

PHARAOH. Strong malt liquor.

PHILISTINES. Bailiffs, or officers of justice; also drunkards.

PHŒNIX-MEN. Firemen belonging to an insurance office, which gave a badge charged with a phœnix: these men were called likewise firedrakes.

PHOS BOTTLE. A bottle of phosphorus: used by housebreakers to light their lanthorns. Ding the phos; throw away the bottle of phosphorus.

PHRASE OF PAPER. Half a quarter of a sheet. See VESSEL.

Physog. The face. A vulgar abbreviation of physiognomy.

Phyz. The face. Rum phyz; an odd face or countenance.

Picaroon. A pirate; also a sharper.

Pickaniny. A young child, an infant. *Negro term.*

Picking. Pilfering, petty larceny.

Pickle. An arch waggish fellow. In pickle, or in the pickling tub; in a salivation. There are rods in brine, or pickle, for him; a punishment awaits him, or is prepared for him. Pickle herring; the zany or merry andrew of a mountebank. See Jack Pudding.

Pickt Hatch. To go to the manor of pickt hatch, a cant name for some part of the town noted for bawdy houses in Shakespeare's time, and used by him in that sense.

Pickthank. A tale-bearer or mischief maker.

Picture Frame. The sheriff's picture frame; the gallows or pillory.

To Piddle. To make water: a childish expression; as, Mammy, I want to piddle. Piddling also means trifling, or doing any thing in a small degree: perhaps from peddling.

Piece. A wench. A damned good or bad piece; a girl who is more or less active and skilful in the amorous congress. Hence the (*Cambridge*) toast, May we never have a *piece* (peace) that will injure the constitution. Piece likewise means at Cambridge a close or spot of ground adjacent to any of the colleges, as Clare-hall Piece, &c. The spot of ground before King's College formerly belonged to Clare-hall. While Clare Piece belonged to King's, the master of Clare-hall proposed a swop, which being refused by the provost of King's, he erected before their gates a temple of *Cloacina*. It will be unnecessary to say that his arguments were soon acceded to.

Pig. A police officer. A China street pig; a Bow-street officer. Floor the pig and bolt; knock down the officer and run away.

Pig. Sixpence, a sow's baby. Pig-widgeon; a simpleton. To pig together; to lie or sleep together, two or more in a bed. Cold pig; a jocular punishment inflicted by the maid servants, or other females of the house, on persons lying over long in bed: it consists in pulling off all the bed clothes, and leaving them to pig or lie in the cold. To buy a pig in a poke; to purchase any thing without seeing. Pig's eyes; small eyes. Pigsnyes; the same: a vulgar term of endearment to a woman. He can have boiled

pig

pig at home; a mark of being master of his own house: an allusion to a well known poem and story. Brandy is Latin for pig and goose; an apology for drinking a dram after either.

PIG-HEADED. Obstinate.

PIG RUNNING. A piece of game frequently practised at fairs, wakes, &c. A large pig, whose tail is cut short, and both soaped and greased, being turned out, is hunted by the young men and boys, and becomes the property of him who can catch and hold him by the tail, above the height of his head.

PIGEON. A weak silly fellow easily imposed on. To pigeon; to cheat. To milk the pigeon; to attempt impossibilities, to be put to shifts for want of money. To fly a blue pigeon; to steal lead off a church.

PIGEONS. Sharpers, who, during the drawing of the lottery, wait ready mounted near Guildhall, and, as soon as the first two or three numbers are drawn, which they receive from a confederate on a card, ride with them full speed to some distant insurance office, before fixed on, where there is another of the gang, commonly a decent looking woman, who takes care to be at the office before the hour of drawing: to her he secretly gives the number, which she insures for a considerable sum: thus biting the biter.

PIGEON'S MILK. Boys and novices are frequently sent on the first of April to buy pigeons milk.

TO PIKE. To run away. Pike off; run away.

PILGRIM'S SALVE. A sirreverence, human excrement.

PILL, or PEELE GARLICK. Said originally to mean one whose skin or hair had fallen off from some disease, chiefly the venereal one; but now commonly used by persons speaking of themselves: as, there stood poor pill garlick: i. e. there stood I.

PILLALOO. The Irish cry or howl at funerals.

PIMP. A male procurer, or cock bawd; also a small faggot used about London for lighting fires, named from introducing the fire to the coals.

PIMP WHISKIN. A top trader in pimping.

PIMPLE. The head.

PIN. In or to a merry pin: almost drunk: an allusion to a sort of tankard, formerly used in the north, having silver pegs or pins set at equal distances from the top to the bottom: by the rules of good fellowship, every person drinking out of one of these tankards, was to swallow the quantity contained between two pins; if he drank

more

more or less, he was to continue drinking till he ended at a pin: by this means persons unaccustomed to measure their draughts were obliged to drink the whole tankard. Hence when a person was a little elevated with liquor, he was said to have drunk to a merry pin.

PIN BASKET. The youngest child.

PIN MONEY. An allowance settled on a married woman for her pocket expences.

PINCH. At a pinch; on an exigency.

PINCH. To go into a tradesman's shop under the pretence of purchasing rings or other light articles, and while examining them to shift some up the sleeve of the coat. Also to ask for change for a guinea, and when the silver is received, to change some of the good shillings for bad ones; then suddenly pretending to recollect that you had sufficient silver to pay the bill, ask for the guinea again, and return the change, by which means several bad shillings are passed.

TO PINCH ON THE PARSON'S SIDE. To defraud the parson of his tithe.

PINCHERS. Rogues who, in changing money, by dexterity of hand frequently secrete two or three shillings out of the change of a guinea. This species of roguery is called the pinch, or pinching lay.

TO PINK. To stab or wound with a small sword: probably derived from the holes formerly cut in both men and women's clothes, called pinking. Pink of the fashion; the top of the mode. To pink and wink; frequently winking the eyes through a weakness in them.

PINKING-DINDEE. A sweater or mohawk. *Irish.*

PINS. Legs. Queer pins; ill shapen legs.

PIPER. A broken winded horse.

PISCINARIANS. A club or brotherhood, A.D. 1743.

PISS. He will piss when he can't whistle; he will be hanged. He shall not piss my money against the wall; he shall not have my money to spend in liquor.

He who once a good name gets,
May piss a bed, and say he sweats.

PISS-BURNED. Discoloured: commonly applied to a discoloured grey wig.

PISS MAKER. A great drinker, one much given to liquor.

PISS POT HALL. A house at Clapton, near Hackney, built by a potter chiefly out of the profits of chamber pots, in the bottom of which the portrait of Dr. Sacheverel was depicted.

PISS PROPHET. A physician who judges of the diseases of his patients solely by the inspection of their urine. PISS-

PISS-PROUD. Having a false erection. That old fellow thought he had an erection, but his —— was only piss-proud; said of any old fellow who marries a young wife.

PISSING DOWN ANY ONE'S BACK. Flattering him.

PISSING PINS AND NEEDLES. To have a gonorrhea.

PIT. A watch fob. He drew a rare thimble from the swell's pit. He took a handsome watch from the gentleman's fob.

PIT. To lay pit and boxes into one; an operation in midwifery or copulation, whereby the division between the anus and vagina is cut through, broken, and demolished: a simile borrowed from the playhouse, when, for the benefit of some favourite player, the pit and boxes are laid together. The pit is also the hole under the gallows, where poor rogues unable to pay the fees are buried.

PITT'S PICTURE. A window stopt up on the inside, to save the tax imposed in that gentleman's administration. *Party wit.*

PIT-A-PAT. The palpitation of the heart: as, my heart went pit-a-pat. Pintledy-pantledy; the same.

PITCH-KETTLED. Stuck fast, confounded.

PITCHER. The miraculous pitcher, that holds water with the mouth downwards: a woman's commodity. She has crack'd her pitcher or pipkin; she has lost her maidenhead.

PIZZY CLUB. A society held, A. D. 1744, at the sign of the Tower, on Tower Hill: president, Don Pizzaro.

PLAISTER OF WARM GUTS. One warm belly clapped to another; a receipt frequently prescribed for different disorders.

PLANT. The place in the house of the fence where stolen goods are secreted. Any place where stolen goods are concealed.

TO PLANT. To lay, place, or hide. Plant your wids and stow them; be careful what you say, or let slip. Also to bury, as, he was planted by the parson.

PLATE. Money, silver, prize. He is in for the plate; he has won the *heat*, i. e. is infected with the venereal disorder: a simile drawn from horse-racing. When the plate fleet comes in; when money comes to hand.

PLATTER-FACED. Broad-faced.

PLAY. To play booty; to play with an intention to lose. To play the whole game; to cheat. To play least in sight; to hide, or keep out of the way. To play the devil; to be guilty of some great irregularity or mismanagement.

PLUCK. Courage. He wants pluck: he is a coward. Against the pluck; against the inclination. Pluck the ribbon; ring the bell. To pluck a crow with one; to settle a dispute, to reprove one for some past transgression. To pluck a rose; an expression said to be used by women for going to the necessary house, which in the country usually stands in the garden. To pluck also signifies to deny a degree to a candidate at one of the universities, on account of insufficiency. The three first books of Euclid, and as far as Quadratic Equations in Algebra, will save a man from being plucked. These unfortunate fellows are designated by many opprobrious appellations, such as the twelve apostles, the legion of honor, wise men of the East, &c.

Plug Tail. A man's penis.

Plumb. An hundred thousand pounds.

Plummy. It is all plummy; i. e. all is right, or as it ought to be.

Plump. Fat, full, fleshy. Plump in the pocket; full in the pocket. To plump; to strike, or shoot. I'll give you a plump in the bread basket, or the victualling office: I'll give you a blow in the stomach. Plump his peepers, or day-lights; give him a blow in the eyes. He pulled out his pops and plumped him; he drew out his pistols and shot him. A plumper; a single vote at an election. Plump also means directly, or exactly: as, it fell plump upon him: it fell directly upon him.

Plump Currant. I am not plump currant; I am out of sorts.

Plumpers. Contrivances said to be formerly worn by old maids, for filling out a pair of shrivelled cheeks.

Plyer. A crutch; also a trader.

Pogy. Drunk.

Point. To stretch a point; to exceed some usual limit, to take a great stride. Breeches were usually tied up with points, a kind of short laces, formerly given away by the churchwardens at Whitsuntide, under the denomination of tags: by taking a great stride these were stretched.

Poisoned. Big with child: that wench is poisoned, see how her belly is swelled. Poison-pated: red-haired.

Poke. A blow with the fist: I'll lend you a poke. A poke likewise means a sack: whence, to buy a pig in a poke, i. e. to buy any thing without seeing or properly examining it.

Poker. A sword. Fore pokers; aces and kings at cards. To burn your poker; to catch the venereal disease.

Pole. He is like a rope-dancer's pole, lead at both ends; a saying of a stupid sluggish fellow.

Polish. To polish the king's iron with one's eyebrows; to

be

be in gaol, and look through the iron grated windows. To polish a bone; to eat a meal. Come and polish a bone with me; come and eat a dinner or supper with me.

POLL. The head, jolly nob, napper, or knowledge box; also a wig.

POLT. A blow. Lend him a polt in the muns; give him a knock in the face.

TO POMMEL. To beat: originally confined to beating with the hilt of a sword, the knob being, from its similarity to a small apple, called *pomelle*; in Spanish it is still called the apple of the sword. As the clenched fist likewis somewhat resembles an apple, perhaps that might occasion the term pommelling to be applied to fisty-cuffs.

POMP. To save one's pomp at whist, is to score five before the adversaries are up, or win the game: originally derived from *pimp*, which is Welsh for five; and should be, I have saved my pimp.

POMPAGINIS. Aqua pompaginis; pump water. See AQUA.

POMPKIN. A man or woman of Boston in America: from the number of pompkins raised and eaten by the people of that country. Pompkinshire; Boston and its dependencies.

PONEY. Money. Post the poney; lay down the money.

PONTIUS PILATE. A pawnbroker. Pontius Pilate's guards, the first regiment of foot, or Royal Scots: so intitled from their supposed great antiquity. Pontius Pilate's counsellor; one who like him can say, *Non invenio causam,* I can find no cause. Also (*Cambridge*) a Mr. Shepherd of Trinity College; who disputing with a brother parson on the comparative rapidity with which they read the liturgy, offered to give him as far as Pontius Pilate in the Belief.

POPE. A figure burned annually every fifth of November, in memory of the gunpowder plot, which is said to have been carried on by the papists.

POPE'S NOSE. The rump of a turkey.

POPS. Pistols. Pop shop: a pawnbroker's shop. To pop; to pawn: also to shoot. I popped my tatler; I pawned my watch. I popt the cull; I shot the man. His means are two pops and a galloper; that is, he is a highwayman.

POPLERS. Pottage. *Cant.*

PORK. To cry pork; to give intelligence to the undertaker of a funeral; metaphor borrowed from the raven, whose note sounds like the word *pork.* Ravens are said to smell carrion at a distance.

PORKER. A hog: also a Jew.

Porridge. Keep your breath to cool your porridge; i. e. hold your tongue.

Porridge Island. An alley leading from St. Martin's church-yard to Round-court, chiefly inhabited by cooks, who cut off ready-dressed meat of all sorts, and also sell soup.

Posey, or Poesy. A nosegay. I shall see you ride backwards up Holborn-hill, with a book in one hand, and a posey in t'other; i. e. I shall see you go to be hanged. Malefactors who piqued themselves on being properly equipped for that occasion, had always a nosegay to smell to, and a prayer book, although they could not read.

Posse Mobilitatis. The mob.

Post Master General. The prime minister, who has the patronage of all posts and places.

Post Nointer. A house painter, who occasionally paints or anoints posts. Knight of the post; a false evidence, one ready to swear any thing for hire. From post to pillar; backwards and forwards.

Postilion of the Gospel. A parson who hurrics over the service.

Pot. The pot calls the kettle black a-se; one rogue exclaims against another.

Pot. On the pot; i. e. at stool.

Pot Converts. Proselytes to the Romish church, made by the distribution of victuals and money.

Pot Hunter. One who hunts more for the sake of the prey than the sport. Pot valiant; courageous from drink. Potwallopers: persons entitled to vote in certain boroughs by having boiled a pot there.

Potatoe Trap. The mouth. Shut your potatoe trap and give your tongue a holiday; i. e. be silent. *Irish wit.*

Pothooks and Hangers. A scrawl, bad writing.

Pot-wabblers. Persons entitled to vote for members of parliament in certain boroughs, from having boiled their pots therein. These boroughs are called pot-wabbling boroughs.

Poulain. A bubo. *French.*

Poulterer. A person that guts letters; i. e. opens them and secretes the money. The kiddey was topped for the poultry rig; the young fellow was hanged for secreting a letter and taking out the contents.

Pound. To beat. How the milling cove pounded the cull for being nuts on his blowen; how the boxer beat the fellow for taking liberties with his mistress.

Pound. A prison. See **Lob's Pound**. Pounded; imprisoned. Shut up in the parson's pound; married. **Powder**

POWDER MONKEY. A boy on board a ship of war, whose business is to fetch powder from the magazine.

POWDERING TUB. The same as pickling tub. See PICKLING TUB.

PRAD LAY. Cutting bags from behind horses. *Cant.*

PRAD. A horse. The swell flashes a rum prad; the gentleman sports a fine horse.

PRANCER. A horse. Prancer's nab; a horse's head, used as a seal to a counterfeit pass. At the sign of the prancer's poll, i. e. the nag's head.

PRATE ROAST. A talkative boy.

PRATING CHEAT. The tongue.

PRATTS. Buttocks; also a tinder box. *Cant.*

PRATTLE BROTH. Tea. See CHATTER BROTH, SCANDAL BROTH, &c.

PRATTLING BOX. The pulpit.

PRAY. She prays with her knees upwards; said of a woman much given to gallantry and intrigue. At her last prayers; saying of an old maid.

PREADAMITE QUACABITES. This great and laudable society (as they termed themselves) held their grand chapter at the Coal-hole.

P——K. The virile member.

PRICK-EARED. A prick-eared fellow; one whose ears are longer than his hair: an appellation frequently given to puritans, who considered long hair as the mark of the whore of Babylon.

PRICKLOUSE. A taylor.

PRIEST-CRAFT. The art of awing the laity, managing their consciences, and diving into their pockets.

PRIEST-LINKED. Married.

PRIEST-RIDDEN. Governed by a priest, or priests.

PRIG. A thief, a cheat: also a conceited coxcomical fellow.

PRIG NAPPER. A thief taker.

PRIGGERS. Thieves in general. Priggers of prancers; horse stealers. Priggers of cacklers: robbers of henroosts.

PRIGGING. Riding; also lying with a woman.

PRIGSTAR. A rival in love.

PRIME. Bang up. Quite the thing. Excellent. Well done. She's a prime piece; she is very skilful in the venereal act. Prime post. She's a prime article.

PRIMINARY. I had like to be brought into a priminary; i. e. into trouble; from *premunire.*

PRINCE PRIG. A king of the gypsies; also the head thief or receiver general.

Princes. When the majesty of the people was a favourite term in the House of Commons, a celebrated wit, seeing chimney sweepers dancing on a May-day, styled them the young princes.

Princod. A pincushion. *Scotch.*---Also a round plump man or woman.

Princox. A pert, lively, forward fellow.

Princum Prancum. Mrs. Princum Prancum; a nice, precise, formal madam.

Prinking. Dressing over nicely: prinked up as if he came out of a bandbox, or fit to sit upon a cupboard's head.

Print. All in print, quite neat or exact, set, screwed up. Quite in print; set in a formal manner.

Priscian. To break Priscian's head; to write or speak false grammar. Priscian was a famous grammarian, who flourished at Constantinople in the year 525; and who was so devoted to his favourite study, that to speak false Latin in his company, was as disagreeable to him as to break his head.

Prittle Prattle. Insignificant talk: generally applied to women and children.

Prog. Provision. Rum prog; choice provision. To prog; to be on the hunt for provision: called in the military term to forage.

Props. Crutches.

Property. To make a property of any one; to make him a conveniency, tool, or cat's paw; to use him as one's own.

Proud. Desirous of copulation. A proud bitch; a bitch at heat, or desirous of a dog.

Provender. He from whom any money is taken on the highway: perhaps providor, or provider. *Cant.*

Prophet. The prophet; the Cock at Temple Bar: so called, in 1788, by the bucks of the town of the inferior order.

Prunella. Mr. Prunella; a parson: parson's gowns being frequently made of prunella.

To Pry. To examine minutely into a matter or business. A prying fellow; a man of impertinent curiosity, apt to peep and inquire into other men's secrets.

Public Man. A bankrupt.

Public Ledger. A prostitute: because, like that paper, she is open to all parties.

Pucker. All in a pucker; in a dishabille. Also in a fright: as, she was in a terrible pucker.

Pucker Water. Water impregnated with alum, or other astringents, used by old experienced traders to counterfeit virginity.

Puddings. The guts: I'll let out your puddings.

Pudding-headed Fellow. A stupid fellow, one whose brains are all in confusion.

Pudding Sleeves. A parson.

Pudding Time. In good time, or at the beginning of a meal: pudding formerly making the first dish. To give the crows a pudding; to die. You must eat some cold pudding, to settle your love.

Puff, or Puffer. One who bids at auctions, not with an intent to buy, but only to raise the price of the lot; for which purpose many are hired by the proprietor of the goods on sale.

Puff Guts. A fat man.

Puffing. Bidding at an auction, as above; also praising any thing above its merits, from interested motives. The art of puffing is at present greatly practised, and essentially necessary in all trades, professions, and callings. To puff and blow; to be out of breath.

Pug. A Dutch pug; a kind of lap-dog, formerly much in vogue; also a general name for a monkey.

Pug Carpenter. An inferior carpenter, one employed only in small jobs.

Pug Drink. Watered cyder.

Pugnosed, or Pugified. A person with a snub or turned up nose.

Pully Hawly. To have a game at pully hawly; to romp with women.

Pull. To be pulled; to be arrested by a police officer. To have a pull is to have an advantage; generally where a person has some superiority at a game of chance or skill.

Pump. A thin shoe. To pump; to endeavour to draw a secret from any one without his perceiving it. Your pump is good, but your sucker is dry; said by one to a person who is attempting to pump him. Pumping was also a punishment for bailiffs who attempted to act in privileged places, such as the Mint, Temple, &c. It is also a piece of discipline administered to a pickpocket caught in the fact, when there is no pond at hand. To pump ship; to make water, and sometimes to vomit. *Sea phrase.*

Pump Water. He was christened in pump water; commonly said of a person that has a red face.

Punch. A liquor called by foreigners Contradiction, from its being composed of spirits to make it strong, water to make it weak, lemon juice to make it sour, and sugar to make it sweet. Punch is also the name of the prince of puppets, the chief wit and support of a puppet-show. To punch it, is a cant term for running away. Punchable; old passable money, anno 1695. A girl that is ripe for man is called a punchable wench. Cobler's Punch. Urine with a cinder in it.

Punk. A whore; also a soldier's trull. See Trull.

Puny. Weak. A puny child; a weak little child. A puny stomach; a weak stomach. Puny, or puisne judge; the last made judge.

Pupil Mongers. Persons at the universities who make it their business to instruct and superintend a number of pupils.

Puppy. An affected or conceited coxcomb.

Purblind. Dim-sighted.

Purl. Ale in which wormwood has been infused, or ale and bitters drunk warm.

Purl Royal. Canary wine; with a dash of tincture of wormwood.

Purse Proud. One that is vain of his riches.

Pursenets. Goods taken up at thrice their value, by young spendthrifts, upon trust.

Purser's Pump. A bassoon: from its likeness to a syphon, called a purser's pump.

Pursy, or Pursive. Short-breathed, or foggy, from being over fat.

Pushing School. A fencing school; also a brothel.

Put. A country put; an ignorant awkward clown. To put upon any one; to attempt to impose on him, or to make him the but of the company.

Puzzle-cause. A lawyer who has a confused understanding.

Puzzle-text. An ignorant blundering parson.

QUA

Quack. An ungraduated ignorant pretender to skill in physic, a vender of nostrums.

Quack-salver. A mountebank: a seller of salves.

Quacking Cheat. A duck.

Quag. Abbreviation of quagmire; marshy moorish ground.

Quall-

Quail-pipe. A woman's tongue; also a device to take birds of that name by imitating their call. Quail pipe boots; boots resembling a quail pipe, from the number of plaits; they were much worn in the reign of Charles II.

Quakers. A religious sect so called from their agitations in preaching.

Quaking Cheat. A calf or sheep.

Quandary. To be in a quandary: to be puzzled. Also one so over-gorged, as to be doubtful which he should do first, sh---e or spew. Some derive the term quandary from the French phrase *qu'en dirai je?* what shall I say of it? others from an Italian word signifying a conjuror's circle.

Quarrel-picker. A glazier: from the small squares in casements, called *carreux*, vulgarly quarrels.

Quarromes, or Quarron. A body. *Cant.*

Quartered. Divided into four parts; to be hanged, drawn, and quartered, is the sentence on traitors and rebels. Persons receiving part of the salary of an office from the holder of it, by virtue of an agreement with the donor, are said to be quartered on him. Soldiers billetted on a publican are likewise said to be quartered on him.

To Quash. To suppress, annul or overthrow; vulgarly pronounced *squash*: they squashed the indictment.

Quean. A slut, or worthless woman, a strumpet.

Queen Dick. To the tune of the life and death of Queen Dick. That happened in the reign of Queen Dick; i.e. never.

Queen Street. A man governed by his wife, is said to live in Queen street, or at the sign of the Queen's Head.

Queer, or Quire. Base, roguish, bad, naught or worthless. How queerly the cull touts; how roguishly the fellow looks. It also means odd, uncommon. *Cant.*

Queer as Dick's Hatband. Out of order, without knowing one's disease.

To Queer. To puzzle or confound. I have queered the old full bottom; i.e. I have puzzled the judge. To queer one's ogles among bruisers; to darken one's day lights.

Queer Wedges. Large buckles.

Queer Bail. Insolvent sharpers, who make a profession of bailing persons arrested: they are generally styled Jew bail, from that branch of business being chiefly carried on by the sons of Judah. The lowest sort of these, who borrow or hire clothes to appear in, are called Mounters, from their mounting particular dresses suitable to the occasion. *Cant.*

Queer Birds. Rogues relieved from prison, and returned to their old trade.

Queer Bit-makers. Coiners. *Cant.*

Queer Bitch. An odd, out-of-the-way fellow.

Queer Bluffer. The master of a public-house the resort of rogues and sharpers, a cut-throat inn or alehouse keeper.

Queer Bung. An empty purse.

Queer Checkers. Among strolling players, door-keepers who defraud the company, by falsely checking the number of people in the house.

Queer Cole Fencer. A putter off, or utterer, of bad money.

Queer Cole Maker. A maker of bad money.

Queer Cove. A rogue. *Cant.*

Queer Cuffin. A justice of the peace; also a churl.

Queer Degen. An ordinary sword, brass or iron hilted.

Queer Ken. A prison. *Cant.*

Queer Kicks. A bad pair of breeches.

Queer Mort. A diseased strumpet. *Cant.*

Queer Nab. A felt hat, or other bad hat.

Queer Plungers. Cheats who throw themselves into the water, in order that they may be taken up by their accomplices, who carry them to one of the houses appointed by the Humane Society for the recovery of drowned persons, where they are rewarded by the society with a guinea each; and the supposed drowned persons, pretending he was driven to that extremity by great necessity, is also frequently sent away with a contribution in his pocket.

Queer Prancer. A bad, worn-out, foundered horse; also a cowardly or faint-hearted horse-stealer.

Queer Rooster. An informer that pretends to be sleeping, and thereby overhears the conversation of thieves in night cellars.

Queer Street. Wrong. Improper. Contrary to one's wish. It is queer street, a cant phrase, to signify that it is wrong or different to our wish.

Qui tam. A qui tam horse; one that will both carry and draw. *Law wit.*

To Quibble. To make subtle distinctions; also to play upon words.

Quick and Nimble. More like a bear than a squirrel. Jeeringly said to any one moving sluggishly on a business or errand that requires dispatch.

Quid. The quantity of tobacco put into the mouth at one time. To quid tobacco; to chew tobacco. *Quid est hoc? hoc est* quid; a guinea. Half a quid; half a guinea.

The

The swell tipped me fifty quid for the prad; the gentleman gave fifty pounds for the horse.

QUIDS. Cash, money. Can you tip me any quids? can you lend me some money?

QUIFFING. Rogering. See To ROGER.

QUIDNUNC. A politician: from a character of that name in the farce of the Upholsterer.

QUILL DRIVER. A clerk, scribe, or hackney writer.

QUIM. The private parts of a woman: perhaps from the Spanish *quemar*, to burn. (*Cambridge*) A *piece's furbelow.*

QUINSEY. Choked by a hempen quinsey; hanged.

QUIPPS. Girds, taunts, jests.

QUIRE, or CHOIR BIRD. A complete rogue, one that has sung in different choirs or cages, i. e. gaols. *Cant.*

QUIRKS AND QUILLETS. Tricks and devices. Quirks in law; subtle distinctions and evasions.

QUIZ. A strange-looking fellow, an odd dog. *Oxford.*

QUOD. Newgate, or any other prison. The dab's in quod; the poor rogue is in prison.

QUOTA. Snack, share, part, proportion, or dividend. Tip me my quota; give me part of the winnings, booty, or plunder. *Cant.*

RAG

RABBIT. A Welch rabbit; bread and cheese toasted, i. e. a Welch rare bit. Rabbits were also a sort of wooden canns to drink out of, now out of use.

RABBIT CATCHER. A midwife.

RABBIT SUCKERS. Young spendthrifts taking up goods on trust at great prices.

RACK RENT. Rent strained to the utmost value. To lie at rack and manger; to be in great disorder.

RACKABACK. A gormagon. See GORMAGON.

RAFFS. An appellation given by the gownsmen of the university of Oxford to the inhabitants of that place.

RAG. Bank notes. Money in general. The cove has no rag; the fellow has no money.

RAG. A farthing.

TO RAG. To abuse, and tear to rags the characters of the persons abused. She gave him a good ragging, or ragged him off heartily.

RAG CARRIER. An ensign.

RAG FAIR. An inspection of the linen and necessaries of a company of soldiers, commonly made by their officers on Mondays or Saturdays.

RAG WATER. Gin, or any other common dram: these liquors seldom failing to reduce those that drink them to rags.

RAGAMUFFIN. A ragged fellow, one all in tatters, a tatterdemallion.

RAILS. See HEAD RAILS. A dish of rails; a lecture, jobation, or scolding from a married woman to her husband.

RAINBOW. Knight of the rainbow; a footman: from being commonly clothed in garments of different colours. A meeting of gentlemen, styled of the most ancient order of the rainbow, was advertised to be held at the Foppington's Head, Moorfields.

RAINY DAY. To lay up something for a rainy day; to provide against a time of necessity or distress.

RAKE, RAKEHELL, or RAKESHAME. A lewd, debauched fellow.

RALPH SPOONER. A fool.

RAM CAT. A he cat.

RAMMISH. Rank. Rammish woman; a sturdy virago.

RAMMER. The arm. The busnapper's kenchin seized my rammer; i. e. the watchman laid hold of my arm. *Cant.*

To RAMP. To snatch, or tear any thing forcibly from the person.

RAMSHACKLED. Out of repair. A ramshackled house; perhaps a corruption of *ransacked,* i. e. plundered.

RANDLE. A set of nonsensical verses, repeated in Ireland by schoolboys, and young people, who have been guilty of breaking wind backwards before any of their companions; if they neglect this apology, they are liable to certain kicks, pinches, and fillips, which are accompanied with divers admonitory couplets.

RANDY. Obstreperous, unruly, rampant.

RANGLING. Intriguing with a variety of women.

RANK. Stinking, rammish, ill-flavoured; also strong, great. A rank knave; a rank coward: perhaps the latter may allude to an ill savour caused by fear.

RANK RIDER. A highwayman.

RANTALLION. One whose scrotum is so relaxed as to be longer than his penis, i. e. whose shot pouch is longer that the barrel of his piece.

RANTIPOLE. A rude romping boy or girl; also a gadabout dissipated woman. To ride rantipole; the same as riding St. George. See ST. GEORGE.

RANTUM SCANTUM. Playing at rantum scantum; making the beast with two backs.

TO RAP. To take a false oath; also to curse. He rapped out a volley; i. e. he swore a whole volley of oaths. To rap, means also to exchange or barter: a rap is likewise an Irish halfpenny. Rap on the knuckles; a reprimand.

RAPPAREES. Irish robbers, or outlaws, who in the time of Oliver Cromwell were armed with short weapons, called in Irish *rapiers*, used for ripping persons up.

RAPPER. A swinging great lie.

RAREE SHEW MEN. Poor Savoyards, who subsist by shewing the magic lantern and marmots about London.

RASCAL. A rogue or villain: a term borrowed from the chase; a rascal originally meaning a lean shabby deer, at the time of changing his horns, penis, &c. whence, in the vulgar acceptation, rascal is conceived to signify a man without genitals: the regular vulgar answer to this reproach, if uttered by a woman, is the offer of an ocular demonstration of the virility of the party so defamed. Some derive it from *rascaglione*, an Italian word signifying a man without testicles, or an eunuch.

RAT. A drunken man or woman taken up by the watch, and confined in the watch-house. *Cant.* To smell a rat; to suspect some intended trick, or unfair design.

RATS. Of these there are the following kinds: a black rat and a grey rat, a py-rat and a cu-rat.

RATTLE. A dice-box. To rattle; to talk without consideration, also to move off or go away. To rattle one off; to rate or scold him.

RATTLE-PATE. A volatile, unsteady, or whimsical man or woman.

RATTLE-TRAPS. A contemptuous name for any curious portable piece of machinery, or philosophical apparatus.

RATTLER. A coach. Rattle and prad; a coach and horses.

RATTLING COVE. A coachman. *Cant.*

RATTLING MUMPERS. Beggars who ply coaches. *Cant.*

RAW HEAD AND BLOODY BONES. A bull beggar, or scarechild, with which foolish nurses terrify crying brats.

READER. A pocket-book. *Cant.*

READER MERCHANTS. Pickpockets, chiefly young Jews, who ply about the Bank to steal the pocket-books of persons who have just received their dividends there.

READY. The ready rhino; money. *Cant.*

REBUS. A riddle or pun on a man's name, expressed in sculpture or painting, thus: a bolt or arrow, and a tun, for Bolton; death's head, and a ton, for Morton.

RECEIVER GENERAL. A prostitute.

RECKON. To reckon with one's host; to make an erroneous judgment in one's own favour. To cast-up one's reckoning or accounts; to vomit.

To RECRUIT. To get a fresh supply of money.

RECRUITING SERVICE. Robbing on the highway.

RED FUSTIAN. Port wine.

RED LANE. The throat. Gone down the red lane; swallowed.

RED RIBBIN. Brandy.

RED LATTICE. A public house.

RED LETTER DAY. A saint's day or holiday, marked in the calendars with red letters. Red letter men; Roman Catholics: from their observation of the saint days marked in red letters.

RED RAG. The tongue. Shut your potatoe trap, and give your red rag a holiday; i. e. shut your mouth, and let your tongue rest. Too much of the red rag; too much tongue.

RED SAIL-YARD DOCKERS. Buyers of stores stolen out of the royal yards and docks.

RED SHANK. A Scotch highlander.

REGULARS. Share of the booty. The coves cracked the swell's crib, fenced the swag, and each cracksman napped his regular; some fellows broke open a gentleman's house, and after selling the property which they had stolen, they divided the money between them.

RELIGIOUS HORSE. One much given to prayer, or apt to be down upon his knees.

RELIGIOUS PAINTER. One who does not break the commandment which prohibits the making of the likeness of any thing in heaven or earth, or in the waters under the earth.

THE RELISH. The sign of the Cheshire cheese.

RELISH. Carnal connection with a woman.

REMEDY CRITCH. A chamber pot, or member mug.

REMEMBER PARSON MELHAM. Drink about: a Norfolk phrase.

RENDEZVOUS. A place of meeting. The rendezvous of the beggars were, about the year 1638, according to the Bellman, St. Quinton's, the Three Crowns in the Vintry, St. Tybs, and at Knapsbury: there were four barns within a mile of London. In Middlesex were four other harbours, called Draw the Pudding out of the Fire, the Cross Keys in Craneford parish, St. Julian's in Isleworth parish, and the house of Pettie in Northall parish. In Kent, the King's Barn near Dartford, and Ketbrooke near Blackheath.

Rep. A woman of reputation.

Repository. A lock-up or spunging-house, a gaol. Also livery stables where horses and carriages are sold by auction.

Rescounters. The time of settlement between the bulls and bears of Exchange-alley, when the losers must pay their differences, or become lame ducks, and waddle out of the Alley.

Resurrection Men. Persons employed by the students in anatomy to steal dead bodies out of church-yards.

Reverence. An ancient custom, which obliges any person easing himself near the highway or foot-path, on the word *reverence* being given him by a passenger, to take off his hat with his teeth, and without moving from his station to throw it over his head, by which it frequently falls into the excrement; this was considered as a punishment for the breach of delicacy. A person refusing to obey this law, might be pushed backwards. Hence, perhaps, the term, *sir-reverence*.

Reversed. A man set by bullies on his head, that his money may fall out of his breeches, which they afterwards by accident pick up. See Hoisting.

Review of the Black Cuirassiers. A visitation of the clergy. See Crow Fair.

Rhino. Money. *Cant.*

Rib. A wife: an allusion to our common mother Eve, made out of Adam's rib. A crooked rib: a cross-grained wife.

Ribaldry. Vulgar abusive language, such as was spoken by ribalds. Ribalds were originally mercenary soldiers who travelled about, serving any master for pay, but afterwards degenerated into a mere banditti.

Ribbin. Money. The ribbin runs thick; i. e. there is plenty of money. *Cant.* Blue ribbin. Gin. The cull lushes the blue ribbin; the silly fellow drinks common gin.

To Ribroast. To beat: I'll ribroast him to his heart's content.

Rich Face, or Nose. A red pimpled face.

Richard Snary. A dictionary. A country lad, having been reproved for calling persons by their christian names, being sent by his master to borrow a dictionary, thought to shew his breeding by asking for a Richard Snary.

Rider. A person who receives part of the salary of a place or appointment from the ostensible occupier, by virtue of an agreement with the donor, or great man appointing.

 The

The rider is said to be quartered upon the possessor, who often has one or more persons thus riding behind him. See QUARTERED.

RIDGE. A guinea. Ridge cully; a goldsmith. *Cant.*

RIDING ST. GEORGE. The woman uppermost in the amorous congress, that is, the dragon upon St. George. This is said to be the way to get a bishop.

RIDING SKIMMINGTON. A ludicrous cavalcade, in ridicule of a man beaten by his wife. It consists of a man riding behind a woman, with his face to the horse's tail, holding a distaff in his hand, at which he seems to work, the woman all the while beating him with a ladle; a smock displayed on a staff is carried before them as an emblematical standard, denoting female superiority: they are accompanied by what is called the *rough music*, that is, frying-pans, bulls horns, marrow-bones and cleavers, &c. A procession of this kind is admirably described by Butler in his Hudibras. He rode private, i. e. was a private trooper.

RIFF RAFF. Low vulgar persons, mob, tag-rag and bob-tail.

RIG. Fun, game, diversion, or trick. To run one's rig upon any particular person; to make him a butt. I am up to your rig; I am a match for your tricks.

RIGGING. Clothing. I'll unrig the bloss; I'll strip the wench. Rum Rigging; fine clothes. The cull has rum rigging, let's ding him and mill him, and pike; the fellow has good clothes, let's knock him down, rob him, and scour off, i.e. run away.

RIGHT. All right! A favourite expression among thieves, to signify that all is as they wish, or proper for their purpose. All right, hand down the jemmy; every thing is in proper order, give me the crow.

RIGMAROLE. Roundabout, nonsensical. He told a long rigmarole story.

RING. Money procured by begging: beggars so called it from its ringing when thrown to them. Also a circle formed for boxers, wrestlers, and cudgel-players, by a man styled Vinegar; who, with his hat before his eyes, goes round the circle, striking at random with his whip to prevent the populace from crowding in.

TO RING A PEAL. To scold; chiefly applied to women. His wife rung him a fine peal!

RING THE CHANGES. When a person receives silver in change to shift some good shillings and put bad ones in their place. The person who gave the change is then requested to give good shillings for these bad ones.

RIP. A miserable rip; a poor, lean, worn-out horse. A shabby mean fellow.

RIPPONS. Spurs: Rippon is famous for a manufactory of spurs both for men and fighting cocks.

ROARATORIOS AND UPROARS. Oratorios and operas.

ROARING BOY. A noisy, riotous fellow.

ROARER. A broken-winded horse.

ROARING TRADE. A quick trade.

TO ROAST. To arrest. I'll roast the dab; I'll arrest the rascal.—Also to jeer, ridicule, or banter. He stood the roast; he was the butt.—Roast meat clothes; Sunday or holiday-clothes. To cry roast meat; to boast of one's situation. To rule the roast; to be master or paramount.

ROAST AND BOILED. A nick name for the Life Guards, who are mostly substantial house-keepers; and eat daily of roast and boiled.

ROBERT'S MEN. The third old rank of the canting crew, mighty thieves, like Robin Hood.

ROBY DOUGLASS, with one eye and a stinking breath. The breech.

ROCHESTER PORTION. Two torn smocks, and what nature gave.

ROCKED. He was rocked in a stone kitchen; a saying meant to convey the idea that the person spoken of is a fool, his brains having been disordered by the jumbling of his cradle.

ROGER. A portmanteau; also a man's yard. *Cant.*

ROGER, or TIB OF THE BUTTERY. A goose. *Cant.* Jolly Roger; a flag hoisted by pirates.

TO ROGER. To bull, or lie with a woman; from the name of Roger being frequently given to a bull.

ROGUES. The fourth order of canters. A rogue in grain; a great rogue, also a corn chandler. A rogue in spirit; a distiller or brandy merchant.

ROGUM POGUM, or DRAGRUM POGRAM. Goat's beard, eaten for asparagus; so called by the ladies who gather cresses, &c. who also deal in this plant.

ROMBOYLES. Watch and ward. Romboyled; sought after with a warrant.

ROME MORT. A queen.

ROMEVILLE. London. *Cant.*

ROMP. A forward wanton girl, a tomrig. Grey, in his notes to Shakespeare, derives it from arompo, an animal found in South Guinea. that is a man eater. See HOYDEN.

ROOK. A cheat: probably from the thievish disposition of the birds of that name. Also the cant name for a crow used in house-breaking. To rook; to cheat, particularly at play.

ROOM. She lets out her fore room and lies backwards: saying of a woman suspected of prostitution.

ROOST LAY. Stealing poultry.

ROPES. Upon the high ropes; elated, in high spirits, cock-a-hoop.

ROSE. Under the rose: privately or secretly. The rose was, it is said, sacred to Harpocrates, the God of silence, and therefore frequently placed in the ceilings of rooms destined for the receiving of guests; implying, that whatever was transacted there, should not be made public.

ROSY GILLS. One with a sanguine or fresh-coloured countenance.

ROTAN. A coach, cart, or other wheeled carriage.

ROT GUT. Small beer; called beer-a-bumble---will burst one's guts before it will make one tumble.

ROVERS. Pirates, vagabonds.

ROUGH. To lie rough; to lie all night in one's clothes: called also roughing it. Likewise to sleep on the bare deck of a ship, when the person is commonly advised to chuse the softest plank.

ROUGH MUSIC. Saucepans, frying-pans, poker and tongs, marrow-bones and cleavers, bulls horns, &c. beaten upon and sounded in ludicrous processions.

ROULEAU. A number of guineas, from twenty to fifty or more, wrapped up in paper, for the more ready circulation at gaming-tables: sometimes they are inclosed in ivory boxes, made to hold exactly 20, 50, or 100 guineas.

ROUND DEALING. Plain, honest dealing.

ROUND HEADS. A term of reproach to the puritans and partizans of Oliver Cromwell, and the Rump Parliament, who it is said made use of a bowl as a guide to trim their hair.

ROUND ROBIN. A mode of signing remonstrances practised by sailors on board the king's ships, wherein their names are written in a circle, so that it cannot be discovered who first signed it, or was, in other words, the ringleader.

ROUND SUM. A considerable sum.

ROUND ABOUT. An instrument used in housebreaking. This instrument has not been long in use. It will cut a round piece about five inches in diameter out of a shutter or door.

ROUND MOUTH. The fundament. Brother round mouth speaks: he has let a fart.

ROUT. A modern card meeting at a private house; also an order from the Secretary at War, directing the march and quartering of soldiers.

Row. A disturbance; a term used by the students at Cambridge.

Row. To row in the same boat; to be embarked in the same scheme.

Rowland. To give a Rowland for an Oliver; to give an equivalent. Rowland and Oliver were two knights famous in romance: the wonderful achievements of the one could only be equalled by those of the other.

Royal Scamps. Highwaymen who never rob any but rich persons, and that without ill treating them See Scamp.

Royal Stag Society. Was held every Monday evening, at seven o'clock, at the Three tuns, near the Hospital Gate, Newgate-street.

Royster. A rude boisterous fellow; also a hound that opens on a false scent.

To Rub. To run away, Don't rub us to the whit; don't send us to Newgate. *Cant.*---To rub up; to refresh: to rub up one's memory. A rub: an impediment. A rubber; the best two out of three. To win a rubber: to win two games out of three.

Ruby faced. Red-faced.

Ruff. An ornament formerly worn by men and women round their necks. Wooden ruff; the pillory.

Ruffian. The devil. *Cant.*---May the ruffian nab the cuffin queer, and let the harmanbeck trine with his kinchins about his colquarren; may the Devil take the justice, and let the constable be hanged with his children about his neck. The ruffian cly thee; the Devil take thee. Ruffian cook ruffian, who scalded the Devil in his feathers; a saying of a bad cook, Ruffian sometimes also means a justice.

Ruffles. Handcuffs. *Cant.*

Rufflers. The first rank of canters; also notorious rogues pretending to be maimed soldiers or sailors.

Ruffmans. The woods, hedges, or bushes. *Cant.*

Rug. It is all rug; it is all right and safe, the game is secure. *Cant.*

Rug. Asleep. The whole gill is safe at rug; the people of the house are fast asleep.

Rum. Fine, good, valuable.

Rum Beck. A justice of the peace. *Cant.*

Rum Bite. A clever cheat, a clean trick.

Rum Bleating Cheat. A fat wether sheep. *Cant.*

Rum Blowen. A handsome wench. *Cant.*

Rum Bluffer. A jolly host. *Cant.*

Rum Bob. A young apprentice; also a sharp trick. Rum

RUM BOOZE. Wine, or any other good liquor. Rum boozing welts; bunches of grapes. *Cant.*

RUM BUBBER. A dexterous fellow at stealing silver tankards from inns and taverns.

RUM BUGHER. A valuable dog. *Cant.*

RUM BUNG. A full purse. *Cant.*

RUM CHUB. Among butchers, a customer easily imposed on, as to the quality and price of meat. *Cant.*

RUM CHANT. A song.

RUM CLOUT. A fine silk, cambric, or holland handkerchief. *Cant.*

RUM COD. A good purse of gold. *Cant.*

RUM COLE. New money, or medals.

RUM COVE. A dexterous or clever rogue.

RUM CULL. A rich fool, easily cheated, particularly by his mistress.

RUM DEGEN. A handsome sword. *Cant.*

RUM DELL. See RUM DOXY.

RUM DIVER. A dextrous pickpocket. *Cant.*

RUM DOXY. A fine wench. *Cant.*

RUM DRAWERS. Silk, or other fine stockings. *Cant.*

RUM DROPPER. A vintner. *Cant.*

RUM DUBBER. An expert picklock.

RUM DUKE. A jolly handsome fellow; also an odd eccentric fellow; likewise the boldest and stoutest fellows lately among the Alsatians, Minters, Savoyards, and other inhabitants of privileged districts, sent to remove and guard the goods of such bankrupts as intended to take sanctuary in those places. *Cant.*

RUM FILE. See RUM DIVER.

RUM FUN. A sharp trick. *Cant.*

RUM GAGGERS. Cheats who tell wonderful stories of their sufferings at sea, or when taken by the Algerines, *Cant.*

RUM GHELT. See RUM COLE. *Cant.*

RUM GLYMMER. King or chief of the link-boys. *Cant.*

RUM KICKS. Breeches of gold or silver brocade, or richly laced with gold or silver. *Cant.*

RUM MAWND. One that counterfeits a fool. *Cant*

RUM MORT. A queen, or great lady. *Cant.*

RUM NAB. A good hat.

RUM NANTZ. Good French brandy. *Cant.*

RUM NED. A very rich silly fellow. *Cant.*

RUM PAD. The highway. *Cant.*

RUM PADDERS. Highwaymen well mounted and armed. *Cant.*

RUM PEEPERS. Fine looking-glasses. *Cant.* RUM

Rum Prancer. A fine horse. *Cant.*
Rum Quids. A great booty. *Cant.*
Rum Ruff Peck. Westphalia ham. *Cant.*
Rum Snitch. A smart fillip on the nose.
Rum Squeeze. Much wine, or good liquor, given among fiddlers. *Cant.*
Rum Tilter. See Rum Degen.
Rum Tol. See Rum Degen.
Rum Topping. A rich commode, or woman's head-dress.
Rum Ville. See Romeville.
Rum Wiper. See Rum Clout.
Rumbo. Rum, water, and sugar ; also a prison.
Rumboyle. A ward or watch.
Rumbumtious. Obstreperous.
Rumford. To ride to Rumford to have one's backside new bottomed: i. e. to have a pair of new leather breeches. Rumford was formerly a famous place for leather breeches. A like saying is current in Norfolk and Suffolk, of Bungay, and for the same reason.—Rumford lion ; a calf. See Essex Lion.
Rump. To rump any one ; to turn the back to him : an evolution sometimes used at court. Rump and a dozen ; a rump of beef and a dozen of claret ; an Irish wager, called also buttock and trimmings. Rump and kidney men ; fiddlers that play at feasts, fairs, weddings, &c. and live chiefly on the remnants.
Rumpus. A riot, quarrel, or confusion.
Run Goods. A maidenhead, being a commodity never entered.
Running Horse, or Nag. A clap, or gleet.
Running Smobble. Snatching goods off a counter, and throwing them to an accomplice, who brushes off with them.
Running Stationers. Hawker of newspapers, trials, and dying speeches.
Runt. A short squat man or woman : from the small cattle called Welsh runts.
Rushers. Thieves who knock at the doors of great houses in London, in summer time, when the families are gone out of town, and on the door being opened by a woman, rush in and rob the house ; also housebreakers who enter lone houses by force.
Russian Coffee-House. The Brown Bear in Bow-street, Covent Garden, a house of call for thief-takers and runners of the Bow street justices.
Rusty. Out of use. To nab the rust ; to be refractory ;

ry; properly applied to a restive horse, and figuratively to the human species. To ride rusty; to be sullen; called also to ride grub.

RUSTY GUTS. A blunt surly fellow: a jocular misnomer of *resticus*.

RUTTING. Copulating. Rutting time; the season when deer go to rut.

SACHEVEREL. The iron door, or blower, to the mouth of a stove: from a divine of that name, who made himself famous for blowing the coals of dissension in the latter end of the reign of queen Ann.

SACK. A pocket. To buy the sack: to get drunk. To dive into the sack; to pick a pocket. To break a bottle in an empty sack; a bubble bet, a sack with a bottle in it not being an empty sack.

SAD DOG. A wicked debauched fellow; one of the ancient family of the sad dogs. Swift translates it into Latin by the words *tristis canis*.

SADDLE. To saddle the spit; to give a dinner or supper. To saddle one's nose; to wear spectacles. To saddle a place or pension; to oblige the holder to pay a certain portion of his income to some one nominated by the donor. Saddle sick; galled with riding, having lost leather.

SAINT. A piece of spoilt timber in a coach-maker's shop, like a saint, devoted to the flames.

SAINT GEOFFREY'S DAY. Never, there being no saint of that name: to-morrow-come-never, when two Sundays come together.

SAINT LUKE'S BIRD. An ox; that Evangelist being always represented with an ox.

SAINT MONDAY. A holiday most religiously observed by journeymen shoemakers, and other inferior mechanics. a profanation of that day, by working, is punishable by a fine, particularly among the gentle craft. An Irishman observed, that this saint's anniversary happened every week.

SAL. An abbreviation of *salivation*. In a high sal: in the pickling tub, or under a salivation.

SALESMAN'S DOG. A barker. Vide BARKER.

SALMON-

SALMON-GUNDY. Apples, onions, veal or chicken, and pickled herrings, minced fine, and eaten with oil and vinegar; some derive the name of this mess from the French words *selon mon goust*, because the proportions of the different ingredients are regulated by the palate of the maker; others say it bears the name of the inventor, who was a rich Dutch merchant; but the general and most probable opinion is, that it was invented by the countess of Salmagondi, one of the ladies of Mary de Medicis, wife of King Henry IV. of France, and by her brought into France.

SALMON, or SALAMON. The beggars' sacrament or oath.

SALT. Lecherous. A salt bitch: a bitch at heat, or proud bitch. Salt eel; a rope's end, used to correct boys, &c. at sea: you shall have a salt eel for supper.

SAMMY. Foolish. Silly.

SANDWICH. Ham, dried tongue, or some other salted meat, cut thin and put between two slices of bread and butter: said to be a favourite morsel with the Earl of Sandwich.

SANDY PATE. A red haired man or woman.

SANGAREE. Rack punch was formerly so called in bagnios.

SANK, SANKY, or CENTIPEE'S. A taylor employed by clothiers in making soldier's clothing.

SAPSCULL. A simple fellow. Sappy; foolish.

SATYR. A libidinous fellow: those imaginary things are by poets reported to be extremely salacious.

SAUCE BOX. A term of familiar raillery, signifying a bold or forward person.

SAVE-ALL. A kind of candlestick used by our frugal forefathers, to burn snuffs and ends of candles. Figuratively, boys running about gentlemen's houses in Ireland, who are fed on broken meats that would otherwise be wasted, also a miser.

SAUNTERER. An idle, lounging fellow; by some derived from *sans terre*; applied to persons, who, having no lands or home, lingered and loitered about. Some derive it from persons devoted to the Holy Land, *saint terre*, who loitered about, as waiting for company.

SAW. An old saw; an ancient proverbial saying.

SAWNY, or SANDY. A general nick-name for a Scotchman, as Paddy is for an Irishman, or Taffy for a Welchman; Sawny or Sandy being the familiar abbreviation or diminution of Alexander, a very favourite name among the Scottish nation.

SCAB. A worthless man or woman.

SCALD MISERABLES. A set of mock masons, who, A. D. 1744, made a ludicrous procession in ridicule of the Free Masons.

SCALDER. A clap. The cull has napped a scalder; the fellow has got a clap.

SCALY. Mean. Sordid. How scaly the cove is; how mean the fellow is.

SCALY FISH. An honest, rough, blunt sailor.

SCAMP. A highwayman. Royal scamp: a highwayman who robs civilly. Royal foot scamp; a footpad who behaves in like manner.

TO SCAMPER. To run away hastily.

SCANDAL BROTH. Tea.

SCANDAL PROOF. One who has eaten shame and drank after it, or would blush at being ashamed.

SCAPEGALLOWS. One who deserves and has narrowly escaped the gallows, a slip-gibbet, one for whom the gallows is said to groan.

SCAPEGRACE. A wild dissolute fellow.

SCARCE. To make one's self scarce; to steal away.

SCARLET HORSE. A high red, hired or hack horse: a pun on the word *hired.*

SCAVEY. Sense, knowledge. " Massa, me no scavey;" master, I don't know (*negro language*) perhaps from the French *scavoir.*

SCHEME. A party of pleasure.

SCHISM MONGER. A dissenting teacher.

SCHISM SHOP. A dissenting meeting house.

A SCOLD'S CURE. A coffin. The blowen has napped the scold's cure; the bitch is in her coffin.

SCHOOL OF VENUS. A bawdy-house.

SCHOOL BUTTER. Cobbing, whipping.

SCONCE. The head, probably as being the fort and citadel of a man: from *sconce*, an old name for a fort, derived from a Dutch word of the same signification. To build a sconce: a military term for bilking one's quarters. To sconce or skonce; to impose a fine. *Academical phrase.*

SCOT. A young bull.

SCOTCH GREYS. Lice. The headquarters of the Scotch greys: the head of a man full of large lice.

SCOTCH PINT. A bottle containing two quarts.

SCOTCH BAIT. A halt and a resting on a stick, as practised by pedlars.

SCOTCH CHOCOLATE. Brimstone and milk.

SCOTCH FIDDLE. The itch.

SCOTCH MIST. A sober soaking rain; a Scotch mist will wet an Englishman to the skin.

Scotch Warming Pan. A wench; also a fart.

Scoundrel. A man void of every principle of honour.

Scour. To scour or score off; to run away: perhaps from *score*; i. e. full speed, or as fast as legs would carry one. Also to wear: chiefly applied to irons, fetters, or handcuffs, because wearing scours them. He will scour the darbies; he will be in fetters. To scour the cramp ring; to wear bolts or fetters, from which, as well as from coffin hinges, rings supposed to prevent the cramp are made.

Scourers. Riotous bucks, who amuse themselves with breaking windows, beating the watch, and assaulting every person they meet: called scouring the streets.

Scout. A college errand-boy at Oxford, called a gyp at Cambridge. Also a watchman or a watch. *Cant.*

Scragged. Hanged.

Scraggy. Lean, bony.

Scragg'em Fair. A public execution.

Scrap. A villainous scheme or plan. He whiddles the whole scrap; he discovers the whole plan or scheme.

Scrape. To get into a scrape; to be involved in a disagreeable business.

Scraper. A fiddler; also one who scrapes plates for mezzotinto prints.

Scraping. A mode of expressing dislike to a person, or sermon, practised at Oxford by the students, in scraping their feet against the ground during the preachment; frequently done to testify their disapprobation of a proctor who has been, as they think, too rigorous.

Scratch. Old Scratch; the Devil: probably from the long and sharp claws with which he is frequently delineated.

Scratch Land. Scotland.

Scratch Platter, or Taylor's Ragout. Bread sopt in the oil and vinegar in which cucumbers have been sliced.

Screen. A bank note. Queer screens; forged bank notes. The cove was twisted for smashing queer screens; the fellow was hanged for uttering forged bank notes.

Screw. A skeleton key used by housebreakers to open a lock. To stand on the screw signifies that a door is not bolted, but merely locked.

To Screw. To copulate. A female screw; a common prostitute. To screw one up; to exact upon one in a bargain or reckoning.

Screw Jaws. A wry-mouthed man or woman.

Scrip. A scrap or slip of paper. The cully freely blotted the

the scrip, and tipt me forty hogs; the man freely signed the bond, and gave me forty shillings.—Scrip is also a Change Alley phrase for the last loan or subscription. What does scrip go at for the next rescounters? what does scrip sell for delivered at the next day of settling?

SCROBY. To be tipt the scroby; to be whipt before the justices.

SCROPE. A farthing. *Cant.*

SCRUB. A low mean fellow, employed in all sorts of dirty work.

SCRUBBADO. The itch.

SCULL. A head of a house, or master of a college, at the universities.

SCULL, or SCULLER. A boat rowed by one man with a light kind of oar, called a scull; also a one-horse chaise or buggy.

SCULL THATCHER. A peruke-maker.

SCUM. The riff-raff, tag-rag, and bob-tail, or lowest order of people.

SCUT. The tail of a hare or rabbit; also that of a woman.

SCUTTLE. To scuttle off; to run away. To scuttle a ship; to make a hole in her bottom in order to sink her.

SEA CRAB. A sailor.

SEA LAWYER. A shark.

SEALER, or SQUEEZE WAX. One ready to give bond and judgment for goods or money.

SECRET. He has been let into the secret: he has been cheated at gaming or horse-racing. He or she is in the grand secret, i. e. dead.

SEEDY. Poor, pennyless, stiver-cramped, exhausted.

SEES. The eyes. See DAYLIGHTS.

SERVED. Found guilty. Convicted. Ordered to be punished or transported. To serve a cull out; to beat a man soundly.

SERAGLIO. A bawdy-house; the name of that part of the Great Turk's palace where the women are kept.

SEND. To drive or break in. Hand down the Jemmy and send it in; apply the crow to the door, and drive it in.

SET. A dead set: a concerted scheme to defraud a person by gaming.

SETTER. A bailiff's follower, who, like a setting dog follows and points out the game for his master. Also sometimes an exciseman.

TO SETTLE. To knock down or stun any one. We settled the cull by a stroke on his nob; we stunned the fellow by a blow on the head.

Seven-sided Animal. A one-eyed man or woman, each having a right side and a left side, a fore side and a back side, an outside, an inside, and a blind side.

Shabbaroon. An ill-dressed shabby fellow; also a mean-spirited person.

Shaftsbury. A gallon pot full of wine, with a cock.

To Shag. To copulate. He is but bad shag; he is no able woman's man.

Shag-bag, or Shake-bag. A poor sneaking fellow; a man of no spirit: a term borrowed from the cock-pit.

Shake. To shake one's elbow; to game with dice. To shake a cloth in the wind; to be hanged in chains.

Shake. To draw any thing from the pocket. He shook the swell of his fogle; he robbed the gentleman of his silk handkerchief.

Shallow Pate. A simple fellow.

Shallow. A *Whip* hat, so called from the want of depth in the crown. Lilly Shallow, a *white* Whip hat.

Sham. A cheat, or trick. To cut a sham; to cheat or deceive. Shams; false sleeves to put on over a dirty shirt, or false sleeves with ruffles to put over a plain one. To sham Abram; to counterfeit sickness.

To Shamble. To walk awkwardly. Shamble-legged: one that walks wide and shuffles about his feet.

Shanker. A venereal wart.

Shanks. Legs, or gams.

Shanks Naggy. To ride shanks naggy: to travel on foot. *Scotch.*

Shannon. A river in Ireland: persons dipped in that river are perfectly and for ever cured of bashfulness.

Shapes. To shew one's shapes; to be stript, or made peel, at the whipping-post.

Shappo, or Shap. A hat: corruption of *chapeau*. *Cant.*

Shark. A sharper: perhaps from his preying upon any one he can lay hold of. Also a custom-house officer, or tide-waiter. Sharks; the first order of pickpockets. *Bow-street term*, A. D. 1785.

Sharp. Subtle, acute, quick-witted; also a sharper or cheat, in opposition to a flat, dupe, or gull. Sharp's the word and quick's the motion with him; said of any one very attentive to his own interest, and apt to take all advantages. Sharp set; hungry.

Sharper. A cheat, one that lives by his wits. Sharpers tools; a fool and false dice.

Shaver. A cunning shaver; a subtle fellow, one who trims close, an acute cheat. A young shaver; a boy. *Sea term.*

SHAVINGS. The clippings of money.

SHE HOUSE. A house where the wife rules, or, as the term is, wears the breeches.

SHE LION. A shilling.

SHE NAPPER. A woman thief-catcher; also a bawd or pimp.

SHEEP'S HEAD. Like a sheep's head, all jaw; saying of a talkative man or woman.

SHEEPISH. Bashful. A sheepish fellow; a bashful or shamefaced fellow. To cast a sheep's eye at any thing; to look wishtfully at it.

SHEEPSKIN FIDDLER. A drummer.

SHELF. On the shelf, i. e. pawned.

SHERIFF'S JOURNEYMAN. The hangman.

SHERIFF'S BALL. An execution. To dance at the sheriff's ball, and loll out one's tongue at the company; to be hanged, or go to rest in a horse's night-cap, i. e. a halter.

SHERIFF'S BRACELETS. Handcuffs.

SHERIFF'S HOTEL. A prison.

SHERIFF'S PICTURE FRAME. The gallows.

TO SHERK. To evade or disappoint: to sherk one's duty.

TO SHERRY. To run away: sherry off.

SHIFTING. Shuffling. Tricking. Shifting cove; i. e. a person who lives by tricking.

SHIFTING BALLAST. A term used by sailors, to signify soldiers, passengers, or any landsmen on board.

SHILLALEY. An oaken sapling, or cudgel: from a wood of that name famous for its oaks. *Irish.*

SHILLY-SHALLY. Irresolute. To stand shilly-shally; to hesitate, or stand in doubt.

SHINDY. A dance. *Sea phrase.*

SHINE. It shines like a shitten barn door.

SHIP SHAPE. Proper, as it ought to be. *Sea phrase,*

SH-T SACK. A dastardly fellow: also a non-conformist. This appellation is said to have originated from the following story:---After the restoration, the laws against the non-conformists were extremely severe. They sometimes met in very obscure places: and there is a tradition that one of their congregations were assembled in a barn, the rendezvous of beggars and other vagrants, where the preacher, for want of a ladder or tub, was suspended in a sack fixed to the beam. His discourse that day being on the last judgment, he particularly attempted to describe the terrors of the wicked at the sounding of the trumpet, on which a trumpeter to a puppet-show, who had taken refuge in that barn, and lay hid under the straw, sounded a charge. The congregation, struck with the utmost con-

consternation, fled in an instant from the place, leaving their affrighted teacher to shift for himself. The effects of his terror are said to have appeared at the bottom of the sack, and to have occasioned that opprobrious appellation by which the non-conformists were vulgarly distinguished.

SH-T-NG THROUGH THE TEETH. Vomiting. Hark ye, friend, have you got a padlock on your a-se, that you sh-te through your teeth? vulgar address to one vomiting.

SHOD ALL ROUND. A parson who attends a funeral is said to be shod all round, when he receives a hat-band, gloves, and scarf: many shoeings being only partial.

SHOEMAKER'S STOCKS. New, or strait shoes. I was in the shoemaker's stocks; i. e. had on a new pair of shoes that were too small for me.

TO SHOOLE. To go skulking about.

TO SHOOT THE CAT. To vomit from excess of liquor; called also catting.

SHOP. A prison. Shopped; confined, imprisoned.

SHOPLIFTER. One that steals whilst pretending to purchase goods in a shop.

SHORT-HEELED WENCH. A girl apt to fall on her back.

SHOT. To pay one's shot; to pay one's share of a reckoning. Shot betwixt wind and water; poxed or clapped.

SHOTTEN HERRING. A thin meagre fellow.

TO SHOVE THE TUMBLER. To be whipped at the cart's tail.

SHOVE IN THE MOUTH. A dram.

SHOVEL. To be put to bed with a shovel; to be buried. He or she was fed with a fire-shovel; a saying of a person with a large mouth.

SHOULDER FEAST. A dinner given after a funeral, to those who have carried the corpse.

SHOULDER CLAPPER. A bailiff, or member of the catch club. Shoulder-clapped; arrested.

SHOULDER SHAM. A partner to a file. See FILE.

SHRED. A taylor.

SHRIMP. A little diminutive person.

TO SHUFFLE. To make use of false pretences, or unfair shifts. A shuffling fellow; a slippery shifting fellow.

SHY COCK. One who keeps within doors for fear of bailiffs.

SICE. Sixpence.

SICK AS A HORSE. Horses are said to be extremely sick at their stomachs, from being unable to relieve themselves by vomiting. Bracken, indeed, in his Farriery, gives an instance of that evacuation being procured, but by a

 means

means which he says would make the Devil vomit. Such as may have occasion to administer an emetic either to the animal or the fiend, may consult his book for the recipe.

SIDE POCKET. He has as much need of a wife as a dog of a side pocket; said of a weak old debilitated man. He wants it as much as a dog does a side pocket; a simile used for one who desires any thing by no means necessary.

SIDLEDYWRY. Crooked.

SIGN OF A HOUSE TO LET. A widow's weeds.

SIGN OF THE { FIVE SHILLINGS. The crown.
TEN SHILLINGS. The two crowns.
FIFTEEN SHILLINGS. The three crowns. }

SILENCE. To silence a man; to knock him down, or stun him. Silence in the court, the cat is pissing; a gird upon any one requiring silence unnecessarily.

SILENT FLUTE. See PEGO, SUGAR STICK, &c.

SILK SNATCHERS. Thieves who snatch hoods or bonnets from persons walking in the streets.

SILVER LACED. Replete with lice. The cove's kickseys are silver laced: the fellow's breeches are covered with lice.

SIMEONITES, (at Cambridge,) the followers of the Rev. Charles Simeon, fellow of King's College, author of Skeletons of Sermons, and preacher at Trinity church; they are in fact rank methodists.

SIMKIN. A foolish fellow.

SIMON. Sixpence. Simple Simon: a natural, a silly fellow; Simon Suck-egg, sold his wife for an addle duck-egg.

To SIMPER. To smile: to simper like a firmity kettle.

SIMPLETON. Abbreviation of simple Tony or Anthony, a foolish fellow.

SIMPLES. Physical herbs; also follies. He must go to Battersea, to be cut for the simples—Battersea is a place famous for its garden grounds, some of which were formerly appropriated to the growing of simples for apothecaries, who at a certain season used to go down to select their stock for the ensuing year, at which time the gardeners were said to cut their simples; whence it became a popular joke to advise young people to go to Battersea, at that time, to have their simples cut, or to be cut for the simples.

To SING. To call out; the coves sing out beef; they call out stop thief.

To SING SMALL. To be humbled, confounded, or abashed, to have little or nothing to say for one's-self. SINGLE

Single Peeper. A person having but one eye.

Singleton. A very foolish fellow; also a particular kind of nails.

Singleton. A corkscrew, made by a famous cutler of that name, who lived in a place called Hell, in Dublin; his screws are remarkable for their excellent temper.

Sir John. The old title for a country parson: as Sir John of Wrotham, mentioned by Shakespeare.

Sir John Barleycorn. Strong beer.

Sir Loin. The sur, or upper loin.

Sir Reverence. Human excrement, a t—d.

Sir Timothy. One who, from a desire of being the head of the company, pays the reckoning, or, as the term is, stands squire. See Squire.

Sitting Breeches. One who stays late in company, is said to have his sitting breeches on, or that he will sit longer than a hen.

Six and Eight-pence. An attorney, whose fee on several occasions is fixed at that sum.

Six and Tips. Whisky and small beer. *Irish.*

Sixes and Sevens. Left at sixes and sevens: i.e. in confusion; commonly said of a room where the furniture, &c. is scattered about; or of a business left unsettled.

Size of Ale. Half a pint. Size of bread and cheese; a certain quantity. Sizings: Cambridge term for the college allowance from the buttery, called at Oxford battles.

To Size. (*Cambridge*) To sup at one's own expence. If a *man* asks you to *sup*, he treats you; if to *size*, you pay for what you eat—liquors *only* being provided by the inviter.

Sizar (*Cambridge*). Formerly students who came to the University for purposes of study and emolument. But at present they are just as gay and dissipated as their fellow collegians. About fifty years ago they were on a footing with the servitors at Oxford, but by the exertions of the present Bishop of Llandaff, who was himself a sizar, they were absolved from all marks of inferiority or of degradation. The chief difference at present between them and the pensioners, consists in the less amount of their college fees. The saving thus made induces many extravagant fellows to become sizars, that they may have more money to lavish on their dogs, pieces, &c.

Skew. A cup, or beggar's wooden dish.

Skewvow, or All askew. Crooked, inclining to one side.

Skin. In a bad skin; out of temper, in an ill humour. Thin-skinned: touchy, peevish.

Skin. A purse. Frisk the skin of the stephen; empty the money out of the purse. Queer skin; an empty purse.

Skin Flint. An avaricious man or woman.

Skink. To skink, is to wait on the company, ring the bell, stir the fire, and snuff the candles; the duty of the youngest officer in the military mess. See Boots.

Skins. A tanner.

Skip Jacks. Youngsters that ride horses on sale, horse-dealers boys. Also a plaything made for children with the breast bone of a goose.

Skip Kennel. A footman.

Skipper. A barn. *Cant.*---Also the captain of a Dutch vessel.

To Skit. To wheedle. *Cant.*

Skit. A joke. A satirical hint.

Skrip. See Scrip.

Skulker. A soldier who by feigned sickness, or other pretences, evades his duty; a sailor who keeps below in time of danger; in the civil line, one who keeps out of the way, when any work is to be done. To skulk; to hide one's self, to avoid labour or duty.

Sky Blue. Gin.

Sky Farmers. Cheats who pretend they were farmers in the isle of Sky, or some other remote place, and were ruined by a flood, hurricane, or some such public calamity: or else called sky farmers from their farms being *in nubibus,*' in the clouds.'

Sky Parlour. The garret, or upper story.

Slabbering Bib. A parson or lawyer's band.

Slag. A slack-mettled fellow, one not ready to resent an affront.

Slam. A trick; also a game at whist lost without scoring one. To slam to a door; to shut it with violence.

Slamkin. A female sloven, one whose clothes seem hung on with a pitch-fork, a careless trapes.

Slang. A fetter. Double slanged; double ironed. Now double slanged into the cells for a crop he is knocked down; he is double ironed in the condemned cells, and ordered to be hanged.

Slang. Cant language.

Slap-bang Shop. A petty cook's shop, where there is no credit given, but what is had must be paid *down with the ready slap-bang*, i. e. immediately. This is a common appellation for a night cellar frequented by thieves, and sometimes for a stage coach or caravan.

Slapdash. Immediately, instantly, suddenly. **Slasher.**

SLASHER. A bullying, riotous fellow. *Irish.*

SLAT. Half a crown. *Cant.*

SLATE. A sheet. *Cant.*

SLATER'S PAN. The gaol at Kingston in Jamaica: Slater is the deputy Provost-marshal.

SLATTERN. A woman sluttishly negligent in her dress.

SLEEPING PARTNER. A partner in a trade, or shop, who lends his name and money, for which he receives a share of the profit, without doing any part of the business.

SLEEPY. Much worn: the cloth of your coat must be extremely sleepy, for it has not had a nap this long time.

SLEEVELESS ERRAND. A fool's errand, in search of what it is impossible to find.

SLICE. To take a slice; to intrigue, particularly with a married woman, because a slice off a cut loaf is not missed.

SLIPGIBBET. See SCAPEGALLOWS.

SLIPPERY CHAP. One on whom there can be no dependance, a shuffling fellow.

SLIPSLOPS. Tea, water-gruel, or any innocent beverage taken medicinally.

SLIPSLOPPING. Misnaming and misapplying any hard word; from the character of Mrs. Slipslop, in Fielding's Joseph Andrews.

SLOP. Tea. How the blowens lush the slop. How the wenches drink tea!

SLOPS. Wearing apparel and bedding used by seamen.

SLOP SELLER. A dealer in those articles, who keeps a slop shop.

SLOUCH. A stooping gait, a negligent slovenly fellow. To slouch; to hang down one's head. A slouched hat: a hat whose brims are let down.

SLUBBER DE GULLION. A dirty nasty fellow.

SLUG. A piece of lead of any shape, to be fired from a blunderbuss. To fire a slug; to drink a dram.

SLUG-A-BED. A drone, one that cannot rise in the morning.

SLUICE YOUR GOB. Take a hearty drink.

SLUR. To slur, is a method of cheating at dice: also to cast a reflection on any one's character, to scandalize.

SLUSH. Greasy dish-water, or the skimmings of a pot where fat meat has been boiled.

SLUSH BUCKET. A foul feeder, one that eats much greasy food.

SLY BOOTS. A cunning fellow, under the mask of simplicity.

SMABBLED, or SNABBLED. Killed in battle.

To SMACK. To kiss. I had a smack at her muns: I kissed her mouth. To smack calves skin; to kiss the book, i. e.

to take an oath. The queer cuffin bid me smack calves skin, but I only bussed my thumb; the justice bid me kiss the book, but I only kissed my thumb.

SMACK SMOOTH. Level with the surface, every thing cut away.

SMACKING COVE. A coachman.

SMALL CLOTHES. Breeches: a gird at the affected delicacy of the present age; a suit being called coat, waistcoat, and articles, or small clothes.

SMART. Spruce, fine: as smart as a carrot new scraped.

SMART MONEY. Money allowed to soldiers or sailors for the loss of a limb, or other hurt received in the service.

SMASHER. A person who lives by passing base coin. The cove was fined in the steel for smashing; the fellow was ordered to be imprisoned in the house of correction for uttering base coin.

SMASH. Leg of mutton and smash: a leg of mutton and mashed turnips. *Sea term.*

TO SMASH. To break; also to kick down stairs. *Cant.* To smash. To pass counterfeit money.

SMEAR. A plasterer.

SMEAR GELT. A bribe. *German.*

SMELLER. A nose. Smellers: a cat's whiskers.

SMELLING CHEAT. An orchard, or garden; also a nosegay. *Cant.*

SMELTS. Half guineas. *Cant.*

SMICKET. A smock, or woman's shift.

SMIRK. A finical spruce fellow. To smirk; to smile, or look pleasantly.

SMITER. An arm. To smite one's tutor; to get money from him. *Academic term.*

SMITHFIELD BARGAIN. A bargain whereby the purchaser is taken in. This is likewise frequently used to express matches or marriages contracted solely on the score of interest, on one or both sides, where the fair sex are bought and sold like cattle in Smithfield.

SMOCK-FACED. Fair faced.

TO SMOKE. To observe, to suspect.

SMOKER. A tobacconist.

SMOKY. Curious, suspicious, inquisitive.

SMOUCH. Dried leaves of the ash tree, used by the smugglers for adulterating the black or bohea teas.

SMOUS. A German Jew.

SMUG. A nick name for a blacksmith; also neat and spruce.

SMUG LAY. Persons who pretend to be smugglers of lace and valuable articles; these men borrow money of publicans by depositing these goods in their hands: they shortly decamp,

decamp, and the publican discovers too late that he has been duped; and on opening the pretended treasure, he finds trifling articles of no value.

SMUGGLING KEN. A bawdy-house.

To SMUSH. To snatch, or seize suddenly.

SMUT. Bawdy. Smutty story; an indecent story.

SMUT. A copper. A grate. Old iron. The cove was lagged for a smut: the fellow was transported for stealing a copper.

SNACK. A share. To go snacks; to be partners.

To SNABBLE. To rifle or plunder; also to kill.

SNAFFLER. A highwayman. Snaffler of prances; a horse stealer.

To SNAFFLE. To steal. To snaffle any ones poll; to steal his wig.

SNAGGS. Large teeth; also snails.

SNAKESMAN. See LITTLE SNAKESMAN.

SNAP DRAGON. A Christmas gambol: raisins and almonds being put into a bowl of brandy, and the candles extinguished, the spirit is set on fire, and the company scramble for the raisins.

To SNAP THE GLAZE. To break shop windows or show glasses.

SNAPPERS. Pistols.

SNAPT. Taken, caught.

SNATCH CLY. A thief who snatches women's pockets.

SNEAK. A pilferer. Morning sneak; one who pilfers early in the morning, before it is light. Evening sneak; an evening pilferer. Upright sneak: one who steals pewter pots from the alehouse boys employed to collect them. To go upon the sneak; to steal into houses whose doors are carelessly left open. *Cant.*

SNEAKER. A small bowl.

SNEAKING BUDGE. One that robs alone.

SNEAKSBY. A mean-spirited fellow, a sneaking cur.

SNEERING. Jeering, flickering, laughing in scorn.

SNICKER. A glandered horse.

To SNICKER, or SNIGGER. To laugh privately, or in one's sleeve.

To SNILCH. To eye, or look at any thing attentively: the cull snilches. *Cant.*

SNIP. A taylor.

SNITCH. To turn snitch, or snitcher; to turn informer.

To SNITE. To wipe, or slap. Snite his snitch; wipe his nose, i. e. give him a good knock.

To SNIVEL. To cry, to throw the snot or snivel about. Snivelling

Snivelling; crying. A snivelling fellow; one that whines or complains.

To Snoach. To speak through the nose, to snuffle.

Snob. A nick name for a shoemaker.

To Snooze, or Snoodge. To sleep. To snooze with a mort; to sleep with a wench. *Cant.*

Snoozing Ken. A brothel. The swell was spiced in a snoozingken of his screens; the gentleman was robbed of his bank notes in a brothel.

Snow. Linen hung out to dry or bleach. Spice the snow; to steal the linen.

Snout. A hogshead. *Cant.*

Snowball. A jeering appellation for a negro.

To Snub. To check, or rebuke.

Snub Devil. A parson.

Snub Nose. A short nose turned up at the end.

Snudge. A thief who hides himself under a bed, in order to rob the house.

Snuff. To take snuff; to be offended.

To Snuffle. To speak through the nose.

Snuffles. A cold in the head, attended with a running at the nose.

Snug. All's snug; all's quiet.

To Soak. To drink. An old soaker; a drunkard, one that moistens his clay to make it stick together.

Socket Money. A whore's fee, or hire: also money paid for a treat, by a married man caught in an intrigue.

Soldier's Bottle. A large one.

Soldier's Mawnd. A pretended soldier, begging with a counterfeit wound, which he pretends to have received at some famous siege or battle.

Soldier's Pomatum. A piece of tallow candle.

Soldier. A red herring.

Solfa. A parish clerk.

Solo Player. A miserable performer on any instrument, who always plays alone, because no one will stay in the room to hear him.

Solomon. The mass. *Cant.*

Son of Prattlement. A lawyer.

Song. He changed his song; he altered his account or evidence. It was bought for an old song, i. e. very cheap. His morning and his evening song do not agree; he tells a different story.

Sooterkin. A joke upon the Dutch women, supposing that, by their constant use of stoves, which they place under their petticoats, they breed a kind of small animal in their

their bodies, called a sooterkin, of the size of a mouse, which when mature slips out.

Sop. A bribe. A sop for Cerberus; a bribe for a porter, turnkey, or gaoler.

Soph. (*Cambridge*) An undergraduate in his second year.

Sorrel. A yellowish red. Sorrel pate; one having red hair.

Sorrow shall be his Sops. He shall repent this. Sorrow go by me; a common expletive used by the presbyterians in Ireland.

Sorry. Vile, mean, worthless. A sorry fellow, or hussy; a worthless man or woman.

Sot Weed. Tobacco.

Soul Case. The body. He made a hole in his soul case; he wounded him.

Soul Doctor, or Driver. A parson.

Sounders. A herd of swine.

Souse. Not a souse; not a penny. *French.*

Sow. A fat woman. He has got the wrong sow by the ear, he mistakes his man. Drunk as David's sow; see David's Sow.

Sow's Baby. A sucking pig.

Sow Child. A female child.

Spado. A sword. *Spanish.*

Spangle. A seven shilling piece.

Spank. (*Whip*) To run neatly along, between a trot and gallop. The tits spanked it to town; the horses went merrily along all the way to town.

Spanish. The spanish; ready money.

Spanish Coin. Fair words and compliments.

Spanish Faggot. The sun.

Spanish Gout. The pox.

Spanish Padlock. A kind of girdle contrived by jealous husbands of that nation, to secure the chastity of their wives.

Spanish, or King of Spain's Trumpeter. An ass when braying.

Spanish Worm. A nail: so called by carpenters when they meet with one in a board they are sawing.

Spanks, or Spankers. Money; also blows with the open hand.

Spanking. Large.

Spark. A spruce, trim, or smart fellow. A man that is always thirsty, is said to have a spark in his throat.

Sparkish. Fine, gay.

Sparking Blows. Blows given by cocks before they close, or

or, as the term is, mouth it: used figuratively for words previous to a quarrel.

SPARROW. Mumbling a sparrow; a cruel sport frequently practised at wakes and fairs: for a small premium, a booby having his hands tied behind him, has the wing of a cock sparrow put into his mouth: with this hold, without any other assistance than the motion of his lips, he is to get the sparrow's head into his mouth: on attempting to do it, the bird defends itself surprisingly, frequently pecking the mumbler till his lips are covered with blood, and he is obliged to desist: to prevent the bird from getting away, he is fastened by a string to a button of the booby's coat.

SPARROW-MOUTHED. Wide-mouthed, like the mouth of a sparrow: it is said of such persons, that they do not hold their mouths by lease, but have it from year to year; i. e. from ear to ear. One whose mouth cannot be enlarged without removing their ears, and who when they yawn have their heads half off.

SPATCH COCK. [Abbreviation of *dispatch cock.*] A hen just killed from the roost, or yard, and immediately skinned, split, and broiled: an Irish dish upon any sudden occasion.

TO SPEAK WITH. To rob. I spoke with the cull on the cherry-coloured prancer; I robbed the man on the black horse. *Cant.*

SPEAK. Any thing stolen. He has made a good speak; he has stolen something considerable.

SPECKED WHIPER. A coloured hankerchief. *Cant.*

SPICE. To rob. Spice the swell; rob the gentleman.

SPICE ISLANDS. A privy. Stink-hole bay or dilberry creek. The fundament.

SPIDER-SHANKED. Thin-legged.

TO SPIFLICATE. To confound, silence, or dumbfound.

SPILT. A small reward or gift.

SPILT. Thrown from a horse, or overturned in a carriage: pray, coachee, don't spill us.

SPINDLE SHANKS. Slender legs.

TO SPIRIT AWAY. To kidnap, or inveigle away.

SPIRITUAL FLESH BROKER. A parson.

SPIT. He is as like his father as if he was spit out of his mouth; said of a child much resembling his father.

SPIT. A sword.

SPIT FIRE. A violent, pettish, or passionate person.

SPLICED. Married: an allusion to joining two ropes ends by splicing. *Sea term.*

SPLIT CROW. The sign of the spread eagle, which being represented with two heads on one neck, gives it somewhat the appearance of being split.

SPLIT

Split Cause. A lawyer.

Split Fig. A grocer.

Spoil Iron. The nick-name for a smith.

Spooney. (*Whip.*) Thin, haggard, like the shank of a spoon; also delicate, craving for something, longing for sweets. Avaricious. That tit is damned spooney. She's a spooney piece of goods. He's a spooney old fellow.

Spoil Pudding. A parson who preaches long sermons, keeping his congregation in church till the puddings are overdone.

To Sport. To exhibit: as, Jack Jehu sported a new gig yesterday: I shall sport a new suit next week. To sport or flash one's ivory; to shew one's teeth. To sport timber; to keep one's outside door shut; this term is used in the inns of court to signify denying one's self. N. B. The word *sport* was in great vogue ann. 1783 and 1784.

Spunge. A thirsty fellow, a great drinker. To spunge; to eat and drink at another's cost. Spunging-house: a bailiff's lock-up-house, or repository, to which persons arrested are taken, till they find bail, or have spent all their money: a house where every species of fraud and extortion is practised, under the protection of the law.

Spunk. Rotten touchwood, or a kind of fungus prepared for tinder; figuratively, spirit, courage.

Spoon Hand. The right hand.

To Spout. To rehearse theatrically.

Spouting Club. A meeting of apprentices and mechanics to rehearse different characters in plays: thus forming recruits for the strolling companies.

Spouting. Theatrical declamation.

Spouted. Pawned.

Spreac. Butter.

Spread Eagle. A soldier tied to the halberts in order to be whipped; his attitude bearing some likeness to that figure, as painted on signs.

Spree. A frolic. Fun. A drinking bout. A party of pleasure.

Spring-ankle Warehouse. Newgate, or any other gaol. *Irish.*

Squab. A fat man or woman: from their likeness to a well-stuffed couch, called also a squab. A new-hatched chicken.

Square. Honest, not roguish. A square cove, i. e. a man who does not steal, or get his living by dishonest means.

Square Toes. An old man: square toed shoes were anciently

anciently worn in common, and long retained by old men.

Squeak. A narrow escape, a chance: he had a squeak for his life. To squeak; to confess, peach, or turn stag. They squeak beef upon us; they cry out thieves after us. *Cant.*

Squeaker. A bar-boy; also a bastard or any other child. To stifle the squeaker; to murder a bastard, or throw it into the necessary house.---Organ pipes are likewise called squeakers. The squeakers are meltable; the small pipes are silver. *Cant.*

Squeeze Crab. A sour-looking, shrivelled, diminutive fellow.

Squeeze Wax. A good-natured foolish fellow, ready to become security for another, under hand and seal.

Squelch. A fall. Formerly a bailiff caught in a barrack-yard in Ireland, was liable by custom to have three tosses in a blanket, and a squelch; the squelch was given by letting go the corners of the blanket, and suffering him to fall to the ground. Squelch-gutted; fat, having a prominent belly.

Squib. A small satirical or political temporary jeu d'esprit, which, like the firework of that denomination, sparkles, bounces, stinks, and vanishes.

Squint-a-pipes. A squinting man or woman; said to be born in the middle of the week, and looking both ways for Sunday; or born in a hackney coach, and looking out of both windows; fit for a cook, one eye in the pot, and the other up the chimney; looking nine ways at once.

Squire of Alsatia. A weak profligate spendthrift, the squire of the company; one who pays the whole reckoning, or treats the company, called standing squire.

Squirish. Foolish.

Squirrel. A prostitute: because she like that animal, covers her back with her tail. *Meretrix corpore corpus alit.* Menagiana, ii. 128.

Squirrel Hunting. See Hunting.

Stag. To turn stag; to impeach one's confederates: from a herd of deer, who are said to turn their horns against any of their number who is hunted.

To Stag. To find, discover, or observe.

Staggering Bob, with his Yellow Pumps. A calf just dropped, and unable to stand, killed for veal in Scotland: the hoofs of a young calf are yellow.

Stall Whimper. A bastard. *Cant.*

Stal-

STALLING. Making or ordaining. Stalling to the rogue; an ancient ceremony of instituting a candidate into the society of rogues, somewhat similar to the creation of a herald at arms. It is thus described by Harman: the upright man taking a gage of bowse, i. e. a pot of strong drink, pours it on the head of the rogue to be admitted; saying,—I, A. B. do stall thee B. C. to the rogue; and from henceforth it shall be lawful for thee to cant for thy living in all places.

STALLING KEN. A broker's shop, or that of a receiver of stolen goods.

STALLION. A man kept by an old lady for secret services.

STAM FLESH. To cant. *Cant.*

STAMMEL, or STRAMMEL. A coarse brawny wench.

STAMP. A particular manner of throwing the dice out of the box, by striking it with violence against the table.

STAMPS. Legs.

STAMPERS. Shoes.

STAND-STILL. He was run to a stand-still; i. e. till he could no longer move.

STAR GAZER. A horse who throws up his head; also a hedge whore.

To STAR THE GLAZE. To break and rob a jeweller's show glass. *Cant.*

STARCHED. Stiff, prim, formal, affected.

STARING QUARTER. An ox cheek.

START, or THE OLD START. Newgate: he is gone to the start, or the old start. *Cant.*

STARTER. One who leaves a jolly company, a milksop; he is no starter, he will sit longer than a hen.

STARVE'EM, ROB'EM, AND CHEAT'EM. Stroud, Rochester, and Chatham; so called by soldiers and sailors, and not without good reason.

STAR LAG. Breaking shop-windows, and stealing some article thereout.

STASH. To stop. To finish. To end. The cove tipped the prosecutor fifty quid to stash the business; he gave the prosecutor fifty guineas to stop the prosecution.

STATE. To lie in state; to be in bed with three harlots.

STAY. A cuckold.

STAYTAPE. A taylor; from that article, and its coadjutor buckram, which make no small figure in the bills of those knights of the needle.

STEAMER. A pipe. A swell steamer; a long pipe, such as is used by gentlemen to smoke.

STEEL. The house of correction.

STELL

STEEL BAR. A needle. A steel bar flinger; a taylor, stay-maker, or any other person using a needle.

STEENKIRK. A muslin neckcloth carelessly put on, from the manner in which the French officers wore their cravats when they returned from the battle of Steenkirk.

STEEPLE HOUSE. A name given to the church by Dissenters.

STEPHEN. Money. Stephen's at home; i. e. has money.

STEPNEY. A decoction of raisins of the sun and lemons in conduit water, sweetened with sugar, and bottled up.

STEWED QUAKER. Burnt rum, with a piece of butter: an American remedy for a cold.

STICKS. Household furniture.

STICKS. Pops or pistols. Stow your sticks; hide your pistols. *Cant*. See POPS.

STICK FLAMS. A pair of gloves.

STIFF-RUMPED. Proud, stately.

STINGBUM. A niggard.

STINGO. Strong beer, or other liquor.

STIRRUP CUP. A parting cup or glass, drank on horseback by the person taking leave.

STITCH. A nick name for a taylor: also a term for lying with a woman.

STITCHBACK. Strong ale.

STIVER-CRAMPED. Needy, wanting money. A stiver is a Dutch coin, worth somewhat more than a penny sterling.

STOCK. A good stock; i. e. of impudence. Stock and block; the whole: he has lost stock and block.

STOCK DRAWERS. Stockings.

STOCK JOBBERS. Persons who gamble in Exchange Alley, by pretending to buy and sell the public funds, but in reality only betting that they will be at a certain price, at a particular time; possessing neither the stock pretended to be sold, nor money sufficient to make good the payments for which they contract: these gentlemen are known under the different appellations of bulls, bears, and lame ducks.

STOMACH WORM. The stomach worm gnaws; I am hungry.

STONE. Two stone under weight, or wanting; an eunuch. Stone doublet; a prison. Stone dead; dead as a stone.

STONE JUG. Newgate, or any other prison.

STONE TAVERN. Ditto.

STOOP-NAPPERS, or OVERSEERS OF THE NEW PAVEMENT. Persons set in the pillory. *Cant*.

STOOP. The pillory. The cull was served for macing and napp'd the stoop; he was convicted of swindling, and put in the pillory.

STOP HOLE ABBEY. The nick name of the chief rendezvous of the canting crew of beggars, gypsies, cheats, thieve , &c. &c.

STOTER. A great blow. Tip him a stoter in the haltering place ; give him a blow under the left ear.

STOUP. A vessel to hold liquor : a vessel containing a size or half a pint, is so called at Cambridge.

STOW. Stow you ; be silent, or hold your peace. Stow your whidds and plant'em, for the cove of the ken can cant'em ; you have said enough, the man of the house understands you.

STRAIT-LACED. Precise, over nice, puritanical.

STRAIT WAISTCOAT. A tight waistcoat, with long sleeves coming over the hand, having strings for binding them behind the back of the wearer : these waistcoats are used in madhouses for the management of lunatics when outrageous.

STRAMMEL. See STAMMEL.

STRANGER. A guinea.

STRANGLE GOOSE. A poulterer.

TO STRAP. To work. The kiddy would not strap, so he went on the scamp ; the lad would not work, and therefore robbed on the highway.

STRAPPER. A large man or woman.

STRAPPING. Lying with a woman. *Cant.*

STRAW. A good woman in the straw ; a lying-in woman. His eyes draw straw ; his eyes are almost shut, or he is almost asleep : one eye draws straw, and t'other serves the thatcher.

STRETCH. A yard. The cove was lagged for prigging a peter with several stretch of dobbin from a drag ; the fellow was transported for stealing a trunk, containing several yards of ribband, from a waggon.

STRETCHING. Hanging. He'll stretch for it ; he will be hanged for it. Also telling a great lie : he stretched stoutly.

STRIKE. Twenty shillings. *Cant.*

STRIP ME NAKED. Gin.

STROKE. To take a stroke : to take a bout with a woman.

STROLLERS. Itinerants of different kinds. Strolling morts ; beggars or pedlars pretending to be widows.

STROMMEL. Straw. *Cant.*

STRONG MAN. To play the part of the strong man, i. e. to push the cart and horses too ; to be whipt at the cart's tail.

STRUM. A perriwig. Rum strum : a fine large wig. (*Cambridge*) To *do* a piece. Fœminam subagitare. *Cant.*

To Strum. To have carnal knowledge of a woman; also to play badly on the harpsichord, or any other stringed instrument. A strummer of wire: a player on any instrument strung with wire.

Strumpet. A harlot.

Stub-faced. Pitted with the small pox: the devil ran over his face with horse stubs (horse nails) in his shoes.

Stubble-it. Hold your tongue. *Cant.*

Stuling Ken. See Stalling Ken. *Cant.*

Stum. The flower of fermenting wine, used by vintners to adulterate their wines.

Stumps. Legs. To stir one's stumps; to walk fast.

Sturdy Beggars. The fifth and last of the most ancient order of canters, beggars that rather demand than ask. *Cant.*

Successfully. Used by the vulgar for *successively:* as three or four landlords of this house have been ruined successfully by the number of soldiers quartered on them. *Irish.*

Such a Reason pist my Goose, or my Goose pist. Said when any one offers an absurd reason.

Suck. Strong liquor of any sort. To suck the monkey; see Monkey. Sucky; drunk.

To Suck. To pump. To draw from a man all he knows. The file sucked the noodle's brains: the deep one drew out of the fool all he knew.

Sucking Chicken. A young chicken.

Suds. In the suds; in trouble, in a disagreeable situation, or involved in some difficulty.

Sugar Stick. The virile member.

Sugar Sops. Toasted bread soked in ale, sweetened with sugar, and grated nutmeg: it is eaten with cheese.

Suit and Cloak. Good store of brandy, or other strong liquor, let down gutter lane.

Sulky. A one-horse chaise or carriage, capable of holding but one person: called by the French a *desobligeant.*

Sun. To have been in the sun; said of one that is drunk.

Sunburnt. Clapped; also having many male children.

Sunday Man. One who goes abroad on that day only, for fear of arrests.

Sunny Bank. A good fire in winter.

Sunshine. Prosperity.

Supernaculum. Good liquor, of which there is not even a drop left sufficient to wet one's nail.

Supouch. A landlady of an inn, or hostess.

Surveyor of the Highways. One reeling drunk.

Surveyor of the Pavement. One standing in the pillory.

Sus. per Coll. Hanged: persons who have been hanged are thus entered into the jailor's books.

Suspence. One in a deadly suspence; a man just turned off at the gallows.

Sutler. A camp publican: also one that pilfers gloves, tobacco boxes, and such small moveables.

Swabbers. The ace of hearts, knave of clubs, ace and duce of trumps, at whist: also the lubberly seamen, put to swab and clean the ship.

Swad, or Swadkin. A soldier. *Cant.*

To **Swaddle.** To beat with a stick.

Swaddlers. The tenth order of the canting tribe, who not only rob, but beat, and often murder passenges. *Cant* — Swaddlers is also the Irish name for methodist.

Swag. A shop. Any quantity of goods. As, plant the swag; conceal the goods. Rum swag; a shop full of rich goods. *Cant.*

Swagger. To bully, brag, or boast, also to strut.

Swannery. He keeps a swannery; i. e. all his geese are swans.

Sweating. A mode of diminishing the gold coin, practised chiefly by the Jews, who corrode it with aqua regia. Sweating was also a diversion practised by the bloods of the last century, who styled themselves Mohocks: these gentlemen lay in wait to surprise some person late in the night, when surroudning him, they with their swords pricked him in the posteriors, which obliged him to be constantly turning round; this they continued till they thought him sufficiently sweated.

Sweet. Easy to be imposed on, or taken in: also expert. dexterous clever. Sweet's your hand; said of one dexterous at stealing.

Sweet Heart. A term applicable to either the masculine or feminine gender, signifying a girl's lover, or a man's mistress: derived from a sweet cake in the shape of a heart.

Sweetners. Guinea droppers, cheats, sharpers To sweeten: to decoy, or draw in. To be sweet upon; to coax, wheedle, court, or allure. He seemed sweet upon that wench; he seemed to court that girl.

Swell. A gentleman. A well dressed man. The flashman bounced the swell of all his blunt; the girl's bully frightened the gentleman out of all his money

Swelled Head. A disorder to which horses are extremely liable, particularly those of the subalterns of the army.

 This

This disorder is generally occasioned by remaining too long in one livery-stable or inn, and often arises to that height that it prevents their coming out at the stable door. The most certain cure is the *unguentum aureum*---not applied to the horse, but to the palm of the master of the inn or stable. N. B. Neither this disorder, nor its remedy, is mentioned by either Bracken, Bartlet, or any of the modern writers on farriery.

Swig. A hearty draught of liquor.

Swigmen. Thieves who travel the country under colour of buying old shoes, old clothes, &c. or selling brooms, mops, &c. *Cant.*

To Swill. To drink greedily.

Swill Tub. A drunkard, a sot.

Swimmer. A counterfeit old coin.

Swimmer. A ship. I shall have a swimmer; a cant phrase used by thieves to signify that they will be sent on board the tender.

To Swing. To be hanged. He will swing for it; he will be hanged for it.

Swing Tail. A hog.

To Swinge. To beat stoutly.

Swinging. A great swinging fellow; a great stout fellow. A swinging lie; a lusty lie.

Swindler. One who obtains goods on credit by false pretences, and sells them for ready money at any price, in order to make up a purse. This name is derived from the German word *schwindlin*, to totter, to be ready to fall; these arts being generally practised by persons on the totter, or just ready to break. The term *swindler* has since been used to signify cheats of every kind.

Swipes. Purser's swipes; small beer: so termed on board the king's ships, where it is furnished by the purser.

Swish Tail. A pheasant; so called by the persons who sell game for the poachers.

To Swive. To copulate.

Swivel-eyed. Squinting.

Swizzle. Drink, or any brisk or windy liquor. In North America, a mixture of spruce beer, rum, and sugar, was so called. The 17th regiment had a society called the Swizzle Club, at Ticonderoga, A. D. 1760.

Sword Racket. To enlist in different regiments, and on receiving the bounty to desert immediately.

Swop. An exchange.

Syebuck. Sixpence.

Syntax. A schoolmaster.

TABBY. An old maid; either from Tabitha, a formal antiquated name; or else from a tabby cat, old maids being often compared to cats. To drive Tab; to go out on a party of pleasure with a wife and family.

TACE. Silence, hold your tongue. *Tace* is Latin for a candle; a jocular admonition to be silent on any subject.

TACKLE. A mistress; also good clothes. The cull has tipt his tackle rum gigging; the fellow has given his mistress good clothes. A man's tackle: the genitals.

TAFFY, i. e. Davy. A general name for a Welchman, St. David being the tutelar saint of Wales. Taffy's day; the first of March, St. David's day.

TAG-RAG AND BOBTAIL. An expression meaning an assemblage of low people, the mobility of all sorts. To tag after one like a tantony pig: to follow one wherever one goes, just as St. Anthony is followed by his pig.

TAIL. A prostitute. Also, a sword.

TAKEN IN. Imposed on, cheated.

TALE TELLERS. Persons said to have been formerly hired to tell wonderful stories of giants and fairies, to lull their hearers to sleep. Talesman; the author of a story or report: I'll tell you my tale, and my talesman. Tale bearers; mischief makers, incendiaries in families.

TALL BOY. A bottle, or two-quart pot.

TALLY MEN. Brokers that let out clothes to the women of the town. See RABBIT SUCKERS.

TALLYWAGS, or TARRYWAGS. A man's testicles.

TAME. To run tame about a house; to live familiarly in a family with which one is upon a visit. Tame army; the city trained bands.

TANDEM. A two-wheeled chaise, buggy, or noddy, drawn by two horses, one before the other: that is, *at length.*

TANGIER. A room in Newgate, where debtors were confined, hence called Tangerines.

TANNER. A sixpence. The kiddey tipped the rattling cove a tanner for luck; the lad gave the coachman sixpence for drink.

TANTADLIN TART. A sirreverence, human excrement.

TANTRUMS. Pet, or passion: madam was in her tantrums.

TANTWIVY. Away they went tantwivy; away they went full speed. Tantwivy was the sound of the hunting horn in full cry, or that of a post horn.

TAP. A gentle blow. A tap on the shoulder; - an- arrest. To tap a girl; to be the first seducer: in allusion to a beer barrel. To tap a guinea; to get it changed.

TAPPERS. Shoulder tappers: bailiffs.

TAPE. Red tape; brandy. Blue or white tape; gin.

TAPLASH. Thick and bad beer.

TAR. Don't lose a sheep for a halfpennyworth of tar: tar is used to mark sheep. A jack tar; a sailor.

TARADIDDLE. A fib, or falsity.

TARPAWLIN. A coarse cloth tarred over: also, figuratively, a sailor.

TARRING AND FEATHERING. A punishment lately inflicted by the good people of Boston on any person convicted, or suspected, of loyalty: such delinquents being stripped naked, were daubed all over with tar, and afterwards put into a hogshead of feathers.

TART. Sour, sharp, quick, pert.

TARTAR. To catch a Tartar; to attack one of superior strength or abilities. This saying originated from a story of an Irish soldier in the Imperial service, who, in a battle against the Turks, called out to his comrade that he had caught a Tartar. 'Bring him along then,' said he. 'He won't come,' answered Paddy. 'Then come along yourself,' replied his comrade. 'Arrah,' cried he, 'but he won't let me.'---A Tartar is also an adept at any feat, or game: he is quite a Tartar at cricket, or billiards.

TAT. Tit for tat; an equivalent.

TATS. False dice.

TATLER. A watch. To flash a tatler: to wear a watch.

TATMONGER. One that uses false dice.

TATTERDEMALLION. A ragged fellow, whose clothes hang all in tatters.

TATTOO. A beat of the drum, or signal for soldiers to go to their quarters, and a direction to the sutlers to close the tap, and draw no more liquor for them; it is generally beat at nine in summer and eight in winter. The devil's tattoo; beating with one's foot against the ground, as done by persons in low spirits.

TAW. A schoolboy's game, played with small round balls made of stone dust, called marbles. I'll be one upon your taw presently; a species of threat.

TAWDRY. Garish, gawdy, with lace or staring and discordant colours: a term said to be derived from the shrine and altar of St. Audrey (an Isle of Ely saintess), which for finery exceeded all others thereabouts, so as to become proverbial; whence any fine dressed man or woman was said to be all St. Audrey, and by contraction all tawdry.

Tawed. Beaten.

Tayle. See Tail.

Tayle Drawers. Thieves who snatch gentlemens swords from their sides. He drew the cull's tayle rumly; he snatched away the gentleman's sword cleverly.

Taylor. Nine taylors make a man; an ancient and common saying, originating from the effeminacy of their employment; or, as some have it, from nine taylors having been robbed by one man; according to others, from the speech of a woollendraper, meaning that the custom of nine taylors would make or enrich one man.—A London taylor, rated to furnish half a man to the Trained Bands, asking how that could possibly be done? was answered, By sending four journeymen and an apprentice.—Put a taylor, a weaver, and a miller into a sack, shake them well, and the first that puts out his head is certainly a thief.—A taylor is frequently styled pricklouse, from their assaults on those vermin with their needles.

Taylor's Goose. An iron with which, when heated, they press down the seams of clothes.

Tea Voider. A chamber pot.

Teagueland. Ireland. Teaguelanders; Irishmen.

Tears of the Tankard. The drippings of liquor on a man's waistcoat.

Teddy my Godson. An address to a supposed simple fellow, or nysey.

Teize. To nap the teize; to receive a whipping. *Cant.*

Temple Pickling. Pumping a bailiff: a punishment formerly administered to any of that fraternity caught exercising their functions within the limits of the Temple.

Ten Toes. See Bayard of ten Toes.

Ten in the Hundred. An usurer: more than five in the hundred being deemed usurious interest.

Tenant at Will. One whose wife usually fetches him from the alehouse.

Tenant for Life. A married man; i. e. possessed of a woman for life.

Tender Parnell. A tender creature, fearful of the least puff of wind or drop of rain. As tender as Parnell, who broke her finger in a posset drink.

Termagant. An outrageous scold: from Termagantes, a cruel Pagan, formerly represented in divers shows and entertainments, where being dressed *a la Turque*, in long clothes, he was mistaken for a furious woman.

Terra Firma. An estate in land.

TESTER. A sixpence: from *teston*, a coin with a head on it

TETBURY PORTION. A **** and a clap.

THAMES. He will not find out a way to set the Thames on fire; he will not make any wonderful discoveries, he is no conjuror.

THATCH-GALLOWS. A rogue, or man of bad character.

THICK. Intimate. They are as thick as two inkle-weavers.

THIEF. You are a thief and a murderer, you have killed a baboon and stole his face; vulgar abuse.

THIEF IN A CANDLE. Part of the wick or snuff, which falling on the tallow, burns and melts it, and causing it to gutter, thus steals it away.

THIEF TAKERS. Fellows who associate with all kinds of villains, in order to betray them, when they have committed any of those crimes which entitle the persons taking them to a handsome reward, called blood money. It is the business of these thief takers to furnish subjects for a handsome execution, at the end of every sessions.

THIMBLE. A watch. The swell flashes a rum thimble; the gentleman sports a fine watch.

THINGSTABLE. Mr. Thingstable; Mr. Constable: a ludicrous affectation of delicacy in avoiding the pronunciation of the first syllable in the title of that officer, which in sound has some similarity to an indecent monosyllable.

THINGUMBOB. Mr. Thingumbob; a vulgar address or nomination to any person whose name is unknown, the same as Mr. What-d'ye-call'em. Thingumbobs; testicles.

THIRDING. A custom practised at the universities, where two thirds of the original price is allowed by the upholsterers to the students for household goods returned to them within the year.

THIRTEENER. A shilling in Ireland, which there passes for thirteen pence.

THOMOND. Like Lord Thomond's cocks, all on one side. Lord Thomond's cock-feeder, an Irishman, being entrusted with some cocks which were matched for a considerable sum, the night before the battle shut them all together in one room, concluding that as they were all on the same side, they would not disagree: the consequence was, they were most of them either killed or lamed before the morning.

THOMAS. Man Thomas; a man's penis.

THORNS. To be or sit upon thorns; to be uneasy, impatient, anxious for an event.

THORNBACK. An old maid.

THOROUGH CHURCHMAN. A person who goes in at one door of a church, and out at the other, without stopping.

THOROUGH-

THOROUGH-GOOD-NATURED WENCH. One who being asked to sit down, will lie down.

THOROUGH GO NIMBLE. A looseness, a violent purging.

THOROUGH COUGH. Coughing and breaking wind backwards at the same time.

THOROUGH STITCH. To go thorough stitch; to stick at nothing; over shoes, over boots.

THOUGHT. What did thought do? lay in bed and beshit himself, and thought he was up; reproof to any one who excuses himself for any breach of positive orders, by pleading that he thought to the contrary.

THREE TO ONE. He is playing three to one, though sure to lose; said of one engaged in the amorous congress.

THREE-PENNY UPRIGHT. A retailer of love, who, for the sum mentioned, dispenses her favours standing against a wall.

THREE-LEGGED MARE, or STOOL. The gallows, formerly consisting of three posts, over which were laid three transverse beams. This clumsy machine has lately given place to an elegant contrivance, called the *new drop*, by which the use of that vulgar vehicle a cart, or mechanical instrument a ladder, is also avoided; the patients being left suspended by the dropping down of that part of the floor on which they stand. This invention was first made use of for a peer. See DROP.

THREE THREADS. Half common ale, mixed with stale and double beer.

THREPS. Threepence.

TO THROTTLE. To strangle.

THROTTLE. The throat, or gullet.

TO THRUM. To play on any instrument stringed with wire. A thrummer of wire: a player on the spinet, harpsichord or guitar.

THRUMS. Threepence.

THUMB By rule of thumb: to do any thing by dint of practice. To kiss one's thumb instead of the book; a vulgar expedient to avoid perjury in taking a false oath.

THUMMIKINS. An instrument formerly used in Scotland, like a vice, to pinch the thumbs of persons accused of different crimes, in order to extort confession.

THUMP. A blow. This is better than a thump on the back with a stone; said on giving any one a drink of good liquor on a cold morning. Thatch, thistle, thunder, and thump; words to the Irish, like the Shibboleth of the Hebrews.

THUMPING. Great: a thumping boy.

THWACK. A great blow with a stick across the shoulders.

TIB. A young lass

TIBBY.

TIBBY. A cat.

TIB OF THE BUTTERY. A goose. *Cant.*---Saint Tibb's evening; the evening of the last day, or day of judgment: he will pay you on St. Tibb's eve. *Irish.*

TICK. To run o'tick; take up goods upon trust, to run in debt. Tick; a watch. See *Sessions Papers.*

TICKLE TEXT. A parson.

TICKLE PITCHER. A thirsty fellow, a sot.

TICKLE TAIL. A rod, or schoolmaster. A man's penis.

TICKRUM. A licence.

TIDY. Neat.

TIFFING. Eating or drinking out of meal time, disputing or falling out; also lying with a wench. A tiff of punch, a small bowl of punch.

TILBURY. Sixpence; so called from its formerly being the fare for crossing over from Gravesend to Tilbury fort.

TILT. To tilt; to fight with a sword. To run full tilt against one: allusion to the ancient tilting with the lance.

TILTER. A sword.

TIM WHISKY. A light one-horse chaise without a head.

TIMBER TOE. A man with a wooden leg.

TINY. Little.

TO TIP. To give or lend. Tip me your daddle; give me your hand. Tip me a hog; give me a shilling. To tip the lion; to flatten a man's nose with the thumb, and at the same time to extend his mouth with the fingers, thereby giving him a sort of lion-like countenance. To tip the velvet; tonguing a woman. To tip all nine; to knock down all the nine pins at once, at the game of bowls or skittles: tipping, at these games, is slightly touching the tops of the pins with the bowl. Tip; a draught; don't spoil his tip.

TIP-TOP. The best: perhaps from fruit, that growing at the top of the tree being generally the best, as partaking most of the sun. A tip-top workman; the best, or most excellent workman.

TIPPERARY FORTUNE. Two town lands, stream a town, and ballinocack; said of Irish women without fortune.

TIPPLE. Liquor.

TIPPLERS. Sots who are continually sipping.

TIPSEY. Almost drunk.

TIRING. Dressing: perhaps abbreviation of *attiring.* Tiring women, or tire women: women that used to cut ladies hair, and dress them.

TIT. A horse; a pretty little tit; a smart little girl. A tit, or tid bit; a delicate morsel. Tommy tit; a smart lively little fellow.

TIT FOR TAT. An equivalent.

TO TITTER. To suppress a laugh.

TITTER TATTER. One reeling, and ready to fall at the least touch; also the childish amusement of riding upon the two ends of a plank, poised upon the prop underneath its centre, called also see-saw. Perhaps tatter is a rustic pronunciation of totter.

TITTLE-TATTLE. Idle discourse, scandal, women's talk, or small talk.

TITTUP. A gentle hand gallop, or canter.

TIZZY. Sixpence.

TOAD EATER. A poor female relation, and humble companion, or reduced gentlewoman, in a great family, the standing butt, on whom all kinds of practical jokes are played off, and all ill humours vented. This appellation is derived from a mountebank's servant, on whom all experiments used to be made in public by the doctor, his master; among which was the eating of toads, formerly supposed poisonous. Swallowing toads is here figuratively meant for swallowing or putting up with insults, as disagreeable to a person of feeling as toads to the stomach.

TOAD. Toad in a hole; meat baked or boiled in pye-crust. He or she sits like a toad on a chopping-block; a saying of any who sits ill on horseback. As much need of it as a toad of a side-pocket; said of a person who desires any thing for which he has no real occasion. As full of money as a toad is of feathers.

TOAST. A health; also a beautiful woman whose health is often drank by men. The origin of this term (as it is said) was this: a beautiful lady bathing in a cold bath, one of her admirers out of gallantry drank some of the water: whereupon another of her lovers observed, he never drank in the morning, but he would kiss the toast, and immediately saluted the lady.

TOASTING IRON, or CHEESE TOASTER. A sword.

TOBY LAY. The highway. High toby man; a highwayman. Low toby man; a footpad.

TOBACCO. A plant, once in great estimation as a medicine:

> Tobacco hic
> Will make you well if you be sick.
> Tobacco hic
> If you be well will make you sick.

TODDY. Originally the juice of the cocoa tree, and afterwards rum, water, sugar, and nutmeg.

TODDLE. To walk away. The cove was touting, but stagging the traps he toddled; he was looking out, and seeing the officers he walked away.

TODGE.

TODGE. Beat all to a todge: said of any thing beat to mash.

TOGE. A coat. *Cant.*

TOGEMANS. The same. *Cant.*

TOGS Clothes. The swell is rum-togged. The gentleman is handsomely dressed.

TOKEN. The plague: also the venereal disease. She tipped him the token; she gave him a clap or pox.

TOL, or TOLEDO. A sword: from Spanish swords made at Toledo, which place was famous for sword blades of an extraordinary temper.

TOLLIBAN RIG. A species of cheat carried on by a woman, assuming the character of a dumb and deaf conjuror.

TOM T—DMAN. A night man, one who empties necessary houses.

TOMBOY. A romping girl, who prefers the amusement used by boys to those of her own sex.

TOM OF BEDLAM. The same as Abram man.

TOM CONY. A simple fellow.

TOM LONG. A tiresome story teller. It is coming by Tom Long, the carrier; said of any thing that has been long expected.

TOM THUMB. A dwarf, a little hop-o'my-thumb.

TOMMY. Soft Tommy, or white Tommy; bread is so called by sailors, to distinguish it from biscuit. Brown Tommy; ammunition bread for soldiers; or brown bread given to convicts at the hulks.

TO-MORROW COME NEVER. When two Sundays come together; never.

TONGUE. Tongue enough for two sets of teeth: said of a talkative person. As old as my tongue, and a little older than my teeth; a dovetail in answer to the question, How old are you? Tongue pad; a scold, or nimble-tongued person.

TONY. A silly fellow, or ninny. A mere tony: a simpleton.

TOOLS. The private parts of a man.

TOOL. The instrument of any person or faction, a cat's paw. See CAT'S PAW.

TOOTH MUSIC. Chewing.

TOOTH-PICK. A large stick. An ironical expression.

TOPPER. A violent blow on the head.

TOP ROPES. To sway away on all top ropes; to live riotously or extravagantly.

TO TOP. To cheat, or trick: also to insult: he thought to have topped upon me. Top; the signal among taylors for snuffing the candles: he who last pronounces that word, is obliged to get up and perform the operation.—to be topped, to be hanged. The cove was topped for smashing queer screens; he was hanged for uttering forged bank notes.

TOP DIVER. A lover of women. An old top diver; one who has loved old hat in his time.

TOP HEAVY. Drunk.

TOP LIGHTS. The eyes. Blast your top lights. See CURSE.

TOP SAIL. He paid his debts at Portsmouth with the top-sail; i. e. he went to sea and left them unpaid. So soldiers are said to pay off their scores with the drum; that is, by marching away.

TOPER. One that loves his bottle, a soaker. See TO SOAK.

TOPPING FELLOW. One at the top or head of his profession.

TOPPING CHEAT. The gallows. *Cant.*

TOPPING COVE. The hangman. *Cant.*

TOPPING MAN. A rich man.

TOPSY-TURVY. The top side the other way; i. e. the wrong side upwards; some explain it, the top side turf ways, turf being always laid the wrong side upwards.

TORCHECUL. Bumfodder.

TORMENTER OF SHEEP SKIN. A drummer.

TORMENTER of CATGUT. A fiddler.

TORY. An advocate for absolute monarchy and church power; also an Irish vagabond, robber, or rapparee.

TOSS POT. A drunkard.

TOSS OFF. Manual pollution.

TOTTY-HEADED. Giddy, hare-brained.

TOUCH. To touch; to get money from any one; also to arrest. Touched in the wind; broken-winded. Touched in the head; insane, crazy. To touch up a woman; to have carnal knowledge of her. Touch bone and whistle; any one having broken wind backwards, according to the vulgar law, may be pinched by any of the company till he has touched bone (i. e. his teeth) and whistled.

TOUCH BUN FOR LUCK. See BUN.

TOUT. A look-out house, or eminence.

TOUTING. (From *tueri*, to look about.) Publicans forestalling guests, or meeting them on the road, and begging their custom; also thieves or smugglers looking out to see that the coast is clear. Touting ken; the bar of a public house.

TOW ROW. A grenadier. The tow-row club; a club or society of the grenadier officers of the line.

TOWEL. An oaken towel, a cudgel. To rub one down with an oaken towel; to beat or cudgel him.

TOWER. Clipped money: they have been round the tower with it. *Cant.*

TO TOWER. To overlook, to rise aloft as in a high tower.

TOWER HILL PLAY. A slap on the face, and a kick on the breech.

TOWN. A woman of the town; a prostitute. To be on the town; to live by prostitution.

TOWN BULL. A common whoremaster. To roar like a town bull; to cry or bellow aloud.

TO TRACK. To go. Track up the dancers; go up stairs. *Cant.*

TRADING JUSTICES. Broken mechanics, discharged footmen, and other low fellows, smuggled into the commission of the peace, who subsist by fomenting disputes, granting warrants, and otherwise retailing justice: to the honour of the present times, these nuisances are by no means so common as formerly.

TRADESMEN. Thieves. Clever tradesmen; good thieves.

TRANSLATORS. Sellers of old mended shoes and boots, between coblers and shoemakers.

TO TRANSMOGRAPHY, or TRANSMIGRIFY. To patch up, vamp, or alter.

TO TRANSNEAR. To come up with any body.

TRANTER. See CROCKER.

TRAP. To understand trap; to know one's own interest.

TRAP STICKS. Thin legs, gambs: from the sticks with which boys play at trap-ball.

TRAPS. Constables and thief-takers. *Cant.*

TO TRAPAN. To inveigle, or ensnare.

TRAPES. A slatternly woman, a careless sluttish woman.

TRAVELLER. To tip the traveller; to tell wonderful stories, to romance.

TRAVELLING PIQUET. A mode of amusing themselves, practised by two persons riding in a carriage, each reckoning towards his game the persons or animals that pass by on the side next them, according to the following estimation:

A parson riding a grey horse, with blue furniture; game.
An old woman under a hedge; ditto.
A cat looking out of a window; 60.
A man, woman, and child, in a buggy; 40.
A man with a woman behind him; 30.
A flock of sheep; 20.

A flock

A flock of geese; 10.
A post chaise; 5.
A horseman; 2.
A man or woman walking; 1.

TRAY TRIP. An ancient game like Scotch hop, played on a pavement marked out with chalk into different compartments.

TRENCHER CAP. The square cap worn by the collegians. at the universities of Oxford and Cambridge.

TRENCHER MAN. A stout trencher man; one who has a good appetite, or, as the term is, plays a good knife and fork.

TRESWINS. Threepence.

TRIB. A prison: perhaps from tribulation.

TRICKUM LEGIS. A quirk or quibble in the law.

TRIG. The point at which schoolboys stand to shoot their marbles at taw; also the spot whence bowlers deliver the bowl.

TO TRIG IT. To play truant. To lay a man trigging; to knock him down.

TRIGRYMATE. An idle female companion.

TRIM. State, dress. In a sad trim; dirty.—Also spruce or fine: a trim fellow.

TRIM TRAM. Like master, like man.

TRIMMING. Cheating, changing side, or beating. I'll trim his jacket; I'll thresh him. To be trimmed; to be shaved; I'll just step and get trimmed.

TRINE. To hang; also Tyburn.

TRINGUM TRANGUM. A whim, or maggot.

TRINING. Hanging.

TRINKETS. Toys, bawbles, or nicknacks.

TRIP. A short voyage or journey, a false step or stumble, an error in the tongue, a bastard. She has made a trip; she has had a bastard.

TRIPE. The belly, or guts. Mr. Double Tripe; a fat man. Tripes and trullibubs; the entrails: also a jeering appellation for a fat man.

TO TROLL. To loiter or saunter about.

TROLLY LOLLY. Coarse lace once much in fashion.

TROLLOP. A lusty coarse sluttish woman.

TROOPER. You will die the death of a trooper's horse. that is, with your shoes on; a jocular method of telling any one he will be hanged.

TROT. An old trot; a decrepit old woman. A dog trot; a gentle pace.

Trotters. Feet. To shake one's trotters at Bilby's ball, where the sheriff pays the fiddlers; perhaps the Bilboes ball, i. e. the ball of fetters: fetters and stocks were anciently called the bilboes.

To Trounce. To punish by course of law.

Truck. To exchange, swop, or barter; also a wheel such as ship's guns are placed upon.

Trull. A soldier or a tinker's trull; a soldier or tinker's female companion.—*Guteli*, or *trulli*, are spirits like women, which shew great kindness to men, and hereof it is that we call light women trulls. *Randle Holms's Academy of Armory.*

Trumpery. An old whore, or goods of no value; rubbish.

Trumpet. To sound one's own trumpet; to praise one's self.

Trumpeter. The king of Spain's trumpeter; a braying ass. His trumpeter is dead, he is therefore forced to sound his own trumpet. He would make an excellent trumpeter, for he has a strong breath; said of one having a fœtid breath.

Trumps. To be put to one's trumps: to be in difficulties, or put to one's shifts. Something may turn up trumps; something lucky may happen. All his cards are trumps: he is extremely fortunate.

Trundlers. Peas.

Trunk. A nose. How fares your old trunk? does your nose still stand fast? an allusion to the proboscis or trunk of an elephant. To shove a trunk: to introduce one's self unasked into any place or company. Trunk-maker like; more noise than work.

Trusty Trojan, or Trusty Trout. A true friend.

Try on. To endeavour. To live by thieving. Coves who try it on; professed thieves.

Tryning. See Trining.

Tu Quoque. The mother of all saints.

Tub Thumper. A presbyterian parson.

Tucked up. Hanged. A tucker up to an old bachelor or widower; a supposed mistress.

Tuft Hunter. An anniversary parasite, one who courts the acquaintance of nobility, whose caps are adorned with a gold tuft.

Tumbler. A cart; also a sharper employed to draw in pigeons to game; likewise a posture-master, or rope-dancer. To shove the tumbler, or perhaps tumbril; to be whipt at the cart's tail.

To Tune. To beat: his father tuned him delightfully: perhaps from fetching a tune out of the person beaten, or from a comparison with the disagreeable sounds of instruments when tuning.

To Tup. To have carnal knowledge of a woman.

Tup. A ram: figuratively, a cuckold.

Tup Running. A rural sport practised at wakes and fairs in Derbyshire; a ram, whose tail is well soaped and greased, is turned out to the multitude; any one that can take him by the tail, and hold him fast, is to have him for his own.

T—d. There were four t—ds for dinner: stir t—d, hold t—d, tread t—d, and mus-t—d: to wit, a hog's face, feet and chitterlings, with mustard. He will never sh—e a seaman's t—d; i. e. he will never make a good seaman.

Turf. On the turf; persons who keep running horses, or attend and bet at horse-races, are said to be on the turf.

Turk. A cruel, hard-hearted man. Turkish treatment; barbarous usage. Turkish shore; Lambeth, Southwark, and Rotherhithe side of the Thames.

Turkey Merchant. A poulterer.

Turncoat. One who has changed his party from interested motives.

Turned up. Acquitted; discharged.

Turnip-pated. White or fair-haired.

Turnpike Man. A parson; because the clergy collect their tolls at our entrance into and exit from the world.

Tuzzy-muzzy. The monosyllable.

Twaddle. Perplexity, confusion, or any thing else: a fashionable term that for a while succeeded that of *bore*. See Bore.

Twangey, or Stangey. A north country name for a taylor.

Tweague. In a great tweague: in a great passion. Tweaguey; peevish, passionate.

To Tweak. To pull: to tweak any one's nose.

Twelver. A shilling.

Twiddle-diddles. Testicles.

Twiddle poop. An effeminate looking fellow.

In Twig. Handsome; stilish. The cove is togged in twig; the fellow is dressed in the fashion.

To Twig. To observe. Twig the cull, he is peery; observe the fellow, he is watching us. Also to disengage, snap asunder, or break off. To twig the darbies; to knock off the irons.

Twiss. (*Irish*) A jordan, or pot de chambre. A Mr. Richard

Twiss

Twiss having in his "Travels" given a very unfavourable description of the Irish character, the inhabitants of Dublin, by way of revenge, thought proper to christen this utensil by his name—suffice it to say that the baptismal rites were not wanting at the ceremony. On a nephew of this gentleman the following epigram was made by a friend of ours:

> Perish the country, yet my name
> Shall ne'er in *story* be forgot,
> But still the more increase in fame,
> The more the *country goes to pot.*

TWIST. A mixture of half tea and half coffee; likewise brandy, beer, and eggs. A good twist; a good appetite. To twist it down apace; to eat heartily.

TWISTED. Executed, hanged.

TO TWIT. To reproach a person, or remind him of favours conferred.

TWITTER. All in a twitter; in a fright. Twittering is also the note of some small birds, such as the robin, &c.

TWITTOC. Two. *Cant.*

TWO HANDED PUT. The amorous congress.

TWO THIEVES BEATING A ROGUE. A man beating his hands against his sides to warm himself in cold weather; called also beating the booby, and cuffing Jonas.

TWO TO ONE SHOP. A pawnbroker's: alluding to the three blue balls, the sign of that trade: or perhaps to its being two to one that the goods pledged are never redeemed.

TWO-HANDED. Great. A two-handed fellow or wench; a great strapping man or woman.

TYE. A neckcloth.

TYBURN BLOSSOM. A young thief or pickpocket, who in time will ripen into fruit borne by the deadly never-green.

TYBURN TIPPET. A halter; see Latimer's sermon before Edward VI. A. D. 1549.

TYBURN TOP, or FORETOP. A wig with the foretop combed over the eyes in a knowing style; such being much worn by the gentlemen pads, scamps, divers, and other knowing hands.

TYKE. A dog, also a clown; a Yorkshire tyke.

TYNEY. See TINEY.

VAI

VAGARIES. Frolics, wild rambles.

VAIN-GLORIOUS, or OSTENTATIOUS MAN. One who boasts

boasts without reason, or, as the canters say, pisses more than he drinks.

VALENTINE. The first woman seen by a man, or man seen by a woman, on St. Valentine's day, the 14th of February, when it is said every bird chuses his mate for the ensuing year.

TO VAMP. To pawn any thing. I'll vamp it, and tip you the cole: I'll pawn it, and give you the money. Also to refit, new dress, or rub up old hats, shoes or other wearing apparel; likewise to put new feet to old boots. Applied more particularly to a quack bookseller.

VAMPER. Stockings.

VAN. Madam Van; see MADAM.

VAN-NECK. Miss or Mrs. Van-Neck; a woman with large breasts; a bushel bubby.

VARDY. To give one's vardy; i. e. verdict or opinion.

VARLETS. Now rogues and rascals, formerly yeoman's servants.

VARMENT. (*Whip* and *Cambridge*.) Natty, dashing. He is quite varment, he is quite the go. He sports a varment hat, coat, &c.; he is dressed like a gentleman Jehu.

VAULTING SCHOOL. A bawdy-house; also an academy where vaulting and other manly exercises are taught.

VELVET. To tip the velvet; to put one's tongue into a woman's mouth. To be upon velvet; to have the best of a bet or match. To the little gentleman in velvet, i. e. the mole that threw up the hill that caused Crop (King William's horse) to stumble; a toast frequently drank by the tories and catholics in Ireland.

VENERABLE MONOSYLLABLE. *Pudendum muliebre.*

VENUS'S CURSE. The venereal disease.

VESSELS OF PAPER. Half a quarter of a sheet.

VICAR OF BRAY. See BRAY.

VICE ADMIRAL OF THE NARROW SEAS. A drunken man that pisses under the table into his companions' shoes.

VICTUALLING OFFICE. The stomach.

VINCENT'S LAW. The art of cheating at cards, composed of the following associates: bankers, those who play booty; the gripe, he that betteth; and the person cheated, who is styled the vincent; the gains acquired, termage.

VINEGAR. A name given to the person who with a whip in his hand, and a hat held before his eyes, keeps the ring clear, at boxing-matches and cudgel-playing; also, in cant terms, a cloak.

VIXEN. A termagant; also a she fox, who, when she has cubs, is remarkably fierce.

 To

To Vowel. A gamester who does not immediately pay his losings, is said to vowel the winner, by repeating the vowels I. O. U. or perhaps from giving his note for the money according to the Irish form, where the acknowledgment of the debt is expressed by the letters I. O. U. which, the sum and name of the debtor being added, is deemed a sufficient security among gentlemen.

Uncle. Mine uncle's; a necessary house. He is gone to visit his uncle; saying of one who leaves his wife soon after marriage. It likewise means a pawnbroker's: goods pawned are frequently said to be at mine uncle's, or laid up in lavender.

Understrapper. An inferior in any office, or department.

Under'dubber. A turnkey.

Unfortunate Gentlemen. The horse guards, who thus named themselves in Germany, where a general officer seeing them very awkward in bundling up their forage, asked what the devil they were; to which some of them answered, unfortunate gentlemen.

Unfortunate Women. Prostitutes: so termed by the virtuous and compassionate of their own sex.

Ungrateful Man. A parson, who at least once a week abuses his best benefactor, i. e. the devil.

Unguentum aureum. A bribe.

Unicorn. A coach drawn by three horses.

Unlicked Cub. A rude uncouth young fellow.

Unrigged. Undressed, or stripped. Unrig the drab; strip the wench.

Untruss. To untruss a point; to let down one's breeches in order to ease one's self. Breeches were formerly tied with points, which till lately were distributed to the boys every Whit Monday by the churchwardens of most of the parishes in London, under the denomination of tags: these tags were worsteds of different colours twisted up to a size somewhat thicker than packthread, and tagged at both ends with tin. Laces were at the same given to the girls.

Untwisted. Undone, ruined, done up.

Unwashed Bawdry. Rank bawdry.

Up to their Gossip. To be a match for one who attempts to cheat or deceive; to be on a footing, or in the secret. I'll be up with him; I will repay him in kind.

Uphills. False dice that run high.

Upper Benjamin. A great coat. *Cant.*

Upper Story, or Garret. Figuratively used to signify the

 head.

head. His upper story or garrets are unfurnished; i. e. he is an empty or foolish fellow.

UPPING BLOCK. [Called in some counties a leaping stock, in others a jossing block.] Steps for mounting a horse. He sits like a toad on a jossing block; said of one who sits ungracefully on horseback.

UPPISH. Testy, apt to take offence.

UPRIGHT. Go upright; a word used by shoemakers, taylors and their servants, when any money is given to make them drink, and signifies, Bring it all out in liquor, though the donor intended less, and expects change, or some of his money, to be returned. Three-penny upright. See THREEPENNY UPRIGHT.

UPRIGHT MAN. An upright man signifies the chief or principal of a crew. The vilest, stoutest rogue in the pack is generally chosen to this post, and has the sole right to the first night's lodging with the dells, who afterwards are used in common among the whole fraternity. He carries a short truncheon in his hand, which he calls his filchman, and has a larger share than ordinary in whatsoever is gotten in the society. He often travels in company with thirty or forty males and females, abram men, and others, over whom he presides arbitrarily. Sometimes the women and children who are unable to travel, or fatigued, are by turns carried in panniers by an ass or two, or by some poor jades procured for that purpose.

UPSTARTS. Persons lately raised to honours and riches from mean stations.

URCHIN. A child, a little fellow; also a hedgehog.

URINAL OF THE PLANETS. Ireland: so called from the frequent rains in that island.

USED UP. Killed: a military saying, originating from a message sent by the late General Guise, on the expedition at Carthagena, where he desired the commander in chief to order him some more grenadiers, for those he had were all used up.

WABLER. Foot wabler; a contemptuous term for a foot soldier, frequently used by those of the cavalry.

TO WADDLE. To go like a duck. To waddle out of Change alley as a lame duck; a term for one who has not been able to pay his gaming debts, called his differences, on the Stock Exchange, and therefore absents himself from it.

Wag. An arch frolicsome fellow.

Waggish. Arch, gamesome, frolicsome.

Wagtail. A lewd woman.

Waits. Musicians of the lower order, who in most towns play under the windows of the chief inhabitants at midnight, a short time before Christmas, for which they collect a christmas-box from house to house. They are said to derive their name of waits from being always in waiting to celebrate weddings and other joyous events happening within their district.

Wake. A country feast, commonly on the anniversary of the tutelar saint of the village, that is, the saint to whom the parish church is dedicated. Also a custom of watching the dead, called Late Wake, in use both in Ireland and Wales, where the corpse being deposited under a table, with a plate of salt on its breast, the table is covered with liquor of all sorts; and the guests, particularly the younger part of them, amuse themselves with all kinds of pastimes and recreations: the consequence is generally more than replacing the departed friend.

Walking Cornet. An ensign of foot.

Walking Poulterer. One who steals fowls, and hawks them from door to door.

Walking Stationer. A hawker of pamphlets, &c.

Walking the Plank. A mode of destroying devoted persons or officers in a mutiny or ship-board, by blindfolding them, and obliging them to walk on a plank laid over the ship's side; by this means, as the mutineers suppose, avoiding the penalty of murder.

Walking up against the Wall. To run up a score, which in alehouses is commonly recorded with chalk on the walls of the bar.

Wall. To walk or crawl up the wall; to be scored up at a public-house. Wall-eyed, having an eye with little or no sight, all white like a plaistered wall.

To Wap. To copulate, to beat. If she wont wap for a winne, let her trine for a make; if she won't lie with a man for a penny, let her hang for a halfpenny. Mort wap-apace; a woman of experience, or very expert at the sport.

Wapper-eyed. Sore-eyed.

Ware. A woman's ware; her commodity.

Ware Hawk. An exclamation used by thieves to inform their confederates that some police officers are at hand.

Warm. Rich, in good circumstances. To warm, or give a man a warming; to beat him. See **Chafed.**

Warm-

WARMING-PAN. A large old-fashioned watch. A Scotch warming-pan; a female bedfellow.

WARREN. One that is security for goods taken up on credit by extravagant young gentlemen. Cunny warren; a girl's boarding-school, also a bawdy-house.

WASH. Paint for the face, or cosmetic water. Hog-wash; thick and bad beer.

WASP. An infected prostitute, who like a wasp carries a sting in her tail.

WASPISH. Peevish, spiteful.

WASTE. House of waste; a tavern or alehouse, where idle people waste both their time and money.

WATCH, CHAIN, AND SEALS. A sheep's head and pluck.

WATER-MILL. A woman's private parts.

WATER SNEAKSMAN. A man who steals from ships or craft on the river.

WATER. His chops watered at it; he longed earnestly for it. To watch his waters; to keep a strict watch on any one's actions. In hot water: in trouble, engaged in disputes.

WATER BEWITCHED. Very weak punch or beer.

WATERPAD. One that robs ships in the river Thames.

WATERY-HEADED. Apt to shed tears.

WATER SCRIGER. A doctor who prescribes from inspecting the water of his patients. See PISS PROPHET.

WATTLES. Ears. *Cant.*

WEAR A---E. A one-horse chaise.

WEASEL-FACED. Thin, meagre-faced. Weasel-gutted; thin-bodied; a weasel is a thin long slender animal with a sharp face.

WEDDING. The emptying of a necessary-house, particularly in London. You have been at an Irish wedding, where black eyes are given instead of favours; saying to one who has a black eye.

WEDGE. Silver plate, because melted by the receivers of stolen goods into wedges. *Cant.*

To WEED. To take a part. The kiddey weeded the swell's screens; the youth took some of the gentleman's bank notes.

WEEPING CROSS. To come home by weeping cross; to repent.

WELCH COMB. The thumb and four fingers.

WELCH FIDDLE The itch. See SCOTCH FIDDLE.

WELCH MILE. Like a Welch mile, long and narrow. His story is like a Welch mile, long and tedious.

WELCH RABBIT. [i.e. a Welch rare-bit.] Bread and cheese toasted, See RABBIT.---The Welch are said to be so remark-

remarkably fond of cheese, that in cases of difficulty their midwives apply a piece of toasted cheese to the *janua vitæ* to attract and entice the young Taffy, who on smelling it makes most vigorous efforts to come forth.

Welch Ejectment. To unroof the house, a method practised by landlords in Wales to eject a bad tenant.

To Well. To divide unfairly. To conceal part. A cant phrase used by thieves, where one of the party conceals some of the booty, instead of dividing it fairly amongst his confederates.

Well-hung. The blowen was nutts upon the kiddey because he is well-hung; the girl is pleased with the youth because his genitals are large.

Westminster Wedding. A match between a whore and a rogue.

Wet Parson. One who moistens his clay freely, in order to make it stick together.

Wet Quaker. One of that sect who has no objection to the spirit derived from wine.

Whack. A share of a booty obtained by fraud. A paddy whack; a stout brawney Irishman.

Whapper. A large man or woman.

Wheedle. A sharper. To cut a wheedle; to decoy by fawning or insinuation. *Cant.*

Wheelband in the nick. Regular drinking over the left thumb.

Whelp. An impudent whelp; a saucy boy.

Whereas. To follow a whereas; to become a bankrupt, to figure among princes and potentates: the notice given in the Gazette that a commission of bankruptcy is issued out against any trader, always beginning with the word whereas. He will soon march in the rear of a whereas.

Whet. A morning's draught, commonly white wine, supposed to whet or sharpen the appetite.

Whetstone's Park. A lane between Holborn and Lincoln's-inn Fields, formerly famed for being the resort of women of the town.

Whids. Words. *Cant.*

To Whiddle. To tell or discover. He whiddles; he peaches. He whiddles the whole scrap; he discovers all he knows. The cull whiddled because they would not tip him a snack: the fellow peached because they would not give him a share. They whiddle beef, and we must brush; they cry out thieves, and we must make off. *Cant.*

Whiddler. An informer, or one that betrays the secrets of the gang.

Whiffles. A relaxation of the scrotum.

WHIFFLERS. Ancient name for fifers; also persons at the universities who examine candidates for degrees. A whiffling cur, a small yelping cur.

WHIMPER, or WHINDLE. A low cry.

To WHINE. To complain.

WHINYARD. A sword.

To WHIP THE COCK. A piece of sport practised at wakes, horse-races, and fairs in Leicestershire: a cock being tied or fastened into a hat or basket, half a dozen carters blindfolded, and armed with their cart whips, are placed round it, who, after being turned thrice about, begin to whip the cock, which if any one strikes so as to make it cry out, it becomes his property; the joke is, that instead of whipping the cock they flog each other heartily.

WHIP JACKS. The tenth order of the canting crew, rogues who having learned a few sea terms, beg with counterfeit passes, pretending to be sailors shipwrecked on the neighbouring coast, and on their way to the port from whence they sailed.

To WHIP OFF. To run away, to drink off greedily, to snatch. He whipped away from home, went to the alehouse, where he whipped off a full tankard, and coming back whipped off a fellow's hat from his head.

WHIP-BELLY VENGEANCE, or pinch-gut vengeance, of which he that gets the most has the worst share. Weak or sour beer.

WHIPPER-SNAPPER. A diminutive fellow.

WHIPSHIRE. Yorkshire.

WHIPSTER. A sharp or subtle fellow.

WHIPT SYLLABUB. A flimsy, frothy discourse or treatise without solidity.

WHIRLYGIGS. Testicles.

WHISKER. A great lie.

WHISKER SPLITTER. A man of intrigue.

WHISKIN. A shallow brown drinking bowl.

WHISKY. A malt spirit much drank in Ireland and Scotland; also a one-horse chaise. See TIM WHISKY.

WHISTLE. The throat. To wet one's whistle; to drink.

WHISTLING SHOP. Rooms in the King's Bench and Fleet prison where drams are privately sold.

WHIT. [i. e. Whittington's.] Newgate. *Cant.*---Five rumpadders are rubbed in the darkmans out of the whit, and are piked into the deuseaville; five highwaymen broke out of Newgate in the night, and are gone into the country.

WHITE RIBBIN. Gin.

WHITE FEATHER. He has a white feather; he is a coward: an allusion to a game cock, where having a white feather is a proof he is not of the true game breed.

WHITE-

White-livered. Cowardly, malicious.

White Lie. A harmless lie, one not told with a malicious intent, a lie told to reconcile people at variance.

White Serjeant. A man fetched from the tavern or ale house by his wife, is said to be arrested by the white serjeant.

White Swelling. A woman big with child is said to have a white swelling.

White Tape. Geneva.

White Wool. Geneva.

Whitechapel. Whitechapel portion; two smocks, and what nature gave. Whitechapel breed; fat, ragged, and saucy: see St. Giles's Breed. Whitechapel beau; one who dresses with a needle and thread, and undresses with a knife. To play at whist Whitechapel fashion; i. e. aces and kings first.

Whitewashed. One who has taken the benefit of an act of insolvency, to defraud his creditors, is said to have been whitewashed.

Whitfielite. A follower of George Whitfield, a Methodist.

Whither-go-ye. A wife: wives being sometimes apt to question their husbands whither they are going.

Whittington's College. Newgate: built or repaired by the famous lord mayor of that name.

Whore's Bird. A debauched fellow, the largest of all birds. He sings more like a whore's bird than a canary bird; said of one who has a strong manly voice.

Whore's Curse. A piece of gold coin, value five shillings and three pence, frequently given to women of the town by such as professed always to give gold, and who before the introduction of those pieces always gave half a guinea.

Whore's Kitling, or Whore's Son. A bastard.

Whore-monger. A man that keeps more than one mistress. A country gentleman, who kept a female friend, being reproved by the parson of the parish, and styled a whoremonger, asked the parson whether he had a cheese in his house; and being answered in the affirmative, 'Pray,' says he, 'does that one cheese make you a cheese-monger?'

Whore pipe. The penis.

Whow Ball. A milk-maid: from their frequent use of the word *whow*, to make the cow stand still in milking. Ball is the supposed name of the cow.

Wibble. Bad drink.

Wibling's Witch. The four of clubs: from one James Wib-

Wibling, who in the reign of King James I. grew rich by private gaming, and was commonly observed to have that card, and never to lose a game but when he had it not.

Wicket. A casement; also a little door.

Widow's Weeds. Mourning clothes of a peculiar fashion, denoting her state. A grass widow; a discarded mistress. A widow bewitched; a woman whose husband is abroad, and said, but not certainly known, to be dead.

Wife. A fetter fixed to one leg.

Wife in Water Colours. A mistress, or concubine; water colours being, like their engagements easily effaced, or dissolved.

Wigannowns. A man wearing a large wig.

Wigsby. Mr. Wigsby; a man wearing a wig.

Wild Rogues. Rogues trained up to stealing from their cradles.

Wild Squirt. A looseness.

Wild-goose Chase. A tedious uncertain pursuit, like the following a flock of wild geese, who are remarkably shy.

Willing Tit. A free horse, or a coming girl.

Willow. Poor, and of no reputation. To wear the willow; to be abandoned by a lover or mistress.

Win. A penny.

To Win. To steal. The cull has won a couple of rum glimsticks; the fellow has stolen a pair of fine candlesticks.

Wind. To raise the wind; to procure mony.

Winder. Transportation for life. The blowen has napped a winder for a lift; the wench is transported for life for stealing in a shop.

Wind-mill. The fundament. She has no fortune but her mills; i. e. she has nothing but her **** and a*se.

Windfall. A legacy, or any accidental accession of property.

Windmills in the Head. Foolish projects.

Window peeper. A collector of the window tax.

Windward Passage. One who uses or navigates the windward passage; a sodomite.

Windy. Foolish. A windy fellow; a simple fellow.

Wink. To tip one the wink; to give a signal by winking the eye.

Winnings. Plunder, goods, or money acquired by theft.

Winter Cricket. A taylor.

Winter's Day. He is like a winter's day, short and dirty.

Wipe. A blow, or reproach. I'll give you a wipe on the chops. That story gave him a fine wipe. Also a handkerchief.

Wiper. A handkerchief. *Cant.*

Wiper Drawer. A pickpocket, one who steals handkerchiefs. He drew a broad, narrow, cam, or specked wiper; he picked a pocket of a broad, narrow, cambrick, or coloured handkerchief.

To Wiredraw. To lengthen out or extend any book, letter, or discourse.

Wise. As wise as Waltham's calf, that ran nine miles to suck a bull.

Wise Men of Gotham. Gotham is a village in Nottinghamshire; its magistrates are said to have attempted to hedge in a cuckow; a bush, called the cuckow's bush, is still shewn in support of the tradition. A thousand other ridiculous stories are told of the men of Gotham.

Wiseacre. A foolish conceited fellow.

Wiseacre's Hall. Gresham college.

Wit. He has as much wit as three folks, two fools and a madman.

Witcher. Silver. Witcher bubber; a silver bowl. Witcher tilter; a silver-hilted sword. Witcher cully; a silversmith.

To Wobble. To boil. Pot wobbler; one who boils a pot.

Wolf in the Breast. An extraordinary mode of imposition, sometimes practised in the country by strolling women, who have the knack of counterfeiting extreme pain, pretending to have a small animal called a wolf in their breasts, which is continually gnawing them.

Wolf in the Stomach. A monstrous or canine appetite.

Wood. In a wood; bewildered, in a maze, in a peck of troubles, puzzled, or at a loss what course to take in any business. To look over the wood; to ascend the pulpit, to preach: I shall look over the wood at St. James's on Sunday next. To look through the wood; to stand in the pillory. Up to the arms in wood; in the pillory.

Wood Pecker. A bystander, who bets whilst another plays.

Woodcock. A taylor with a long bill.

Wooden Habeas. A coffin. A man who dies in prison is said to go out with a wooden habeas. He went out with a wooden habeas; i. e. his coffin.

Wooden Spoon. (*Cambridge.*) The last junior optime. See Wrangler, Optime.

Wooden Horse. To ride the wooden horse was a military punishment formerly in use. This horse consisted of two or more planks about eight feet long, fixed together so as to form a sharp ridge or angle, which answered to the body

body of the horse. It was supported by four posts, about six feet long, for legs. A head, neck, and tail, rudely cut in wood, were added, which completed the appearance of a horse. On this sharp ridge delinquents were mounted, with their hands tied behind them; and to steady them (as it was said), and lest the horse should kick them off, one or more firelocks were tied to each leg. In this situation they were sometimes condemned to sit an hour or two; but at length it having been found to injure the soldiers materially, and sometimes to rupture them, it was left off about the time of the accession of King George I. A wooden horse was standing in the Parade at Portsmouth as late as the year 1750.

WOODEN RUFF. The pillory. See NORWAY NECKCLOTH.

WOODEN SURTOUT. A coffin.

WOMAN OF THE TOWN, or WOMAN OF PLEASURE. A prostitute.

WOMAN AND HER HUSBAND. A married couple, where the woman is bigger than her husband.

WOMAN'S CONSCIENCE. Never satisfied.

WOMAN OF ALL WORK. Sometimes applied to a female servant, who refuses none of her master's commands.

WOOLBIRD. A sheep. *Cant.*

WOOL GATHERING. Your wits are gone a wool gathering; saying to an absent man, one in a reverie, or absorbed in thought.

WOOLLEY CROWN. A soft-headed fellow.

WORD GRUBBERS. Verbal critics, and also persons who use hard words in common discourse.

WORD PECKER. A punster, one who plays upon words.

WORD OF MOUTH. To drink by word of mouth, i. e. out of the bowl or bottle instead of a glass.

WORLD. All the world and his wife: every body, a great company.

WORM. To worm out; to obtain the knowledge of a secret by craft, also to undermine or supplant. He is gone to the diet of worms; he is dead and buried, or gone to Rothisbone.

WRANGLERS. At *Cambridge* the first class (generally of twelve) at the annual examination for a degree. There are three classes of honours, wranglers, senior optimes, and junior optimes. Wranglers are said to be born with golden spoons in their mouths, the senior optimes with silver, and the junior with leaden ones. The last junior optime is called the wooden spoon. Those who are not qualified for honors are either in the *Gulf* (that is, meritorious,

rious,but not deserving of being in the three first classes) or among the οι πολλοι, *the many*. See PLUCK, APOSTLES,&c.

WRAP RASCAL. A red cloak, called also a roquelaire.

WRAPT UP IN WARM FLANNEL. Drunk with spirituous liquors. He was wrapt up in the tail of his mother's smock; saying of any one remarkable for his success with the ladies. To be wrapt up in any one: to have a good opinion of him, or to be under his influence.

WRINKLE. A wrinkle-bellied whore; one who has had a number of bastards: child-bearing leaves wrinkles in a woman's belly. To take the wrinkles out of any one's belly; to fill it out by a hearty meal. You have one wrinkle more in your a-se; i. e. you have one piece of knowledge more than you had, every fresh piece of knowledge being supposed by the vulgar naturalists to add a wrinkle to that part.

WRY MOUTH AND A PISSEN PAIR OF BREECHES. Hanging.

WRY NECK DAY. Hanging day.

WYN. See WIN.

XAN

XANTIPPE. The name of Socrates's wife: now used to signify a shrew or scolding wife.

YEA

YAFFLING. Eating. *Cant.*

TO YAM. To eat or stuff heartily.

YANKEY, or YANKEY DOODLE. A booby, or country lout: a name given to the New England men in North America. A general appellation for an American.

YARMOUTH CAPON. A red herring: Yarmouth is a famous place for curing herrings.

YARMOUTH COACH. A kind of low two-wheeled cart drawn by one horse, not much unlike an Irish car.

YARMOUTH PYE. A pye made of herrings highly spiced, which the city of Norwich is by charter bound to present annually to the king.

YARUM. Milk. *Cant.*

YEA AND NAY MAN. A quaker, a simple fellow, one who can only answer yes, or no.

Yellow. To look yellow; to be jealous. I happened to call on Mr. Green, who was out: on coming home, and finding me with his wife, he began to look confounded blue, and was, I thought, a little yellow.

Yellow Belly. A native of the Fens of Licolnshire; an allusion to the eels caught there.

Yellow Boys. Guineas.

To Yelp. To cry out. Yelper; a town cryer, also one apt to make great complaints on trifling occasions.

Yest. A contraction of yesterday.

Yoked. Married. A yoke; the quantum of labour performed at one spell by husbandmen, the day's work being divided in summer into three yokes. *Kentish term.*

Yorkshire Tyke. A Yorkshire clown. To come Yorkshire over any one; to cheat him.

Young One. A familiar expression of contempt for another's ignorance, as "ah! I see you're a young one." How d'ye do, *young one?*

To Yowl. To cry aloud, or howl.

Zad. Crooked like the letter Z. He is a mere zad, or perhaps zed; a description of a very crooked or deformed person.

Zany. The jester, jack pudding, or merry andrew, to a mountebank.

Zedland. Great part of the west country, where the letter Z is substituted for S; as zee for see, zun for sun, &c. &c. This prevails through the counties of Devonshire, Dorsetshire, and Somersetshire.

Znees. Frost or frozen. Zneesy weather; frosty weather.

Znuz. The same as znees.

Zoc, or Soc. A blow. I gid him a zoc; I gave him a blow. *West country.*

Zouch, or Slouch. A slovenly ungenteel man, one who has a stoop in his gait. A slouched hat; a hat with its brims let down, or uncocked.

Zounds. An exclamation, an abbreviation of *God's wounds.*

Zucke. A withered stump of a tree.

FINIS.

W. N. Jones, Printer, Green Arbour Court, Old Bailey, London.

THE

SCOUNDRELS DICTIONARY:

OR, AN

EXPLANATION

OF THE

CANT WORDS used by THIEVES, HOUSE-BREAKERS, STREET ROBBERS, and PICKPOCKETS about Town.

TO WHICH ARE PREFIXED

Some CURIOUS DISSERTATIONS on the ART of WHEEDLING,

AND A

Collection of their FLASH SONGS, with a PROPER GLOSSARY.

The whole printed from a *Copy taken on one of their Gang*, in the late Scuffle between the Watchmen and a Party of them on Clerkenwell Green; which Copy is now in the Custody of one of the Constables of that Parish.

LONDON:
Printed for J. BROWNNELL, in Pater-noster-row.
M.DCC.LIV.

[Price Sixpence.]

Advertisement reproduced from the second edition of "A Classical Dictionary Of The Vulgar Tongue," 1788.

A

C A V E A T

FOR

COMMON CURSETORS,

VULGARLY CALLED

V A G A B O N E S;

SET FORTH BY

THOMAS HARMAN, Esquier,

FOR THE

Utilitie and Proffyt of hys Naturall Countrey.

Newly Augmented and Imprinted, Anno Domini M.D.LXVII.

Viewed, Examined, and Allowed according unto the Queen's Majeſtye's Injunctions.

Imprinted at London, in Flete-ſtreet, at the Signe of the Faulcon, by William Gryffith; and are to be ſolde at his Shoppe in Saynt Dunſtone's Churche Yarde, in the Weſt.

Advertisement reproduced from the second edition of "A Classical Dictionary Of The Vulgar Tongue," 1788.